Dilemmas of Reform in Jiang Zemin's China

Dilemmas of Reform in Jiang Zemin's China

edited by
Andrew J. Nathan
Zhaohui Hong
Steven R. Smith

LYNNE
RIENNER
PUBLISHERS

BOULDER
LONDON

Published in the United States of America in 1999 by
Lynne Rienner Publishers, Inc.
1800 30th Street, Boulder, Colorado 80301

and in the United Kingdom by
Lynne Rienner Publishers, Inc.
3 Henrietta Street, Covent Garden, London WC2E 8LU

Library of Congress Cataloging-in-Publication Data
Dilemmas of Reform in Jiang Zemin's China / Andrew J. Nathan,
    Zhaohui Hong, Steven Smith, editors.
    Includes bibliographical references and index.
    ISBN 1-55587-851-2 (alk. paper)
    1. China—Economic conditions—1976–   2. China—Economic
policy—1976–   I. Nathan, Andrew J. (Andrew James) II. Hong,
    Zhaohui. III. Smith, Steven
HC427.92.D55   1999
338.951—dc21   99-19294
                                                                    CIP

British Cataloguing in Publication Data
A Cataloguing in Publication record for this book
is available from the British Library.

Printed and bound in the United States of America

    The paper used in this publication meets the requirements
∞   of the American National Standard for Permanence of
    Paper for Printed Library Materials Z39.48-1984.

    5 4 3 2 1

Contents

Part 3 Economic Strategies for the Future

Foreword

Hungdah Chiu

China's economic reforms since 1978 have led to economic, political, social, and cultural changes. Economic reform originated in the agricultural sector with the elimination of the people's commune and establishment of the household responsibility system. This stimulated the enthusiasm of farmers and led to a rapid increase of agricultural production. The rise of township and village enterprises successfully absorbed more than 120 million surplus laborers in the countryside. The initial success of economic reform in the rural areas led to urban reforms. Over 100 million laborers released from the agricultural sector accelerated the movement of laborers that sped up the development of a nonstate economy. Now, private enterprises exceed the performance of the state-owned enterprises (SOEs) by contributing more than 70 percent of the gross national production. At the same time, SOEs began to carry out ownership reforms, introducing shareholding and cooperative shareholding.

Economic reform has led to the transformation of a predominantly state-owned and centrally planned economy to a market economy. A stock market, real estate market, and labor market have emerged, and all the crucial elements for a market economy have come into being. Pushed by economic freedom and the market economy, the government has begun to recognize the legitimacy of private ownership and freedom of choice in the economy. The development of a market economy has become irreversible.

The rise of a market economy has led to political changes. As the central government reduced the size of its bureaucracy and curtailed its own authority, local governments strengthened their power in finance, banking, and personnel management. With the emergence of local economies, relations between the central and local governments have become increasingly tense, and local authorities are able to influence and restrain the central government in policymaking and implementation. As a result, the centralized leadership of the Chinese Communist Party (CCP) faces an unprecedented challenge. Additionally, the rise of localism has accelerated the separation between the government and enterprises, as well as between the party and the government. Because an increasing number of factory directors and managers have become contractors, many enterprises have become independent; this economic independence has become the symbol and driving force for democracy, freedom, and pluralism.

Despite problems, county-level elections have been held since 1980. Many nonofficial candidates have won elections through campaigning, while many government-endorsed candidates have been defeated. These grass-roots elections have strengthened the sense of participation of the public, spread the ideas and theories of democracy, and shaken the foundation of the authoritarian system. Grass-roots democracy has further enhanced the democratic function of the People's Congress and gradually changed it from a "rubber stamp" to a representative institution with basic supervisory and check-and-balance functions. As the supreme authority established by the constitution, the People's Congress has begun to participate in the policymaking process, utilizing the legal power provided by the constitution, and resisting pressure from the CCP. As the People's Congress becomes more independent, it represents a challenge to the authoritarian power of the executive branch and the CCP.

While the economy has been modernized, reform has also created political, economic, social, and cultural crises. Because the market system is still in a primitive stage and the modern enterprise system not fully established, many people have been hurt by unemployment. Extensive corruption exists and the social security system is inadequate.

Political reform has become the bottleneck of institutional transformation and social development, but transformation of the political system is the key to further reform. The success or failure of political reform will largely determine whether China will be able to achieve growth, prosperity, and stability in the twenty-first century. The existing political system limits the development of the country. The serious problems in population control, environment, education, relations between nationalities, social order, the judicial system, and the cultural crises are immediately related to the mistakes and miscalculations of the government. Although the CCP began to pay lip service to political reform in 1985 so as to match the economic reforms and eliminate political obstacles to economic development, the Tiananmen Square incident interrupted healthy experimentation and development and caused a deeper political crisis.

With no internal divisions and no external checks, the power of the CCP has created the prerequisite for nationwide corruption. The practice of trading money for power has become so common that it threatens the legitimacy of the regime and may become the spark that ignites mass protest and social instability. Drawing from historical lessons that people's revolts have been driven by misgovernment, it seems likely that without political reform the existing government may be in danger. Political instability would threaten all economic and social reforms.

Although the cry for political reforms has never stopped, reforms have been few. Demand for political change has clashed with political reality and has cost some people their lives. Reforming the political system has become the key link as well as the biggest problem. How to effectively promote and achieve political democracy has become the most challenging task and the greatest test of the wisdom and ability of Jiang Zemin's China.

With the goal of promoting a market economy and political democracy in China, the Center for Modern China, established in 1990, is recognized as one of the leading institutions of China studies. With a "liberal, pragmatic, scientific, creative, and cooperative" spirit, the center brings together social scientists to study the issues essential to the success of China's institutional transition. The center has three hundred active members residing in eighteen countries and areas, each specializing in one of the social sciences or in the humanities. In several major countries outside the United States, the center has branch/liaison offices. It maintains regular exchanges with approximately three hundred scholarly organizations and with nearly two thousand scholars around the world. One unusual feature of the center is that its research associates were born in China and maintain contact with different segments of Chinese society. Some have been active for many years in promoting reform, while others have personally participated in making important decisions regarding reform. Most members of the center have received formal doctoral training in the West and now teach and conduct research in Western universities and research institutions. Some members are recognized as leading specialists in their fields; these scholars are regarded as China specialists by governmental agencies, research institutions, universities, and the mass media in China and elsewhere.

Since 1990, the Center for Modern China has sponsored about two hundred research projects, twenty-five international conferences and seminars, approximately six hundred public lectures around the world, and several study missions to China, the former Soviet Union, and eastern Europe. Its members have participated in approximately two thousand interviews by media organizations from different countries. The center has published approximately eighty issues of its Chinese and English journals, as well as initiated and funded several writing and publishing projects, including thirty volumes of its popular book series and eighteen specialized studies. The fourteen volumes of Market Economy Popular Reader Series, for instance, sold 400,000 copies in the first three months of its publication in China and won the grand prize for the 1994 Chinese Books Award.

Organized by the center with the support of other organizations, an international conference on "The Fifteenth Communist Party Congress and China's Development" was held in New York City in November 1997. The conference featured papers on the significance of the Fifteenth Congress of the CCP for China's political direction, the reform of state-owned enterprises, social problems, cultural reconstruction, China's reunification, ethnic problems, and U.S.–China relations. This book is an outgrowth of that conference; most of its authors were participants and are research fellows of the center.

The editors of this volume have selected ten essays focused on economic reform and political challenges that they believe address the toughest issues, offer the sharpest analyses, and will be of most interest to a wide audience of English-speaking readers. The authors write with the insight that comes from having lived and worked within the Chinese communist system, while at the same time trying to answer the questions they know will be on the minds of their North American colleagues and students. All who are interested in modern China will benefit from the expertise and insight of the authors.

1

Introduction:
Dilemmas of Development

Andrew J. Nathan

The current moment presents choices for China as dramatic as any that important country has ever faced. As the nation enters a new stage of economic reform more challenging and risky than those that have gone before, the pressure for political change also grows. As Guoguang Wu argues in Chapter 2, until now the ruling Chinese Communist Party has been able to legitimize its rule on the basis of economic performance. But the new phase of economic reform bears a price that must be paid by ordinary people, and thus challenges the legitimacy of Communist Party rule in a new way. Wu's insight sets the theme for all the essays in this volume, which explore from varying perspectives the dilemmas of China's new phase of reform.

No Chinese citizen, at home or abroad, supportive or critical of the regime, takes these dilemmas lightly. While economic reform is imperative and political strains inevitable, no one wishes to see the nation suffer political disorder. Many hope for a transition to democratic institutions; all wish that any transition occur without violence or instability. What choices the government faces—how it should handle the next phase of transition and the key economic policy choices within it—are the questions addressed by the essays in this volume.

This book is distinctive because the contributors are at once Western-based social scientists, with all the objectivity and technical expertise that implies, and in most cases Chinese citizens, with the engagement, insight, and personal involvement such a status brings. The essays have been selected from among those presented at the International Conference on the Fifteenth Communist Party Congress and China's Development, held from November 7 to 9, 1997, in Flushing, New York, under the auspices of the Center for Modern China, the *World Journal*, the China Development Foundation, the "Chinese American Voice" radio station in New York, and the Foundation for China in the 21st Century.

The Center for Modern China, headed by Yizi Chen, sponsors research that brings to bear the expertise of Chinese citizens holding academic appointments in the United States on policy choices facing China. Mr. Chen was director of the Economic System Reform Institute of China in the years leading up to 1989. After the Tiananmen incident of June 4, 1989, he founded the Center for Modern China in Princeton, New Jersey. Despite the intense political disputes over China's future conducted since then within and outside China, Mr. Chen has succeeded in engaging a wide-ranging group of Chinese intellectuals abroad to cooperate with him in conducting research on policy issues facing China. Besides organizing conferences and conducting research projects, the center launched the publication of a widely respected academic and policy-oriented journal, the *Journal of Contemporary China*, which is now independent, and still sponsors a Chinese-language journal, *Dangdai Zhongguo yanjiu* (*Modern China Studies*). The center's funding comes from the National Endowment for Democracy and other foundations.

The conference at which the papers were first presented was convened to discuss the significance of the Fifteenth Congress of the Chinese Communist Party (CCP), held in September 1997, for China's economic, political, social, and economic development. Since this was the first CCP congress after the death of Deng Xiaoping, China's paramount leader for the past twenty years, observers watched it closely for signs of new leadership alignments and for evidence of proposed solutions to China's problems. The congress marked the consolidation of power by Deng's chosen successor, Jiang Zemin, who serves not only as party general secretary but as national president (head of state) and chairman of the Central Military Commission. In his report to the congress, Jiang elevated "Deng Xiaoping Theory" to the status of the party's guiding ideology for the reform period, called for bold steps in the reform of troubled state-owned enterprises (SOEs), and made ambiguous promises about political reform and legal construction. All these developments are analyzed and interpreted in the chapters that follow.

The other leaders around Jiang fit the profile of technocrats. The long-time premier, Li Peng, a conservative, was nearing the end of his term in office at the time of the congress and was soon to be shifted to the less powerful post of chairman of the Standing Committee of the National People's Congress. Jiang's colleague and rival, Zhu Rongji, continued to rise in stature. This forceful economic reformer from Shanghai succeeded Li as premier in March 1998. Several chapters in this volume discuss the backgrounds of these and other leaders and the significance of their shifts in power.

The rest of the world has almost as large a stake in the future of China's reforms as do the Chinese themselves. Economic policy, political institutions, and foreign policy have been linked at every stage of contemporary Chinese history. In 1949, when Mao Zedong set China on a course of economic development through Stalinist-style socialism, it was in an international context of antagonistic relations with the West, while in domestic politics his decision brought in train the construction of a Soviet-style system of party control and state economic planning. Less than a decade later, in 1957, Mao's Great Leap Forward propelled the nation into a new phase of self-reliant, mobilizational autarky. This economic strategy was associated in domestic politics with a system of campaign-based mass mobilization, and in foreign policy with a two-pronged confrontation against both the West and the Soviet Union. In both of these periods, China sacrificed the potential fruits of international economic cooperation for economic and political autonomy and self-reliance.

Deng Xiaoping's domestic economic reforms, his program of limited political liberalization, and his open-door foreign economic policies, all of which began in late 1978, were likewise intimately linked, not merely coincidentally compatible. Deng's strategy was not (and could not have been) to marketize and liberalize the economy while keeping it cut off from the world economy, but to use foreign markets, capital, technology, and management techniques to invigorate the domestic economy, and correspondingly to restructure the domestic economy to make use of its comparative advantage in the world trading system. One can even argue that the open-door foreign policy preceded the domestic economic reform policy, both chronologically and logically. Relaxation of tensions with the West (in effect, starting with Richard Nixon's epochal 1972 visit to China) was a necessary precondition for Deng's reforms from 1978 on, because the reforms involved an easing of domestic discipline and a reshaping of domestic ideology, both premised on a less hostile view of the West. Moreover, the reforms would have been unthinkable without an assurance of access to the technology, capital, and markets of the market economies.

The political requirement for making this new economic orientation and foreign policy work was domestic liberalization in its various dimensions—freeing the peasants to move about the country in search of work, the intellectuals to have slightly greater freedoms, the consumer to purchase, the factory manager to invest, and the technical specialist to make decisions on the basis of expertise rather than politics. These changes, however, fell short of democratization. The sustainability of such a self-limitation is one of the leading issues addressed by contributors to this volume.

Given such intimate links among economic policy, domestic politics, and foreign policy, it is not surprising that decisions on economic change have always raised deep political issues for China. In the early years of Deng's open door, policymakers worried about four problems and often, because of them, resisted the expansion of Deng's policies.[1]

The first was *dependency*, the worry that China was allowing itself to be used as a source for raw materials and labor power, but not being given access to first-rate technology and losing the ability to protect its markets and its producers. Policymakers reflected this concern in the Joint Venture

Law of 1979, which demanded majority Chinese control and top-flight technology transfer; in the policy of Special Economic Zones, which for a time tried to sequester international economic actors in special zones of China; in continued forms of direct and indirect protectionism; and in restricted lists of sectors in which foreign direct investment was permitted. Yet over time most of these fire walls against economic integration fell, and the rest are under attack at home and abroad.

A second concern of policymakers has been overcompromises to Chinese *sovereignty*, as foreigners gained the rights to own (strictly speaking, enter into long-term leases for) Chinese land, hire and fire Chinese workers, and control majority or 100 percent interests in enterprises on Chinese soil. Although there was no revival of the old and much-reviled practice of extraterritoriality (the application of foreign law to foreigners on Chinese soil), China now found that every arrest, trial, and imprisonment of a foreign national brought attention and criticism and often the need to deal more lightly with the foreigner than with a native offender. China found itself revising its laws and even its constitution to meet foreign concerns over copyright protection, nonnationalization of private enterprises, health and safety standards, and so on.

Third, Chinese leaders worried about *economic distortion* to their own priorities in national construction. Critics argued that the open-door policy pushed development in unwanted directions and produced undesired side effects. Some viewed the preferential promotion of foreign direct investment in the coastal regions as harming the interests of the interior as well as the nation's macro-interest in regionally balanced development. Some feared that long-term oil and coal development projects that committed future production for foreign sale threatened the stability of domestic supply. Some deplored the allocation of hard-earned capital to the hotels, transport facilities, and site development needed for tourism. Many worried that the open door encouraged an emphasis on capital-intensive industry that was expensive and did not help to alleviate China's labor surplus.

Finally, many Chinese leaders worried about the *social distortion* introduced by Deng's economic policies. In some ways this has been the most enduring concern. Rightly or wrongly, many perceived corruption as a direct consequence of opening to the outside, rather than a domestically produced ill. Many of the cases exposed in the press were those of officials bribed by foreign or overseas Chinese businessmen. More generally, there was the concern that the open door involved Westernization, the adoption of non-Chinese ways of thinking and living that were the opposite of all that the socialist leaders had sacrificed and fought for. Thus a series of four campaigns from 1981 through the late 1980s opposed "bourgeois liberalization," meaning the introduction of non-Chinese, nonsocialist ways of thinking and living consequent upon the turn to the West and the market.

Less was heard about these worries after Deng Xiaoping's 1992 "Southern tour," which revived the momentum of reform after the setback of the 1989 political crackdown. In his speeches and sayings while visiting the southern open zones, Deng set market reform and the open-door policy beyond political cavil by insisting that policymakers should no longer ask whether a policy was "socialist or capitalist in nature" but whether it served to advance the economy and citizens' economic welfare. Among post-Deng leaders, Jiang Zemin and Zhu Rongji have been resolutely pro–open-door, while even conservatives like Li Peng have refrained from mounting any explicit challenge to the policies sanctified by Deng.

However, Deng's policies alone are unlikely to suffice in the next stage of reform. In Chapter 3, Zhaohui Hong and Yi Sun recommend that the deepening of economic reform be accompanied with a new "ideology of modernization" that combines Chinese cultural beliefs and Western ideas. They counsel that the leaders need to establish an effective legal system to guard against problems such as official corruption, loss of public assets, unemployment, and tax evasion. By reshaping the belief system and reconstructing social order, Hong and Sun believe, the post-Deng leadership has the opportunity to offer China a historic and comprehensive ideological, economic, and political "New Deal."

Part 2 addresses the core of successful economic reform, the long-standing problem of inefficient SOEs. At the Fifteenth Party Congress, the party embarked on an ambitious intensification of reform in this, the most problematic sector of the economy. Experimentation over the course of Deng's reform has proven to the leadership's satisfaction that privatization makes firms more efficient. Shaomin Li explores why this is the case under Chinese conditions. His data demonstrate that state ownership continues to damage firm performance, and that industries owned by local governments are more efficient than those owned by more-protective higher levels of government. Even though privatization of enterprises is the only way to achieve thorough, widespread improvement in performance, ideological resistance remains, and he points out that privatization would also require changes in the legal system that would have rebound effects on political life.

Further addressing the privatization of state enterprises, Guoqiang Tian and Hong Liang argue in favor of full privatization rather than the disguised perpertuation of state ownership through a stock system. The line adopted at the Fifteenth Party Congress was to reform state-owned enterprises through a shareholding system (*gufen zhi*). Tian and Liang believe the reform cannot be effective until individual shareholders hold the controlling shares, and they explain why. However, they worry that the rapid expansion of employees in government organs and agencies may consume the gains from even the most successful SOE reform. They suggest that SOE reform must go hand in hand with a resolution of this problem, or be undertaken in vain.

SOE reform is closely linked with China's posture toward the world economy. To deepen reform in one of these areas requires deepening reform in the other, and by the same token the paralysis will be mutually reinforcing if either SOE reform or integration into the world economy ceases to progress. This logic emerges clearly in Jason Yin's chapter on China's negotiations for entry into the World Trade Organization (WTO). Since initiating the application for membership in 1986, China has reduced SOEs' contribution to industrial output from 62 percent to 30 percent (as of 1996); lowered tariffs from an average 36 percent in 1993 to an average of 17 percent in 1997 with a target of 10 percent in 2005; removed many nontariff barriers, including many import quotas, licenses, export subsidies, and restrictions of foreign trading privileges; improved its policies with regard to "national treatment" (the principle that a country is required to treat foreign products the same as domestic products once they are inside the country); and made significant improvements in the legal provisions for and enforcement of intellectual property rights.

As extensive as they are, these changes are far from having brought China into full interdependence with the world economy. Even though China has jumped to tenth place as a world trading economy with a total import and export value of $325 billion, it remains less of a world trader than Canada ($394 billion), Hong Kong ($397 billion), Japan ($761 billion), Germany ($949 billion), or the United States ($1,578 billion). Even Taiwan, a political unit a fraction of China's size, has a total import and export value of $232 billion. At official numbers, China's foreign trade ratio of 36 percent (in 1990–1994) is only about the same as that of other large developing countries such as Indonesia, Brazil, and Nigeria. But in "purchasing power parity" terms it is less, at about 10 percent of GDP.[2] China is still a mercantilist state with plenty of nonmarket, state-directive tools in its tool kit and an incomplete transition to market norms.

The United States is demanding further reforms as the price of WTO accession: further lowering of tariff rates, further dismantlement of nontariff barriers, further opening of the service sector, and reduction of barriers to foreign investment. Yin argues that the cost of further concessions may not be worth the benefits to be gained. The cost of membership will be paid chiefly by the protected SOEs, which are already in a fragile state and facing the challenges of Zhu Rongji's intensified reforms. Any trade deficits resulting from WTO entry will hurt China's foreign exchange reserves and its financial stability at a time when the Asian financial crisis presents unknowable dangers.

The WTO story remains part of the ongoing story of Chinese concessions made on many fronts as it has joined the world economy, and of the domestic political and human costs of these concessions (which parallel the more often-noted political and human gains). For besides the weakening of China's international autonomy, economic reform today, as in the past, exerts direct and indirect impacts on China's domestic political economy. When one opens former pillar industries—among them steel, automobiles, machinery, electronics, and heavy chemicals—to foreign competition and submits them to the mercies of the international market, the potential impact is great on employment, state tax and profit remittances, and on the banks.

Several of our authors argue that the crises arising from these pressures could eventually make political reform irresistible. Xiaonong Cheng's chapter shows how privatization will hurt the interests of workers, thus undercutting part of the political support for the regime and contributing to a political crisis. Under the long-standing, tacit Chinese social contract, the state protected the interests of many urban residents, most of whom were employed in the state sector, and received their political loyalty in return. Now this arrangement blocks state sector reform by tying political stability to the state's capacity to deliver welfare to the politically strategic industrial working class. If the reconstruction of the state sector is to succeed, it must break this social contract, and, in doing so, it is likely to damage the cooperation between urban people and the regime and undermine political stability.

Cheng's concerns are echoed by Wei Yu in his analysis of the financing of two major urban social welfare programs—unemployment insurance and pension insurance. According to Yu, middle-aged and older workers in SOEs who spent most or all of their working lives during the period of planned economy are now suffering from the economic shortcomings of that system. With few savings and no training for today's job market, they have parents to support and children to raise. Policies on unemployment insurance and insurance for retirement must take this situation into account or face opposition in a crucial sector of society. During the transition from plan to market, however, the financial burden of such insurance is too much for enterprises and local governments to bear. Yu recommends that the national government step in and share the cost, using taxes, SOE assets, or even public debt to finance its share.

Yang Zhong, Jie Chen, and John M. Scheb II confirm the political sensitivity of economic reform by showing on the basis of survey research that Beijing residents tend to base their support for the government on economic performance and worry that economic change will affect their livelihoods. A majority of the people in Beijing have enjoyed improvements in their living conditions and social status during reform. Their high level of life satisfaction leads to relatively high levels of confidence in the future economic development of China. If political support is premised on economic welfare, then a growing body of urban poor, consisting of former employees of bankrupt state-owned enterprises, could be a source of instability for China in the future.

Domestic instability or international tensions will have unpredictable effects on China's reform course. They could lead either to an acceleration of reform, or to its deceleration or abandonment. Despite all the difficulties that it faces, China is probably too far integrated into the world economy to get out easily. The economy has expanded more than fourfold since 1978, in the process lifting 200 million people out of poverty.[3] Only South Korea and Taiwan have comparable records of growth. Having been forced into a wide-ranging change of its economic and political systems by the economic and political crises of the late Mao years, China would not lightly give up what are at least perceived to be and probably are the direct benefits of integration into the world economy.

Yet the lesson of history is that in extremis, China does have the capability to revert to relative autarky. In a "China-threat" scenario in which China was drawn into war or found itself facing active containment, or in an instance of domestic turmoil caused by rapid social change, China does have the capability to reverse its reform course. Its natural resources, technological base, and economic scale and complexity make economic self-reliance a possible although costly option. Alternatively, if reform stalls, China could continue to pursue its current relatively dirigiste economic policies at home and mercantilist policies abroad for an indefinite period into the future.

Assuming the continuing enlargement of the open-door policy and deepening of state enterprise reform, however, as most contributors to this volume do, China still has a variety of options. Part 3 of the book addresses China's choice of macroeconomic strategies for the future. Gene Hsin Chang's contribution shows that the leadership group in charge of the economy today was formed starting in 1992, and that it consists for the first time in Chinese history of economists knowledgeable about modern market systems and international finance. In light of this personnel continuity, Chang expects post-Deng economic policies to continue in the spirit of the policies since 1992. Macroeconomic policies will be cautious enough to maintain economic stability while aiming at a growth rate adequate to provide jobs. The objectives of a GDP growth rate of 8–9 percent and an inflation rate of 4–6 percent for the coming decade are challenging, according to Chang, but not impossible.

The contribution by C. W. Kenneth Keng points to the geographic unevenness of development under the reforms. Growth under reform has created nine regional economies that he thinks are likely to consolidate into four. To the often-asked question of whether reform leads to regionalization or integration, Keng in effect answers "both"—in fact, the two trends are not in conflict. Like Europe, greater China will be both one and many, integrated to differing degrees at different geographic levels. One important implication of this argument is that continued fast growth presents an opportunity to solve the vexing problem of Taiwan's relations to the mainland. In a high-growth scenario Taiwan will face powerful incentives to integrate its economy with those of Fujian and Guangdong, thus conceivably dissolving the political suspicions of the past. Keng suggests a number of institutional models that could accommodate this kind of multiregional politico-economic relationship.

The contributors to this volume are by no means unified in either their prognoses or their proposals for China's future. Some express pessimistic attitudes toward the political dilemmas of economic reform, while others more optimistically suggest ways that these dilemmas can be alleviated. While all the authors who address SOE reform believe in privatization, they differ in their judgment about the speed with which the transition from a mixed property rights regime should be accomplished.

What most worries China's citizens and foreign friends alike is how China's navigation of the shoals of economic reform will affect its fragile political system. Even if it hews to its present course, it is by no means clear that China is heading toward capitalist democracy. That is the globalist, optimistic orthodoxy in the world today that lies behind the approving commentaries on the op-ed pages and many of the programs in support of reform mounted by governments and foundations worldwide. But the alternative is that economic reform will lead China into "communist corporatism," a Chinese version of the Japanese and Korean *chaebol* economy in which the government works hand in hand with a small number of favored conglomerates to promote national economic interests abroad and elite political control at home. Indeed, a major plank of Zhu Rongji's reform plan is to concentrate state resources on the five hundred largest state firms, aiding them with favorable interest rates, protection against import competition, tax and price concessions, preferential access to supplies, and protection from unofficial fiscal levies. While our contributors all support bold forward movement on China's reform course, some worry that the regime may at some point respond to its political choices with intensified repression.

Against this prospect, the contributors offer a variety of suggestions for assuring that China's leap into the future ends in an economic and political soft landing. Their recommendations include re-ideologization (Hong and Sun), improvement of state-society relations (Cheng), political democracy (Wu), property rights reform (Li, Tian, and Liang), social welfare reform (Yu), and regional economic integration (Keng). Such thinking is informed by and influences debates going on within China. While we cannot predict what choices the leaders will make, the essays in this volume offer a sense of the options that thoughtful Chinese see before them.

Notes

1. See Andrew J. Nathan, *China's Crisis: Dilemmas of Reform and Prospects for Democracy* (New York: Columbia University Press, 1990), chapter 3.

    2. World Bank, *China Engaged: Integration with the World Economy* (Washington, DC: World Bank, 1997), p. 6.
    3. World Bank, *China 2020: Development Challenges in the New Century* (Washington, DC: World Bank, 1997), p. 1.

PART 1

The Party Congress
and China's Dilemmas

2

Legitimacy Crisis, Political Economy, and the Fifteenth Party Congress

Guoguang Wu

Designated as the "highest decisionmaking body," the Congress of the Chinese Communist Party (CCP), which meets every five years, is always an important event and its pronouncements can indicate China's direction. It also allows China watchers to probe into the behind-door politics in Zhongnanhai. The Fifteenth Congress of the CCP, held in September 1997, represents three "transitions." First, it marks a generational transition as no Long March and Civil War revolutionaries were elected to the Central Committee at this Congress.[1] Second, the death of Deng Xiaoping in February 1997 brought the transition of political power into its final stage, which was settled at this party congress. The succession of power in China has never been easy or insignificant; a shift in leadership could bring about abrupt changes of policy.[2] The third transition is the transition from communism, a change presented as economic reform. In the past, reform has meant the transition from the state-planning economy to the market economy, while political liberalization and democratization were deliberately postponed.[3] Calls for comprehensive political reform and democratization, however, have never disappeared though they have often been suppressed. Just on the eve of the Fifteenth Congress, they arose again to challenge the will and the resolution of the government and party on this critical issue.[4]

How did the Fifteenth Party Congress manage these transitions? Did the party congress map any guidelines for the future? Various interpretations have been presented in the English-speaking media. The pessimistic perspective concludes that this party congress failed "both politically and economically," and that it was a "disappointment."[5] Others see a bright picture in reading party chief Jiang Zemin's report to the congress. The latter perspective regards the reform measures proposed by the general secretary of the CCP as "the boldest economic transition attempted by Beijing since the early 1980s," as the *New York Times* commented in an editorial, although, at the same time, it realized that "Mr. Jiang and his party colleagues showed no parallel interest in political liberalization."[6] Similarly, the *Washington Post* found that the policies Jiang embraced "go well be-yond the market reforms identified with the late Deng Xiaoping and bear the stamp of capitalism at its rawest."[7] One commentator said "Mr. Jiang's speech was still a big step in the right direction. It constituted a remarkable acceptance of the realities of the modern world and the globalization process."[8]

This chapter offers political-economy analysis of the reform policies endorsed by the party congress, roughly defining "political economy" as the interrelationship between the political and the economic affairs of the state.[9] In terms of the generational transition, the Fifteenth Party Congress faced the problem of how to treat Deng's legacy, which is a combination of economic liberalization and political suppression. Similarly, in the transition of power, Deng's successor must be capable of convincing not only the party, but also the country and the world, that the new leadership is able to deal with the gap between the political and the economic realms. Finally, this political-economic relationship is certainly the most challenging aspect of the transition from communism. This transition in China differs from that in the former Soviet Union and other former communist countries in Eastern Europe where democratic revolutions and rapid economic marketizations occurred simultaneously; the Chinese communist regime sustains itself in liberalizing its economy.

How can the Chinese communist regime maintain its legitimacy in economic liberalization? According to the classification by Max Weber, there are three major types of legitimate domination. His theory states that

> The validity of the claims to legitimacy may be based on: 1. Rational grounds—resting on a belief in the legality of enacted rules and the right of those elevated to authority under such rules to issue command (legal authority). 2. Traditional grounds—resting on an established belief in the sanctity of immemorial traditions and the legitimacy of those exercising authority under them (traditional authority); or finally. 3. Charismatic grounds—resting on devotion to the exceptional sanctity, heroism or exemplary character of an individual person, and of the normative patterns or order revealed or ordained by him (charismatic authority).[10]

In addition to these three types, in Third World countries, legitimacy is often based on economic performance.[11]

This chapter argues that the political legitimacy of the Chinese regime is shifting from the communist revolution and revolutionary ideology to the regime's economic performance. The further transition of legitimacy from economic development to what Weber called "rational grounds" has not occurred, creating a crisis of legitimacy for the CCP's party-state system. The Fifteenth Party Congress did more to create a paradox than to offer an answer to the problem of legitimacy. The party congress charis-matized Deng and ideologized his legacy by "upholding the banner" of the so-called Deng Xiaoping Theory, in order to resist political reform and democratization. Yet, such reform could lead China to stability with rationalized authority. As always, the regime with the Dengist mentality sees political reform as dangerous to a stable political environment, which is regarded as a precondition to the expected economic performance. The party congress showed that the CCP is not capable of dealing with the two sides of the paradox at the same time. In terms of political restructuring, the party clearly understands the importance of authority and, accordingly, the importance of stability, state capacities, and the role of the government in socioeconomic transition, but the problem of legitimate authority was ignored.

To develop the above argument in detail, this chapter is divided into three sections corresponding to themes addressed at the party congress. First, the official claim of the congress making Deng Xiaoping Theory the "soul," the "banner," and "guiding ideology to action" of the CCP is examined. It will be interpreted as an effort to make Deng a new spokesman of communist ideology and a charismatic leader who laid down the basis for the current reform policies. This effort, however, is self-contradictory, because authentic Marxist ideology is anticapitalist, while it was Deng who led China toward capitalist development and it is his "theory," if there is such a thing, that offers to stimulate China's economic liberalization. Why does the CCP ignore this contradiction? The secret lies in its thirst for legitimacy: on the one hand, it needs an ideological weapon, which is traditionally powerful for mobilizing the Communist Party; on the other hand, the legitimacy of the current regime is becoming more and more dependent on its economic performance and, accordingly, its policies of promoting economic liberalization, which need to be defended by ideologizing Deng Xiaoping Theory, which is nothing more than a pragmatist doctrine stressing economic development.

The second section will focus on the policy of state-owned enterprise reform, which is widely thought to be the most important policy initiative of the congress. "Privatization," it seems, will be introduced. Can the policy meet the challenges facing China in economic transition? Even though the reform of state-owned enterprises is not simply privatization in the Western meaning, it does seem to contradict traditional Marxism. But this reform, which has already been conducted for several years without full ideological justification, has encountered serious difficulties. Since the overall reform program began two decades ago, the "soft meat" of the economy has already been eaten and now it is the "hard bones" that are left for the next meal. Why did the party congress choose the strategy of "eating bones" in the economy rather than taking cautious but substantial measures to reform political institutions, which lag behind economic reform? The answer is that economic performance is so critical for the regime to sustain its legitimate authority that it has to take risks both in ideological contradiction and in an attempt to produce better economic achievements. Political reform, however, could be dangerous in terms of stimulating political instability and threatening the CCP's power. Even though political reform could bear fruit, the fruit could be bitter to the CCP itself while benefiting the country as a whole.

Finally, the discussion will turn to the Fifteenth Party Congress's policy of political reform. The regime still pays more attention to stability than to a political system that can match and support the economy. The congress, however, did respond in its way to the calls for political reform and even to those for democratization. But it did so by offering lip service instead of substantial measures. By talking about "rule by law" and "socialist democracy," the leadership managed to avoid critical issues like the reevaluation of the 1989 Tiananmen crackdown and democratization of the CCP's own internal political life. With the rise of technocracy in the leadership,[12] the party congress took a technocratic approach rather than a political one.

Dengist Marxism or De-Marxism?
De-ideologization Based on Re-ideologization

Deng, who dominated politics for almost two decades before his death in February 1997, was perhaps the only person who lacked ideological and theoretical concerns among the first-rank communist leaders: Lenin, Stalin, Mao, and others. Ironically, at the party congress held six months after his death, Deng was finally worshipped as a great theoretical contributor to Marxist-Leninist ideology. According to the official description by the CCP itself, the most distinctive characteristic of this congress was its ideological legitimization of the political legacy of Deng. In the first paragraph of his report to the congress on behalf of the Fourteenth Central Committee, General Secretary Jiang opened his three-hour speech with these words:

> The theme of the congress is to hold high the great banner of Deng Xiaoping Theory for an all-round advancement of the cause of building socialism with Chinese characteristics into the 21st century. The issue of the banner is of the utmost importance. The banner represents our orientation and image. . . . After the death of Comrade Deng Xiaoping, it is all the more necessary for the whole Party to keep a high level of consciousness and staunchness on this issue.[13]

Jiang's speech devoted several pages to the "historical status and guiding significance" of Deng Xiaoping Theory, defining that theory with Marxism-Leninism and Mao Zedong Thought together as the "guiding ideology" of the party. Jiang compared Deng Xiaoping Theory with Mao Zedong Thought in this way:

The integration of Marxism-Leninism with China's reality has experienced two historic leaps, resulting in two great theories. The result of the first leap was the theoretical principles concerning the revolution and construction in China. . . . Its principal founder being Mao Zedong, our Party has called it Mao Zedong Thought. The result of the second leap was the theory of building socialism with Chinese characteristics. Its principal founder being Deng Xiaoping, our Party has called it Deng Xiaoping Theory.[14]

Accordingly, the party congress approved an amendment to the party constitution, adding Deng as one of the guides to action. Explaining this addition, the congress stated,

The Chinese Communists, with Comrade Deng Xiaoping as their chief representative, have reviewed the experience gained through their successes and failures since the founding of the People's Republic, emancipated their minds, sought truth from facts, shifted the focus of the work of the whole Party to economic development, introduced reform and opened China to the outside world, thus ushering in a new period of development of the socialist course. They have gradually formulated the line, principles and policies for building socialism with Chinese characteristics, expounded the fundamental issues concerning how to build, consolidate and develop socialism in China and created Deng Xiaoping Theory.[15]

It emphasized that this theory is "a product of the integration of the fundamental tenets of Marxism-Leninism with the practice in present-day China and the features of the times and is a continuation and development of Mao Zedong Thought under the new historical conditions."[16]

Making Deng Xiaoping Theory a guiding ideology was paralleled to defining Mao Zedong Thought as the "guiding ideology" at the Seventh Party Congress. The Fifteenth Congress defined Mao Thought as the "integration of the theory of Marxism-Leninism with the practice of the Chinese revolution" and the Deng Theory a "continuation and development of Mao Zedong Thought." It explained that Deng's theory "had been tested in practice for nearly 20 years during the reform and opening-up."[17]

Those statements cited above are enough to stimulate discussion: Why did the CCP make such great efforts to ideologize the ideas and policies of Deng? Do those statements make sense for the CCP, which is experiencing and even leading a capitalist revolution? The answer seems to be that when the CCP says, "Marxism-Leninism, Mao Zedong Thought, and Deng Xiaoping Theory constitute a unified scientific system," it is trying to use traditional communist ideological weapons to defend projects of capitalistization. It may seem illogical, but it works against both the so-called Leftists and Rightists. In the claim that "in present-day China adhering to Deng Xiaoping Theory means genuinely adhering to Marxism-Leninism and Mao Zedong Thought; holding high the banner of Deng Xiaoping Theory means genuinely holding high the banner of Marxism-Leninism and

Mao Zedong Thought," one can find an ideological dilemma faced by Deng and Jiang as political leaders and by the CCP: de-ideologization based on ideologization, reforms rooted in dogmas.

Before Deng's death, Jiang once signaled a left turn by resuming "talking politics,"[18] which seemed to signal a move away from the "central point" of the Dengist line of "putting emphasis on economic construction." Also, in discussing the "twelve great relationships" in late 1995 in an effort to outline his own policy,[19] Jiang embraced Mao's way of thinking,[20] while affirming his intention of keeping the balance between Deng's policies and Deng's Leftist critics. The latter, however, soon showed their opposition to the central authority endorsed by Deng, to Jiang himself as its "core," and to the legitimate position of Jiang as the interpreter of Marxist-Leninist ideology. When a series of "ten-thousand-character letters" attacking the Dengist reforms were circulated among high-ranking officials in late 1996, they attracted attention both overseas and at home as a signal for a possible post-Deng debate over current policies.[21] These activities apparently threatened the position of Jiang as the "core" of the current leadership and accordingly as the highest authoritative spokesman for interpreting official ideology, forcing Jiang to make a slight right turn to distance himself from the Leftists. When China's central television (CCTV) chose to broadcast a biographic documentary of Deng in early 1997, it seemed that Jiang had made up his mind to stand firmly with Deng. When Deng died in February, Jiang's change was more obvious than before. In the official documents of mourning for Deng, both Jiang himself and the CCP (now that Jiang was the real leader of its organizations) praised the dead patriarch.[22]

This can be read as a preface to Jiang's report to the Fifteenth Party Congress. As the death of Deng in February 1997 and the Fifteenth Party Congress in September are among the most important events in recent Chinese domestic politics, montages could organize the two together like this: at the same place, the People's Great Hall in Beijing, Jiang's tearful face at Deng's funeral turned into the same face at the party congress, but this time with a smile. Praising the dead leader brought Jiang a remarkable harvest. By making Deng Xiaoping Theory the "guiding ideology" of the CCP, Jiang ensured his position as the successor to Deng, both in terms of exercising political power as *a* leading figure among his comrades and of interpreting official ideology as *the* spokesman of the party.

Further, for the CCP and its current leadership, Jiang being its core, this action of ideologization of Deng Theory was a rediscovery of traditional weapons to strengthen the party's legitimacy. First, it again mobilized ideological resources, which are always significant for a communist revolutionary party but which had been dormant for a long time under the economic-centered approach of Deng himself. Second, it helped to charismatize Deng, expanding another resource for the authority of the CCP party-state, which also had been scarce since the death of Mao. As Franz Schurmann defines it in his now-classic study of Chinese communist politics, an ideology is a "systematic set of ideas with action consequences serving the purpose of creating and using organization."[23] The strong organization of the CCP was created long ago, but now, just after and because of Deng's reform, there was a question of how to use this organizational system. Deng's strategy to decrease the importance of ideology had brought about "emancipation of the mind" and, accordingly, the weakening of control over the organization. Now Jiang has had to take the strategy of re-ideologization for reorganizing, mobilizing, and, ideally for him, revitalizing the party.

Re-ideologization, however, can be harmful to economic liberalization, which the party is taking on, and therefore the improvement in economic performance, which the party is seeking passionately. Ideologization, with emphasis on Deng Xiaoping Theory, thus became the choice to the Fifteenth Party Congress.

During the past twenty years, Dengist reform has already had serious negative effects, as well as more positive ones. Governmental corruption, the increasing gap between the rich and the poor, and uneven development of the East Coast areas and the inner regions are the most frequently mentioned and condemned. Those problems and the brutal crackdown on student demonstrations at Tiananmen Square in 1989 have made the legacy of Deng controversial. To ideologize this legacy is one way to eliminate obstacles for insisting on Deng's line.

At the same time, the ideologization of Deng Xiaoping Theory further eliminates obstacles for Jiang. This sounds contradictory, but it is not. Franz Schurmann made a distinction between "pure ideology" and "practical ideology." "Pure ideology," according to Schurmann, "is a set of ideas designed to give the individual a unified and conscious world view." In contrast, "practical ideology is a set of ideas designed to give the individual rational instruments for action." He argues that "without pure ideology, the ideas of practical ideology have no legitimization. But without practical ideology an organization cannot transform its *Weltanschauung* into consistent action."[24] Did Deng Theory become "pure" or "practical ideology" at the party congress?[25] Either way, Jiang enlarged his room for action in the future. Taking Deng Theory as "pure ideology," the CCP could take a pragmatic perspective, leaving wide room for action. If it is "practical" ideology, practical Marxism in China would be Marxism "without Marx," as predicted by some Western scholars.[26] China would have developed Dengist Marxism. Jiang felt the necessity of creating his own "practical ideology" instead of Deng Xiaoping Theory. He told the congress, "the task we are undertaking is a new one. Marx did not speak of it, our predecessors did not do it, and other socialist countries have not done it. We can only study as we act, to find our way through practice."[27] This implies that Jiang and his comrades need to find a new way other than those developed by Marx, Lenin, Mao, and Deng. The function of Dengist Marxism, which could be read as De-Marxism, is to offer legitimacy to the CCP while resisting the fundamentalist criticism from the authentic perspective of communist ideology.

Better Economic Performance, for Whom?
The Dilemma of SOE Reform

The CCP and its leadership understand that ideology, while not as powerful as it once was, is still useful in mobilizing legitimate resources. In fact, ideology can be harmful to good economic performance, which is the critical legitimate resource the regime rests on today. The party does not really want to use the virtues of capitalism to "save China," but to use those virtues as the remedy to save the state-owned enterprises (SOEs), which have become an unbearable burden for the government, even while the economy generally has performed well over the past several years. It is reported that about 70 percent of more than 100,000 SOEs are losing money, and the losses have been growing steadily.[28]

To remedy this, the CCP took a "bold step" at the party congress by introducing the "cooperative share holding system" for privatizing the SOEs. Only a year ago, the experts both overseas and at home expected that privatization of SOEs was ideologically unacceptable to the regime.[29] But scholars underestimated the CCP's need to break out of the restriction of ideology for the sake of better economic performance. In late May 1997, Jiang delivered a speech at the Central Party School and, for the first time, approved privatizing the SOEs.[30] It was regarded as "extremely important" and as the so-called third wave of emancipation of the mind ("*di san ci sixiang jiefang*").[31] The initiation of reforms and the open-door policy in the late 1970s were the first wave, and the south China tour of Deng in 1992 was the second. As Deng's trip called for ending the debate over "socialism versus capitalism" (*xing she xing zi*), now the government thought that it already had the conclusion for the polemics over "public versus private" (*xing gong xing si*) ownership of properties,[32] indicating that the reformers achieved a triumph in adapting private ownership into the revisionist concept of "public ownership." Through a complicated process of negotiating within the CCP itself and with other interest groups, Jiang's report to the party congress confirmed the position presented in his Party School speech in a modest way. Local cadres commented, with some disappointment, that Jiang's report to the party congress was not so "bold and open" as his speech to the Party School.[33] Still, Jiang announced in the report to the congress:

> Public ownership can and should take diversified forms. All management
> methods and organizational forms that mirror the laws governing social-
> ized production may be utilized boldly. We should strive to seek various
> forms for materializing public ownership that can greatly promote the
> growth of the productive forces. The joint stock system is a form of capi-
> tal organization of modern enterprises, which is favorable for separating
> ownership from management and raising the efficiency of the operation of
> enterprises and capital. It can be used both under capitalism and socialism.
> We cannot say in general that the joint stock system is public or private.[34]

In this way, Jiang redefined the nature of "public ownership" and
"public sector." As one Chinese economist put it, "The reform started with
no intention of abolishing public ownership. But, it has been directed by a
new doctrine which potentially conflicts with the conventional doctrine of
public ownership."[35] According to one vice-minister, the CCP "believes diversified ownership is the public sector's way out." China used to define
public ownership as state and collective ownership. "Despite a projected
decline in state ownership, collective ownership, rather than private investment, will continue to dominate China's economy, maintaining socialist principles." This official denied that China was going to privatize its
economy, but, according to an official news weekly, the official compared
China with Britain because "Britain is internationally renowned for its successful privatization drive during the 1980s and 1990s" and "analysts believe China and Britain have much in common."[36]

Whether those arguments are plausible or not, for the working class
such a reform program holds a miserable prospect: under the proletarian
dictatorship, many of the workers, theoretically the masters of the country,
will be fired. To end the losses means cutting back on extra workers and
trimming their costly cradle-to-grave benefits, known as the "iron rice
bowl." According to *The Washington Post,* about 30 percent of China's
113 million industrial workers are no longer needed.[37] *The New York Times*
has reported that "more than 100 million jobs are at stake in the state-
owned businesses that will be up for sale." "Workers at many companies
are suddenly finding themselves obliged to buy shares if they want to keep
their jobs, and once government support disappears they could be left with
nothing if their factories collapse."[38] A Hong Kong magazine estimated
that roughly 30 million surplus industrial workers could lose their jobs and
that those who remain can forget about receiving lifelong social benefits
free of charge.[39] Also, the Chinese government labor forecasts admitted in
May 1997 that, during the current five-year economic plan, those laid-off
workers would have to compete with 72 million new job seekers and 40
million rural laborers flooding into the cities.[40]

Successful SOE reform will inevitably create a challenge, particularly to
what the regime desires most: political stability. Increased unemployment
is already creating social unrest. Worker protests occurred while the party

congress was pushing forward the reform of the money-losing SOEs,[41] even though President Jiang told them: "Workers should change their ideas about employment." According to *The Washington Post,*

> Protests (of unpaid workers) have spread throughout the country, and several more ominous incidents have involved workers who feel cheated by the government and left behind by China's economic miracle—incidents that may portend what lies ahead as China continues restructuring state enterprises.[42]

Meanwhile, the newly rich are rising in the socioeconomic skyline of "socialism." Many of those who have gotten rich because of earlier reforms are now investing overseas, creating capital flight.[43] While capital inflows have grown dramatically over the past decade, a large portion of this capital has left the country in the form of capital flight. This is one of many financial problems facing China. When a nonmainstream economist criticized the current prosperity as the "banquet of the powerful," she was warning that the gap between the rich and the poor is growing wider.[44] Although supporting liberalization and privatization of the economy, she concluded that further economic reform would lead to the pitfalls of early capitalism.

For the government, money is also a problem. As many have realized, the key elements in the changing approach to reform since 1992 have been the role of banks and credit, the restructuring of the pricing mechanism, and the ongoing development of an effective taxation system.[45] Premier Zhu Rongji revealed soon after the party congress that the connection between SOE reform and the financial situation was critical both for SOE reform itself and for the economy as a whole. At the Fifty-Sixth Meeting of the Development Committee of the World Bank and the International Monetary Fund in Hong Kong in late September 1997, while repeatedly stressing that "the focus of our present economic restructuring is the reform of State-owned enterprises," Zhu added that "the reform of the financial system and the reform of the State-owned enterprises are of great significance to building a socialist market economy in China." According to an official weekly, reform would focus on "strengthening the central bank's currency regulation function and its financial supervisory system, increasing the autonomy of commercial banks, and improving market regulations, the legal system and management." It cited Zhu's comment that "our goal is to gradually institute an efficient and reliable modern financial system."[46]

This represents a slight move away from the focus on SOE reform. Zhu, who once successfully cooled China's overheated economy, now faces the challenge of a possible financial crisis. As observers have noted, the economy shows some of the symptoms of those Asian economies that suffered financial crises—an oversupplied property market, a debt-ridden banking sector, a manufacturing base squeezed by overcapacity and rising fixed costs, and an economy generally hampered by corruption and crony-ism.[47] So far China has avoided the serious financial crisis facing its neigh-bors. Foreign investment continues and much of that is invested for long-term return. The currency, *renminbi,* is not yet convertible on the capital account, and the exchange rate remains strictly government-controlled and defended by over $130 billion in foreign exchange reserves. But, since the monetary upheaval that shook Hong Kong in late October 1997, the Chi-nese government has worried about its own financial situation.[48] Further, the whole economic situation is not as bright as the government reports.[49]

In interpreting the relationship between capitalist development and the communist state, scholars have observed that there is no conflict between the two. Instead, they have highlighted the role of the party-state in eco-nomic structural change.

> It is the party-state which is setting the agenda and leading the way, both economically and socio-politically. A crucial part of that process is de-rived from the party-state's general concentration of infrastructural power. In exercising that power the party-state must emphasize the inter-dependence of government and business, even as the party-state has moved from direct to indirect control and management.[50]

The prominent role of the state in economic development and the close connection between government and business create a dilemma of political economy. Particularly in SOE reform, the state itself is the capitalist who confronts the interests of workers, not merely as the representative of the capitalists under typical capitalist arrangements, as Marxist political econ-omy argues. Further, as urgent matters such as financial reform occupy the governmental agenda, the real suffering of the workers is often neglected. The socialist state becomes the agent of making profits, which implies a resource for its own legitimacy.

As one scholar commented, "When Mr. Jiang's report to the congress made much of the fact that China was at 'the primary stage of socialism,' China was in reality admitting the virtues of its capitalism. . . . When shareholding is described as socialism, there is no limit to how capitalist China can become."[51] Meanwhile capitalism is bringing suffering to the workers. The dominant virtue now is not to "save China," but to "save" the Communist Party, which, as its congress demonstrated, is now dominated by the privileged groups who have benefited from economic liberalization without political constraints.

One Step Forward, Two Steps Back:
Political Reform or Politics of Un-Reform?

Economic liberalization unavoidably produced political consequences, the main one of which has been the loss of power by the state. That is why commentators say, "Even when Jiang Zemin wins, he loses," as *Far Eastern Economic Review* has put it. "In the run-up to the just-ended Fifteenth Party Congress, the Chinese president had been compared unfavorably with his predecessors for his ability to dictate the direction of both China and its ruling Communist Party. The irony is that if Mr. Jiang succeeds with his economic reforms, he and his successors will find themselves with even less power," for Jiang and his allies "have drafted an unequivocal condemnation of June 4, 1989, laid down a roadmap to a democratic China."[52] Western media urged Jiang to seize the chance, after Deng died, "to make policy decisions without nervously glancing over his shoulders," and to lead China into a new era of reform and extend it to the political sphere as well.[53]

Calls to reevaluate the June Fourth event in 1989, in which demonstrators for democracy in Beijing were attacked by the military with tanks and machine guns, did not come only from overseas. The painful topic almost made the agenda of the Fifteenth Party Congress. On the eve of the congress, some representatives to the congress were reported to have issued an open appeal to free from house arrest Zhao Ziyang, the former party chief who was ousted by the hard-liners because of his push for political reform and his sympathy with the 1989 democracy movement.[54] On September 15, 1997, the day the congress opened, Zhao himself reportedly sent an open letter to the central leadership and the congress, suggesting a reevaluation of the Tiananmen event.[55] Memories of Tiananmen, cautiously managed by the regime as irrelevant to current politics, thus again emerged onto the national agenda. Soon after the party congress, Jiang talked about "mistakes" when he answered a question about Tiananmen at Harvard University during his tour of the United States. This was regarded as a hint that he might be moving toward a different view of the crackdown,[56] even though the leadership, of which he is the core, refused to review the tragedy during the course of the congress.

Jiang also spoke sympathetically of democracy when he visited Washington. According to the American media, he told the Asia Society there that China would "expand democracy, improve the legal system, run the country according to law and build a socialist country under the law," promising that his country would "further enlarge democracy." Actually, Jiang was repeating his own words in the report to the Fifteenth Party Congress, where he used the term "democracy" or "democratic" thirty-one times in the section entitled "Reforming Political Structure and Strengthening Democracy and the Legal System." Jiang announced that "it is our Party's persistent goal to develop socialist democracy. Without democracy there would be no socialism or socialist modernization. The essence of socialist democracy is that the people are the masters of the country. All powers of the state belong to the people."[57] "We will ensure that our people hold democratic elections, make policy decisions democratically, carry out democratic management and supervision, and enjoy extensive rights and freedoms under the law."[58]

The president's speech sounded good for democratization and democracy, but this does not mean that the CCP now approves democratic reform. First, Jiang's report did not suggest any substantive measures to restructure the authoritarian political system. Comparing this report with the report made by Zhao to the Thirteenth Party Congress, held ten years ago and at which political reform was a major theme, besides repeating some of Zhao's words about the general meaning of democracy, Jiang also referred to several of Zhao's proposals, including dividing power between the Communist Party, the state, and the economic and social entities, decentralizing administrative power from the national government to local governments and further to economic and social organizations, restricting the role of the CCP's grass-roots organizations, conducting dialogues between the party-state and society, making the decisionmaking processes open to the people, and making trade unions independent of the party-state system. All of those were proposed to the Thirteenth Party Congress, and some of them were put into practice before 1989. In addition, the Thirteenth Congress introduced a series of concrete measures to reform elections, media reporting on state activities, and personnel management, stressing the bottom-up supervision of government officials. Zhao had also criticized the political system, pointing out that its shortcomings were rooted in the communist revolution and the campaigns for "socialist remaking."[59] In Jiang's report, however, slogans replaced measures, and generalities were sounded instead of concrete means of democratization. Jiang indeed emphasized many times that the party and the government "must" do something to improve "supervision" and "efficiency." But, how could one force the powerful party-state system to do that without any institutional reform? There has been no answer to this question.

Instead, political suppression has been strengthened under "talking about political reform and democracy." For example, the policy toward dissidents has not changed, as foreign reporters have observed.[60] Zhao, who was prime minister for ten years and who contributed to economic liberalization and development, is now under strict control, and has lost his previously limited freedom of privately meeting friends.[61] A correspondent for *The New York Times* concluded that

> a central paradox of China today is that such strict political limitations coincide with a tremendous expansion of personal freedom in recent years. Economic growth has brought an ever-wider array of choices when it comes to a job, a place of residence or a spouse—all areas where the Communist Party authorities once wielded near-absolute control.[62]

The U.S. State Department concluded in 1997, the year of the party congress, that open dissent in China had been crushed.[63]

All of this once again shows that the central concern in the political domain is stability rather than change. But it is fair to say that the CCP has never tried to hide this. In his report to the Fifteenth Party Congress, Jiang stressed this point again:

> In the primary stage of socialism, it is of the utmost importance to balance reform, development and stability and maintain a stable political environment and public order. Without stability, nothing could be achieved. We must uphold the leadership of the Party and the people's democratic dictatorship. We should promote material progress and cultural and ethical progress, attaching equal importance to both. We must eliminate all factors jeopardizing stability, oppose bourgeois liberalization and guard against the infiltrating, subversive and splittist activities of international and domestic hostile forces.[64]

If one asks how to achieve this desired stability, the CCP would give no other answer but to continue the methods practiced over the last nine years: to tighten control over media, dissidents, and any factors that would lead to social unrest. The post-Deng leadership did not abandon this authoritarian approach to stability, even though it talked about democracy.

Besides the issues of democratization and the reevaluation of the June Fourth incident, a more realistic question for the party congress was: Without political reform, how can the CCP obtain enough popular support for the painful economic reforms such as SOE reforms? The dilemma, a reflection of the legitimacy paradox, is that the CCP depends more than ever on economic performance to sustain its legitimacy, but the party has less legitimacy than ever for creating satisfying performance. In the East Asian miracle of economic development, the state has played an active and capable role for managing economic intervention in guiding development domestically and in managing economic relations externally.[65] This capacity is rooted in external political alliances, domestic authoritarian rule, and effective economic institutions.[66] China has been taking this path since the Deng era. Despite the possible conceptual challenges to these arguments posed by the East Asian financial crises, can the Chinese regime enjoy an alliance with the West? Does it have effective economic institutions? Besides domestic authoritarian rule, it seems that the regime lacks what it needs even for the purpose of better economic performance.

When Lenin discussed "one step forward, two steps back," he used a subtitle to remind his comrades of "the crisis in our party."[67] Without a substantive policy of political reform, the party congress really indicated that the CCP faced the crisis of dealing with the real problems of China, which include governmental corruption, unfair economic competition by the involvement of officials who are abusing their power, and the increasing gap between the rich and the poor. Any proposal short of political reform could not reduce the seriousness of the problems, but the CCP would not carry out such reform in order to maintain political stability. Taking this "technocratic, bureaucratic approach" to policymaking, rather than a "political approach" through which policies are shaped by economic and political demands from different sectors of society, expressed through such channels as elections, legislatures, political parties, and labor unions,[68] the party congress made the choice to *not* reform the political system to match the reformed economic system due to political reasons; the politics of un-reform overwhelmed political reform.

A Marxist approach to the relationship between politics and the economy, which is the official approach, will certainly not endorse this choice. Marxist political economy criticizes the Western classical interpretation of the relationship between politics and the economy, which argues for the capacity of markets to regulate them and is identified with the policy of laissez-faire. "Their argument for market self-regulation treated the market system as a reality *sui generis*, connected to, but not a subsidiary organ of, the state."[69] Marxist political economy, however, argues that the state is a part of the superstructure, the political shell of the means of production that is ultimately responsive to the economic base.[70] Advocates of political reform often cite this basic argument of Marxism to support their position.[71] The government, however, ignores this "basic principle" while still claiming to uphold the Marxist banner. As suggested earlier, Deng Xiaoping Theory is, at most, half-Marxist. It is Marxist in terms of stressing the role of the state in moving the economic transition forward, but it is obviously not Marxist when it separates politics from the economy and procrastinates on the reform of the former. When Jiang announced that the CCP would carry high the banner of Deng Xiaoping Theory, he carried on the legacy of Dengist Marxism or De-Marxism. In fact, he was even bolder than Deng in pushing forward economic privatization while postponing the political reform.

Conclusions

In a widely circulated joke in China, President Bill Clinton of the United States and his Russian and Chinese counterparts, Boris Yeltsin and Jiang Zemin, were each driving down a road. When they reached a crossroads, Clinton gave a turn-right signal and made a right turn; so did Yeltsin. But Jiang hesitated and asked his passenger, Deng, who was sitting beside the driver, which way to go. Deng answered: "Signal left, and turn right."

The Fifteenth Party Congress did not resolve this duality of mentality and policies in the legacy of Deng; it only tried to legitimize it. The party congress, the first to be dominated by Jiang himself, served as a psychodrama for the CCP by attempting to integrate and streamline the duality by ideologizing the so-called Deng Xiaoping Theory. Ideally for the CCP leadership, this re-equipment with Dengist ideology could open a way to mobilize, again, the ideological resources for maintaining the party organization at work but not interrupting the CCP's ongoing programs of "four modernizations." Now with Deng enshrined in the temple of communism, the CCP could have a powerful defender for its current policy in the ideological battles against Stalinist fundamentalists.

Yet, there is a critical paradox in the work of congress. The paradox lies in the contradiction between the CCP's efforts to reestablish its traditional resources for legitimate authority, namely, revolutionary ideology and leaders' charisma, and its ad hoc resting of legitimacy on the regime's achievements of better economic performance, which offers a new kind of substantive resource for the CCP to maintain political stability and to survive in power. Better economic performance requires the CCP to go beyond Marxist-Leninist ideology, but without political, ideological, and organizational equipment, the economy by its own cannot sustain the party's political legitimacy. Fearing that political reform will bring instability to China and perhaps further cause the CCP to lose power, the party congress denied substantial political reform and only offered lip service to the increasing calls for democratization. According to Jiang, "To strengthen Party building ideologically, it is essential to unswervingly arm the entire Party with Deng Xiaoping Theory and give full play to the ideological and political strength of the Party."[72] It is ideological and political strength, however, that the CCP lacks. The impressive performance of the economy offers the CCP a new base for political legitimacy, but it is not legitimacy itself. More than this, the economy also faces new challenges after twenty years of easygoing strategy; now the "hard bone" has appeared before the regime.

Gradual political reform could be the choice of the CCP, following the example set by its old rival, the Guomindang in Taiwan, or a kind of radical political change could happen, just as occurred in the last years of the Soviet Union, when legitimacy proved too weak to support the regime. But there is a third possibility, in which the regime could utilize economic performance as the carrot and, simultaneously, political suppression as the stick to maintain political stability as long as possible, postponing political reform and reducing the impact of ad hoc political change. The political problems would thus be deliberately avoided and transformed into socioeconomic problems for treatment and possible resolution. Surely strong economic performance can be helpful in reducing the many difficulties facing the communist regime, which range from domestic welfare to diplomacy. While politics and economics run in opposite directions, however, what can keep the country free from instability? As its last congress in this century has shown, the CCP is creating perplexities more than it is facing the future.

Notes

1. Joseph Fewsmith, "Chinese Politics on the Eve of the 15th Party Congress," in *China Review 1997*, ed. Maurice Brosseau, Kuan Hsin-chi, and Y. Y. Kueh (Hong Kong: The Chinese University Press, 1997), p. 4.

2. Valerie Bunce, *Do New Leaders Make a Difference? Executive Succession and Public Policy Under Capitalism and Socialism* (Princeton, NJ: Princeton University Press, 1981); Joseph W. Esherick and Elizabeth J. Perry, "Leadership Succession in the People's Republic of China: 'Crisis' or Opportunity?" *Studies in Comparative Communism* 16, no. 3 (autumn 1983): 171–177; Lowell Dittmer, "Patterns of Élite Strife and Succession in Chinese Politics," *The China Quarterly* 123 (September 1990): 405–430.

3. For this feature of the transition from communism in China, see, for example, Susan Shirk, *The Political Logic of Economic Reform in China* (Berkeley: University of California Press, 1993); Minxin Pei, *From Reform to Revolution: The Demise of Communism in China and the Soviet Union* (Cambridge, MA: Harvard University Press, 1994).

4. Such calls for democratization from society are various, exemplified by an article by Shang Dewen, a professor of economics at Beijing University, which discusses the constitutional designs of the future democratic China. Although the foreign media agencies such as Voice of America (VOA) and the British Broadcasting Company (BBC) reported about his article, it has not been published within China. Also, some scholars with government backgrounds and even a few high-ranking officials commented that China needed political reform and democratization. For example, Liu Ji, a vice president of the Chinese Academy of Social Sciences and a policy adviser to President Jiang Zemin, stressed that the requirements for democracy from the people must be fulfilled, as recorded in *The Hong Kong Economic Journal*, September 1, 1997, p. 10. A senior economist, Wang Jue, a professor at the Central Party School, also realized that economic reform must be matched by political reform, according to a report in *Hong Kong Economic Journal*, August 16, 1997, p. 6.

5. Hugo Restall, "China's Failed Party Congress," *Asian Wall Street Journal*, September 23, 1997, p. 10.

6. Cited from *International Herald Tribune*, September 20–21, 1997, p. 6.

7. Cited from *International Herald Tribune*, September 20, 1997, p. 8.

8. Reginald Dale, "Which Future for China: Threat or Positive Force?" *International Herald Tribune*, September 19, 1997, p. 13.

9. James A. Caporaso and David P. Levine, *Theories of Political Economy* (Cambridge: Cambridge University Press, 1992).

10. Max Weber, *Economy and Society: An Outline of Interpretive Sociology*, ed. Guenther Roth and Claus Wittich (Berkeley: University of California Press, 1978), vol. 1, p. 215.

11. This legitimacy based on economic performance can be defined as a kind of "legitimacy by results," as discussed in W. Phillips Shively, *Power and Choice* (New York: McGraw-Hill, 1995, 4th ed.), p. 110.

12. For the rise of technocracy in the CCP leadership during the reform years, see Li Cheng and Lynn White, "Élite Transformation and Modern Change in Mainland China and Taiwan: Empirical Data and the Theory of Technocracy," *The China Quarterly* 121 (March 1990): 1–35; Li Cheng and Lynn White, "The Thirteenth Central Committee of the Chinese Communist Party: From Mobilizers to Managers," *Asian Survey* 28, no. 4 (April 1988): 371–399; Willy Wo-lap Lam, "Leadership Changes at the Fourteenth Party Congress," in *China Review 1993*, ed. Joseph Cheng Yu-shek and Maurice Brosseau (Hong Kong: The Chinese University

Press, 1993), pp. 2.1–2.50; David Shambaugh, "The CCP's Fifteenth Congress: Technocrats in Command," *Issues & Studies* 34, no. 1 (January 1998): 1–37.

13. Jiang Zemin, *Gaoju Deng Xiaoping lilun weida qizhi, ba jianshe you Zhongguo tese de shehui zhuyi shiye quanmian tuixiang ershiyi shiji: zai Zhongguo Gongchandang di shiwu ci quanguo daibiao dahui shang de baogao* [*Hold High the Great Banner of Deng Xiaoping Theory for All-Around Advancement of the Cause of Building Socialism with Chinese Characteristics into the Twenty-First Century: Report Delivered at the Fifteenth National Congress of the Communist Party of China*], English translation in *Beijing Review,* October 6–12, 1997, p. 10. The quotations from this document hereafter will be indicated as "Jiang's report."

14. Ibid., p. 14.

15. *Beijing Review,* October 13–19, 1997, p. 18.

16. Ibid.

17. Ibid.

18. Jiang Zemin, "Lingdao ganbu bixu jiang zhengzhi" ["Leading Cadres Must Pay Attention to Politics"], excerpted from Jiang Zemin's speech to the fifth plenum of the Fourteenth Central Committee, Xinhua, January 17, 1996.

19. Jiang Zemin, "Zhengque chuli shehui zhuyi xiandaihua jianshe zhong de ruogan zhongda guanxi" ["Correctly Managing Some Great Relationships in Socialist Modernization Construction"], *Renmin ribao (People's Daily),* October 9, 1995, p. 1.

20. Mao Zedong discussed "ten great relationships" in 1956 to outline his policy for the socialist construction. See his "Lun shida guanxi" ["On the Ten Great Relationships"], in *Mao Zedong xuanji* [*Selected Works of Mao Zedong*] (Beijing: Renmin chubanshe, 1977), vol. 5, pp. 267–288.

21. The series of letters consist of four pieces. The first one, entitled "Yingxiang woguo guojia anquan de ruogan yinsu" ["Some Factors to Influence National Security of Our Country"], is the most influential as it was reportedly written by Deng Liqun, a former member of the CCP's Central Secretariat and the former head of the Propaganda Department of the Central Committee, though he informally denied his authorship. For the background and the digests, see Ma Licheng and Ling Zhijun, *Jiaofeng: Dangdai Zhongguo sanci sixiang jiefang shilu* [*Crossing Swords: The Chronicle of Three Mind Emancipations in Contemporary China*] (Beijing: Jinri Zhongguo Chubanshe, 1998), pp. 227–423.

22. *Renmin ribao,* February 20, 1997.

23. Franz Schurmann, *Ideology and Organization in Communist China* (Berkeley: University of California Press, 1968, enlarged ed.), p. 18.

24. Ibid., pp. 22–23.

25. Schurmann distinguishes between "theory" and "thought," and asserts that "for our conceptual terms of pure and practical ideology, the Chinese Communists use the words 'theory' and 'thought' respectively. Theory is pure ideology, and thought is practical ideology" (ibid., p. 23). But I think it is difficult to find evidence in Chinese politics for this conclusion. When the Fifteenth Party Congress uses the term "theory" to describe policies and ideas of Deng Xiaoping and still uses "thought" attached to Mao Zedong, it seems unreasonable to conclude that now the CCP regards Mao Zedong Thought as "practical ideology" but Deng Xiaoping Theory as the "pure" one.

26. Bill Brugger and David Kelly, *Chinese Marxism in the Post-Mao Era* (Stanford, CA: Stanford University Press, 1990), pp. 171–175.

27. Jiang's report, p. 15.

28. Steven Mufson, "China's Factory Cutbacks Feed Idled Workers' Anger," *International Herald Tribune,* September 12, 1997, p. 1.

29. See, for example, Joseph C. H. Chai and George Docwra, "Reform of Large and Medium State Industrial Enterprises: Corporatization and Restructure of State Ownership," in *China Review 1997*, ed. Maurice Brosseau, Kuan Hsin-chi, and Y. Y. Kueh (Hong Kong: The Chinese University Press, 1997), pp. 161–180.

30. Jiang's speech at the Central Party School on May 29, 1997, known as the "May 29 Speech." See *Renmin ribao*, May 30, 1997, p. 1. Also, see Ren Huiwen, "Jiang Zemin wu erjiu jianghua wei gongkai de neirong" ["Unpublished Contents of Jiang Zemin's May 29 Speech"], *Hong Kong Economic Journal,* June 20, 1997, p. 19.

31. Ren Huiwen, "Jiang Zemin tuidong Zhonggong disanci sixiang jiefang" ["Jiang Zemin Is Pushing Forward the CCP's Third Wave of Emancipation of the Mind"], *The Hong Kong Economic Journal,* August 15, 1997, p. 19.

32. "Shiwuda hou fei guoyou jingji jiang guoda, Li Junru zhi tupo xing gong xing si kunhuo" ["The Non-State Economy Will Be Enlarged After the Fifteenth Party Congress, and Li Junru Pointed Out That It Would Make a Breakthrough over the Perplexity Around Public or Private Ownership"], *Hong Kong Economic Journal,* August 14, 1997, p. 9.

33. Interview with Chinese governmental officials from Shandong Province, September 14, 1997, Hong Kong.

34. Jiang's report, p. 19.

35. Weiying Zhang, "Decision Rights, Residual Claim and Performance: A Theory of How the Chinese State Enterprise Reform Works," *China Economic Review* 8, no. 1 (spring 1997): 67.

36. *Beijing Review,* October 20–26, 1997, p. 6.

37. Mufson, "China's Factory Cutbacks."

38. Seth Faison, "Dismay in China Firms as Privatization Looms." Cited from *International Herald & Tribune,* October 6, 1997, p. 13.

39. *Far Eastern Economic Review,* October 16, 1997, p. 62.

40. Ibid.

41. Mufson, "China's Factory Cutbacks"; Faison, "Dismay in China Firms as Privatization Looms."

42. Mufson, "China's Factory Cutbacks."

43. Frank R. Gunter, "Capital Flight from the People's Republic of China: 1984–1994," *China Economic Review* 7, no. 1 (spring 1996): 77–96.

44. He Qinglian, *Zhongguo de xianjing [China's Perplexities]* (Hong Kong: The Mirror Books, 1997), p. 79.

45. Kate Hannan, "Reforming China's State Enterprises, 1984–93," *Journal of Communist Studies and Transition Politics* 11, no. 1 (March 1995): 33–55.

46. *Beijing Review,* October 13–19, 1997, p. 5.

47. James Harding, "Asian Markets Contagion May Unnerve China," *Financial Times,* October 27, 1997, p. 6.

48. Ibid.; and Steven Mufson, "Asian Financial Chaos Shakes Beijing," *International Herald Tribune,* October 24, 1997, p. 18.

49. Peter Hannam, "China's Economic Dynamo Begins to Run Out of System," *International Herald Tribune,* November 15–16, 1997, p. 18.

50. David S. G. Goodman, "Collectives and Connectives, Capitalism and Corporatism: Structural Change in China," *Journal of Communist Studies and Transition Politics* 11, no. 1 (March 1995): 32.

51. Gerald Segal, "Notice How Being Firm with Beijing Helps China to Change," *International Herald Tribune,* October 22, 1997, p. 8.

52. *Far Eastern Economic Review,* October 2, 1997, p. 5.

53. "America and China," *International Herald Tribune,* August 20, 1997, p. 8; and "Jiang's Chance," *International Herald Tribune*, October 25–26, 1997, p. 8.

54. Reuters' report from Beijing, see *International Herald Tribune,* September 11, 1997, p. 4.

55. Zhao's letter was widely reported in Hong Kong media. See, for example, *The Apple Daily,* September 17, 1997.

56. John Pomfret and Lena H. Sun, "Jiang Links 'Mistakes' and Tiananmen," *International Herald Tribune,* November 3, 1997, pp. 1 and 4.

57. Jiang's report, p. 24.

58. Brian Knowlton, "Jiang Vows More Democracy," *International Herald Tribune,* October 31, 1997, pp. 1 and 4.

59. Zhao Ziyang, "Yanzhe you Zhongguo tese de shehui zhuyi daolu qianjin: zai Zhongguo Gongchan Dang di shisan ci quanguo daibiao dahui shang de baogao" ["Advancing Along with the Road of Socialism with Chinese Characteristics: Report to the 13th National Congress of the Chinese Communist Party"], in *Zhongguo Gongchan Dang di shisan ci quanguo daibiao dahui wenjian huibian [Documents of the 13th National Congress of the CCP]* (Beijing: Renmin chubanshe, 1987), pp. 34–49.

60. Seth Faison, "China's 'Time for Silence' Drags On," *International Herald Tribune,* November 20, 1997, pp. 1 and 6.

61. *Hong Kong Economic Journal,* September 29, 1997.

62. Faison, "China's 'Time for Silence' Drags On."

63. *International Herald Tribune,* October 25–26, 1997, p. 8.

64. Jiang's report, p. 17.

65. Frederic C. Deyo (ed.), *The Political Economy of the New Asian Industrialism* (Ithaca: Cornell University Press, 1987); Robert Wade, *Governing the Market: Economic Theory and the Role of Government in East Asian Industrialization* (Princeton, NJ: Princeton University Press, 1990); Gary Gereffi and Donald L. Wyman (eds.), *Manufacturing Miracles: Paths of Industrialization in Latin America and East Asia* (Princeton, NJ: Princeton University Press, 1990).

66. Deyo, *The Political Economy.*

67. See Robert C. Tucker, ed., *The Lenin Anthology* (New York: W. W. Norton, 1975).

68. David Collier, ed., *The New Authoritarianism in Latin America* (Princeton, NJ: Princeton University Press, 1979), p. 4.

69. Caporaso and Levine, *Theories of Political Economy,* p. 3.

70. For original and systematic statements of Marxist political economy, see, for example, Robert C. Tucker, ed., *The Marx-Engels Reader* (New York: W. W. Norton, 1978, 2nd ed.). Also, see Caporaso and Levine, *Theories of Political Economy,* chapter 3.

71. Interviews: Beijing, April 1997; Shenzhen, October 1997; and Hong Kong, throughout 1997. Also, the conclusion is based on the opinions expressed from Chinese audiences in the call-in programs of the Voice of America, in which the author participated many times in 1997 to discuss China's political reform.

72. Jiang's report, p. 31.

3

In Search of Re-ideologization and Social Order

Zhaohui Hong & Yi Sun

At the Fifteenth Congress of the Chinese Communist Party, Jiang Zemin delivered a speech entitled "Hold High the Great Banner of Deng Xiaoping's Theory for All-Round Advancement of the Cause of Building Socialism with Chinese Characteristics into the Twenty-First Century."[1] Using the concept of Deng Xiaoping's Theory (*Deng Xiaoping lilun*), Jiang signaled the beginning of ideological reconstruction in Jiang Zemin's China.

As Guoguang Wu and Xiaonong Cheng mention in this book (in Chapters 2 and 7, respectively), the CCP has relied on economic performance to maintain its political legitimacy since the Tiananman incident in 1989. But due to inevitable fluctuation of the market economy, this legitimacy is tenuous. To sustain its legitimacy and stability, the CCP has to add ideology as a supplementary force in Jiang's China.

A review of the changing roles of ideology since 1949 shows three different stages led by three generations of CCP leaders. Mao's era (1949–1976) was characterized by "ideological fever," in which ideology was an omnipotent and omnipresent force that governed ordinary people's daily lives. In contrast, Deng's era (1978–1997) can be seen as one of ideological deconstruction.[2] Deng's economic pragmatism, expressed through his well-known "cat theory," eroded Maoism and diluted the dominant force of communist ideology.[3] However, frustrated by the widespread new cult of wealth, accompanying value vacuum and money worship, Chinese intellectuals in the 1990s began to reassess the role of ideology in an attempt to rescue a society plagued by declining morality.[4] In response, Jiang called for a "reemphasis on politics" (*jiang zhengzhi*) in 1995[5] and advocated "upholding the banner of Deng Xiaoping's theory" at the Fifteenth Party Congress in 1997. Jiang's China seems to be undergoing a process of ideological reconstruction, which differs from both Mao's intense indoctrination and Deng's expedient pragmatism. The role of ideology, therefore, follows a dialectical circle: belief (thesis)–disbelief (antithesis)–reconstruction of belief (synthesis).[6]

When Deng emerged as the paramount leader twenty years ago, he appeared as an advocate of Maoism, but this never prevented him from making creative policy adjustments. Deng shrewdly urged the public to "comprehensively and accurately" interpret Mao's Thoughts, but to "differentiate Mao's ideas from his mistakes." Attributing "Maoist truth" to collective wisdom rather than to Mao himself, Deng's strategy of championing "Maoism without Mao"[7] enabled him to select the "true essence" of Maoism by his own standard. Maoism became those ideas that Deng applauded, such as the emphasis on CCP leadership. On the other hand, Mao's ideas and practices that Deng disliked became Mao's "personal mistakes" awaiting "correction," such as the initiation of the Cultural Revolution. In so doing, Deng managed to kill three birds with one stone, for he succeeded in pacifying the conservatives and meeting the demands of the liberal reformers, while at the same time creating a comfortable environment in which he could practice his own ideology without negative backlash. As a result, Deng's China was actually governed by a composite ideology; that is, by "Mao's bottle with Deng's wine."

Borrowing a page from Deng's book, Jiang is likely to imitate what his predecessor did two decades ago. As Jiang reiterated in his report, it is the "sacred historical responsibility" of the new CCP leadership not only to uphold the "basic principles" of Dengism, but also to "enrich and develop it consistently through practice."[8] Apparently, Jiang intends to distinguish Deng's "correct ideas" from his "personal mistakes" by understanding Deng's theory "comprehensively and accurately." After all, Deng's ideas were also the product of collective wisdom. Despite his public rhetoric, Jiang intends to create his own alternative ideology by inheriting Deng's "useful" ideologies, updating his outmoded ones, and rectifying his erroneous ones in order to formulate Jiang's own initiatives. By repeating Deng's ingenious approach in dealing with Maoism, Jiang's China may be governed by "Dengism without Deng" or "Deng's bottle without Deng's wine."[9]

In his report, Jiang emphasized the concept of the "preliminary phase of socialism" that he interpreted as an important component of Dengism,[10] although former premier Zhao Ziyang initiated it in 1987. It is worth noting that Jiang intended to extend Zhao's application of the "preliminary phase" theory from the pure economic sphere to other areas as well, including the ideological realm, but it is not clear how Jiang defines the so-called preliminary socialist ideology and adapts it to the needs of the "preliminary socialist economy."[11]

Initially, the theory of the "preliminary phase of socialism" was designed to "justify the economic reforms that had introduced many semicapitalist methods into China's economy,"[12] such as land speculation, class polarization, property privatization, and massive unemployment. According to orthodox Marxism, which advanced the theory of "economic determinism," this "semicapitalist economy" would require a "semicapitalist ideology."

The early stages of China's economic development made necessary the establishment of various types of ownership and different means of distribution, which in turn have called for a corresponding belief system. Obviously, Deng's theory alone is insufficient to meet the new demands of socioeconomic development. The need for a new ideology, combined with the necessity for new legal and ethical codes, makes a period of ideological reconstruction imperative.

China's history and culture have determined that ideology still plays an important role in maintaining political legitimacy and guiding the country's socioeconomic development. Although Deng's approach was de-ideologization, traditional Confucianism and radical communism generated a unique priority: thinking is more important than action, and in practice, "rule by ideology."[13] As Yan Sun pointed out, ideology is "the decisive criterion for determining the degree of empirical change." Analyzing the reasons for sustaining "an ideological hegemony," she argues that ideology has contributed to political and social stability. In particular, "the Chinese concern for ideological and conceptual adaptation," in her view, "is related to the national search for identity and resurrection that has faced the nation since its confrontation with the West in the last century."[14]

Ideological reconstruction in Jiang's China must deal simultaneously with two issues—continuity and change. On the one hand, a modified Dengism will help legitimize the new regime and the power succession against conservative challenges, which will help preserve the fruits of economic reforms. On the other hand, maintaining "Dengism without Deng" will allow new ideas to develop. One of the main principles of Dengism, according to Jiang, is to "emancipate mind and seek truth from the facts." Using this principle, in Jiang's view, will be conducive to "solving new issues, promoting new perspectives, and realizing new leaps," and will enable the creation of a new ideology.[15]

This chapter analyzes Jiang's ideological strategy from a historical and comparative perspective, and discusses the issues concerning the construction of new ideological, economic, and legal systems. This new ideology has to venture beyond the historical boundaries set by both Maoism and Dengism, thereby ushering China into a new age.

The Idea of Balance in the Reconstruction of Chinese Values

Jiang expounded on the urgency to build a "socialist spiritual civilization" by incorporating the rich historical and cultural legacies of China and positive aspects of foreign culture.[16] However, he did not have a clear and feasible proposal on how to accomplish this task.

A reconstruction of Chinese values requires the reevaluation of both Maoism and Dengism. Mao can be seen, to a large measure, as an idealist who was fervently devoted to ideology and revolution, whereas Deng was a realist who valued pragmatism and reform. Mao's policies, such as instigation of the class struggle and the Cultural Revolution, were predominantly political in nature, whereas Deng's polices centered around economic themes. Mao favored egalitarianism as practiced in the People's Communes, whereas Deng liked efficiency and implemented the household responsibility system. Mao stressed spiritual values, whereas Deng paid more attention to economic productivity.[17] Wang Huning, political consultant to Jiang, once commented:

> Mao's strategy was to achieve [economic] development through political means, with mixed results of successes and failures. The main problem for Mao was the lack of economic progress. Following the end of the Cultural Revolution, Deng Xiaoping chose a different strategy with the economy at its center. . . . China's political development has to be molded within this framework.[18]

Jiang pointed out that the CCP must learn how to deal with the intricate relationships "between reform, development and stability, between economy and politics, between material civilization and spiritual civilization, between productivity and relations of production, and between economic foundation and spiritual infrastructure."[19] However, Jiang did not offer any specific and convincing way to deal with these "intricate relationships," which actually requires an approach of the most sophisticated balance.

The idea of balance, supported by the "three-sided coin" theory, is valuable in critiquing both Maoism and Dengism and developing a new perspective. Instead of two sides of a coin, this "three-sided coin" analogy argues that each coin actually has a third dimension, which is the middle side connecting the other two sides—a middle-of-the-road approach that often provides a necessary compromise between two opposing views. This kind of compromise or moderation may be the second-best choice in dealing with the dilemmas of China's economic reform.[20] The three-sided coin theory suggests that Jiang's China needs to maintain a meaningful balance between Maoism and Dengism, that is, a balance between idealism and realism, spiritualism and materialism, politics and economy, and egalitarianism and efficiency. Mutually complementary in nature, the balance will supply certain missing links in both Mao's and Deng's ideologies.

This idea of balance is essential for the development of a new ideology. The renewed emphasis on ideology may mark an initial departure from Deng's ideological destruction, but it is by no means a replica of Mao's ideological indoctrination. Failure to conserve aspects of Dengism will make it difficult to preserve the fruits of economic reforms and dodge criticisms from the left; on the other hand, failure to sustain certain portions of Maoism will render it difficult to tackle the negative aspects of reform such as corruption, and to avoid attacks from the right. Only by adopting a middle-of-the-road approach and skillfully combining both Mao's and Deng's ideologies will the new regime be able to provide effective leadership.

This kind of balance works from a cultural perspective as well. In fact, the essences of Chinese traditional (Confucian) culture are balance, moderation, and compromise. The majority of Chinese probably favor moderation as their ideological orientation. The extreme Leftist fever during the Maoist era left people longing for material benefits; yet rampant official corruption and massive unemployment in Deng's era have made many people look back at the frugality and purity of life during Mao's time. The inherently self-contradictory public sentiments—the desire for change and nostalgia for the past—provide a cultural and psychological condition that will make a balanced ideology and moderate leadership all the more welcome.[21]

Balance will also benefit economic progress. From an economic standpoint, equality and efficiency are, in a sense, in perpetual conflict with each other. Maoist preaching and the practice of egalitarianism were pushed to the extreme and resulted in the "iron bowl" phenomenon without unemployment. Deng chose to experiment with a market economy, which emphasized efficiency rather than full employment. However, the resulting social disparities between the rich and the poor and between the urban and rural areas have given rise to widespread public discontent. The yardstick of productivity alone cannot measure social progress as it involves a multitude of other factors such as social and moral justice. In this sense, the current situation presents an excellent environment in which to create an equilibrium between equality and efficiency, poverty and prosperity, and stability and development through construction of a new ideology.[22]

Balance is a means of making adjustments to existing ideas while creating a new governing philosophy. In the process of balancing, "the ideology of modernization" will be a new belief and value system rooted in traditional culture but incorporating Western ideas. It will fill the spiritual void felt by many, especially the young people. This new ideology selectively combines and incorporates Confucianism, religious beliefs, patriotic sentiments, and Western ideas.

Since the late nineteenth century, various reforms and revolutions, including the Western learning movement, the May Fourth Movement, the Nationalist-Communist struggle, the Cultural Revolution, and recent economic reforms, have leveled severe attacks on Confucianism. However, this ancient philosophy has demonstrated remarkable resilience, for it is ingrained in the Chinese mentality. As the guiding philosophy and code of ethical behavior for centuries, Confucianism still has much to offer.[23] The idea of "self-cultivation and social etiquette," for instance, inculcates common courtesy and helps refine human conduct; the idea of "peace" promotes mutual understanding and cooperation; and the principle of "the golden mean" is conducive to moderation, compromise, and tolerance. The

Confucian emphasis on education enhances respect for knowledge and those who transmit knowledge. The principle of "not doing to others what one does not want done to oneself" encourages treating others as equals and with consideration. Finally, the Confucian teaching of self-sacrifice for the public good is badly needed in a society that is enmired in crises about ethics and public morality.[24]

Another ingredient of the new belief system derives from religion. The concepts of humanism and morality contained in many religions can help cultivate the feeling of love of humanity and generate a sense of optimism. Both Western Christianity and eastern Buddhism teach peace, universal love, and nonviolence. Jiang once asked people to reread Mao's *In Remembrance of Bethune* with the purpose of reeducating the public on the "Bethune spirit"—one of selflessness, honesty, purity, and morality.[25] In a way, the Bethune spirit can be seen as a kind of religious expression of self-sacrifice for a worthy cause. However, if labeled as a "communist spirit," it will probably fail to generate any enthusiasm from the public, which has become deeply disillusioned with communism. Religion must be kept separate from politics and religious freedom should be permitted.[26]

A third component of this "ideology of modernization" is patriotism. Patriotism is an internalizing ideology that can galvanize domestic forces for a national course without jeopardizing the interest of other nations or states. In the past, patriotic education conducted under both Mao and Deng was ineffective because the government equated patriotism with devotion to the Communist Party and socialist system. Deng once said that motherland is not an abstract concept because "if you don't love socialist New China led by the Communist Party, what motherland do you love?"[27] Due to this state-centered "communist patriotism,"[28] patriotism was heavily tainted with politics to the extent that some people now have a negative reaction to the word "patriotism." The new version of patriotism, therefore, must distinguish the state from the party, and separate patriotic education from political indoctrination. At the same time, it needs to accentuate the richness of Chinese history, culture, language, land, and people so as to instill a strong sense of pride in the populace. The concept of the party-state should be replaced by one of the culture-state.

Western ideas should also be incorporated into the "ideology of modernization." Jiang urged China to "open various channels of cultural exchange with foreign countries in order to absorb their best cultural elements."[29] Isaac Newton once made an interesting analogy: if two people, each with an apple, exchange the apples, then each would end up with still one apple; yet if two people, each with an idea, exchange their ideas, then each would end up with two ideas. Today, with modern means of communication, this kind of exchange can often generate multiple ideas instead of two ideas.

Today's young people are quick to embrace modern ideas as well as modern fashions and lifestyles. China can take advantage of this mentality to educate the youth on the characteristics of a "modern" citizen. Certainly, greed, selfishness, lawlessness, and extreme materialism are not the real characteristics of a "modern" individual. On the contrary, people should be law-abiding, hardworking, fair-minded, trustworthy, civilized, and willing to help others. Modernization not only bespeaks advancement of material life, but also connotes a high standard of values and ethics.

Defined as such, modernization thus becomes not merely short-term material gain and economic development as outlined by the CCP's blueprint for "the four modernizations," but also a new way of thinking—an ideology that encompasses the positive elements of Confucianism, religion, patriotism, and Western ideas. This ideology will enable China to balance and integrate existing ideologies, including Maoism and Dengism, in order to "promote social, professional and family morality."[30]

The Idea of Transition in Economic Development

Jiang's report to the Fifteenth Party Congress outlined the government's plan for reforming state-owned enterprises (SOEs) through promoting a shareholding system, but Jiang did not specify ways in which to accomplish this. His vagueness may lead to irresponsible bids for massive privatization and create chaos through mass unemployment. The experience of economic reform over the past twenty years has demonstrated that successful reform must be gradual, and must cross several "bridges" before its final destination. Impatient and radical tactics may be self-defeating.

According to the theory of "transitional development" (zhuanxing fazhan lilun), China must complete both "institutional transition" from a planned to a market economy and "economic development" from an agrarian society to an industrial one.[31] Instead of focusing on the ultimate results of the reform, "transition" places the priority on the specific stages of reform in order to formulate feasible policies and strategies for both institutional and economic changes. Additionally, gradualism is conducive to effective reform. In contrast to the Russian "shock therapy," China needs to emphasize gradual but progressive changes.[32]

To implement this idea of transition, reform of the SOE property rights is urgent. Jiang asserted that "the shareholding system (gufen zhi) is a form of capital organization in modern enterprises . . . , which can be used by either capitalism or socialism."[33] One high-ranking government official has given a timetable to solve the SOEs' problems within three years.[34] This kind of time line in a way resembles the overly ambitious and irrational approach that was adopted during the late 1950s, and might have serious repercussions. Clearly, this reform has to be carried out cautiously in order to prevent a wave of frantic bids for destruction of various SOEs. As pointed out by Guoqiang Tian and Hong Liang in Chapter 5, many experiments with the shareholding system have proven unsuccessful, demonstrating the incompatibility between Chinese culture and the Western concept of property rights.[35]

For instance, the shareholding system stresses the importance of capital rather than human resources. This may conflict with the Chinese way of management, which emphasizes interpersonal relations, family connections, and feelings. Also, the Western shareholding system follows the policy of "one share one vote." Chinese culture, however, does not have a democratic tradition with its principle of the minority following the majority. People are not familiar with this democratic practice; instead, they are accustomed to conforming to a strong leader. Paternalism and communistic mercantilism still constitute the basic principles of Chinese management. Besides, a shareholding system requires that the public have easy access to all the company's records. This "open-door" principle would be alien to Chinese culture, which attaches great importance to "face saving" and favors *guanxi* (connections).[36] Additionally, distribution of the enterprises' capital among workers would create tension and would be detrimental to the cohesiveness and productivity of the enterprise as a whole. If existing capital is divided among current employees, then future employees will be the "working class" whose incomes would never catch up with those of the senior members, despite the fact that the new workers are likely to be better-educated and have more technological skills.

Therefore, instead of implementing radical shareholding reform, it would be sensible to first change the SOEs into the cooperative shareholding system (*gufen hezuo zhi*) as a transitional bridge toward the modern shareholding system. The experience of property rights reform of the township and village enterprises (TVEs) in the 1980s showed that the cooperative shareholding system (CSS) has a unique "collective share" (*jiti gu*), theoretically owned by all shareholders in the enterprise. There are four basic characteristics of CSS, compared with the shareholding system. First, the collective share accounts for about 50 percent of total capital. Second, shareholders have the right to dividend income but do not individually own the shares, which are not transferable or inheritable. Employees who leave the enterprise cannot take the shares with them. Third, collective shares are not open for trading on the stock market, nor are they available for purchase by anyone outside of the enterprise. Finally, its voting policy is "one person one vote" instead of "one share one vote" as is practiced by the Western shareholding system.[37]

By utilizing "one person one vote" and by distributing profits fairly among employees, this type of ownership encourages workers to make maximum contributions to their enterprises. The collective share system would ensure a smooth transition from public ownership. Employees in SOEs have an "iron bowl" mentality; it is unrealistic to expect them to adapt to the practices of private ownership within a short period of time. By retaining some "socialistic" characteristics, CSS can lessen the psychological and political resistance to reform on the part of the workers. In addition, SOEs have accumulated a large amount of public capital over the past half century, which in principle should be redistributed, together with the compounded interest, to the workers by making them the new collective owners. Similar to the principle of "the land to the tiller," it is desirable to create a new concept of "the share to the worker."[38]

However, individual workers' shares are always too few to have a strong voice in the process of decisionmaking. In practice, workers refused to buy their company shares because they suspected that without enough votes their investment might be squandered away by the managers. Many believe that leaders of their enterprises will collect the money in the name of shareholding ownership, and workers themselves will end up shouldering the financial burden of their enterprises.[39] If this is the case, the workers' personal savings are cleverly changed into the enterprise's property, which then will be misused by the officials in one way or another.

James Meade's theory of "share economy" might be helpful in encouraging workers' representatives to involve themselves in the operation of their enterprises. Meade argues that a share economy is designed for both labor and capital to share both revenue and risks. This kind of share approach will maintain workers' "social loyalties," which are more important than "any purely economic incentive relating to the level of the individual worker's pay."[40]

But to share the firm's ownership with capitalists, workers must have enough voting power in the process of decisionmaking. At this point, Meade designed a system, the so-called cooperative voting system between labor and capital. It aims at dividing the company's decisionmaking process into two categories. One is to apply the "one person one vote" principle to those issues that are most relevant to the ordinary workers, which include capital raising and allocation, dividend distribution, and workers' education and training, as well as electing the board of directors. Another is to apply the "one share one vote" principle to issues concerning business operation and management, such as production management, marketing, and sales decisions.[41]

However, to support the voting power for workers in the long term, it is necessary for workers to control meaningful shares that are the fundamental base of voting rights in companies. Therefore, one possible way for workers to participate in SOEs' decisionmaking process is to set up a "group share" that practices "one group one vote" instead of "one share one vote" or "one person one vote." This group share allows a group of workers who cannot afford to purchase a large number of shares individually to buy enterprise shares collectively, and a representative of this group can cast one vote at the shareholders' meeting. In doing so, those who own a small number of shares will have their own group representative participating in the management process with a powerful voice. This may be a happy medium between the system of "one share one vote" and that of "one person one vote." It should be similar to "a labor-managed cooperative," as designed by Meade, "in which the workers own the greater part of the equity of the concern and play the predominant part in the control of the concern's operations."[42]

Thus, the collective shareholding with "one group one vote" principle has many advantages, for it combines the principle of "distribution according to contribution" and "dividend according to share ownership." It is especially conducive to building a favorable relationship between labor and capital. In particular, it synthesizes elements of collective and private ownership, Chinese characteristics and Western practices, and traditional ideology and liberal regulations. CSS best addresses the issue of continuity and change by providing a middle-of-the-road solution.[43]

However, CSS is an expedient appropriate during the transition from state ownership to real privatization, and the ultimate goal of SOE reform is to move to a system that is guided and regulated purely by the market with clarification of property rights.

The Idea of Order in the Legal System

Jiang's report put forward the concept of "ruling the country according to the law," maintaining that "policy-making concerning reform and development must be linked with the establishment of a legal system," and that "by the year 2010, China will have a complete socialist legal system with Chinese characteristics."[44] Jiang also stressed that "the goal of politics is to make sure that the economic and other activities are conducted in the right direction and in an orderly fashion." He argued that "through politics, the legal codes and regulations can be implemented into China's economic construction and various other tasks," including "forcefully attacking criminal activities in various forms."[45] Underlining the importance of systematizing legal control, Jiang said that China "must strive to build and perfect a legal system that can regulate economic activities, preserve economic order, and guarantee the government's macro-management and control of economic operations."[46]

The idea of strengthening the legal system was not Jiang's invention; almost all countries that have undergone the process of modernization have done so. The development of industrialized societies demonstrates that it is imperative to balance the double legacies of industrialization—freedom and disorder—in order to balance both personal liberty and social responsibility, both individualism and social stability, and both personal material desire and social ethics. An individual has the right to liberty and freedom, but must also abide by the law and observe certain moral principles.[47] The experiences of other Asian countries have demonstrated that, following economic progress, a sound legal system is more urgent than political democratization. The "four little dragons" in Asia have largely followed the pattern of "economic development first, followed by legal construction, and political democratization as a final destination."[48] This model suggests that democracy may be premature or even counterproductive for social stability before the establishment of a well-functioning legal system.

The reconstruction of the legal system includes several principles. First, to protect the market economy and promote political democracy, "rule of law" is more important than "rule by law." If Mao insisted on rule by man, Deng began to address rule by law, which issued various legal regulations. But for Deng, "law was a tool of power, not a tool for society."[49] Therefore, the top leader (or king) has rights above the law. Jiang is the first chief of the CCP to declare a "rule of law,"[50] which aims at fair and just enforcement of the laws to everybody, including Jiang himself.[51]

Second, the rules of "playing the game" are more critical than the "right to play the game." While few had the right to participate in a free-market economy under Mao, the right to do so was valuable. Under Deng, however, more people had an incomplete or partial right to "play the game" in the market economy, yet the necessary rules were missing, and this gave rise to injustice, corruption, and monopoly. Therefore, making and improving the "rules of the game" have become all the more urgent.

Third, the idea of order means that care for the underrepresented and underprivileged is important because a healthy social order requires both fairness and caring. Caring for the poor is important in promoting long-term fairness and equality. For example, the principle of affirmative action in the United States may not be universal fairness, but is the result of special care for minorities and women. Absolutely fair regulations may turn out to have negative results as far as the underprivileged are concerned because, in practice, fairness to "everybody" is very likely to be harmful to "some." While one emphasizes equal opportunity, equal results also should be of concern. Therefore, new rules have to be designed to minimize the current wide disparity between the rich and the poor, and between the urban and rural areas.[52]

To implement the idea of order, priority should be given to building a legal mechanism to fight against rampant corruption in order to maintain fair competition and equal opportunities. Along with legal stipulations, a regulatory system and the use of public opinion are also necessary in combating corruption.[53] In light of these objectives, officials from the county level and up, first of all, should be required by law to publicize their personal net worth annually and explain periodically the reasons for certain increases. This will put strong psychological pressure on those who are involved in corruption and may curb further corruption. Additionally, every county needs to set up a special anticorruption committee placed under direct leadership of the Standing Committee of the People's Congress rather than party organizations. These committees, combining the powers of the public security bureau, the procurators' offices, and the judicial court, will be entrusted with the responsibility of registering and investigating corruption cases so that penalties can be imposed on the guilty. Also, the power of the mass media and public opinion should be used. Currently, there are no effective means to discourage corrupt officials except for damaging their "face" through the mass media. Major nationwide newspapers should open special anticorruption columns and the local radio and TV networks need to set up anticorruption hotlines to encourage people to get involved in exposing and denouncing corrupt activities. In particular, the power of the CCP Political and Legal Committee (*zhengfa weiyuanhui*) at various levels needs to be reduced and eventually eliminated. Receiving direct instructions from the CCP, these committees were designed to guarantee the party's control of major criminal cases, and their existence has severely jeopardized the independence of the judicial court, since they give the party supremacy over the law.[54]

In addition to anticorruption efforts, China must also set up rules governing the transfer of SOEs' assets to avoid property losses. As Jiang announced, "It is crucial to establish a system to manage and protect national assets, guarantee their value and prevent their loss."[55] But Jiang did not specify how to reach this goal.

Now that large-scale privatization of SOEs is imminent, there may be frantic scrambling for the "Last Supper." Failure to set up a comprehensive system to preserve and control public assets will result in losses of state capital, rampant official corruption, and massive unemployment. A special task force responsible for appraising assets of the SOEs seems to be one necessary way to curtail public property losses. Currently those in charge of such appraisals are generally officials and accountants from the evaluated SOEs, or those from the same local area. These people may find it difficult to avoid the influence of departmentalism or regionalism or the temptation of material incentives in the forms of bribery or favoritism. As a result, appraisers sometimes deliberately underestimate the value of some SOEs, forcing them to sell their shares below their true value. Another additional danger is that those who lose high-ranking official positions due to the administrative reform of 1998 are going to be the government representatives who supervise the SOEs' operation. Without official position and with no sense of loyalty, those former administrators will be likely to trade their power for private profit by underestimating the SOEs' assets.[56] To remedy this situation, the appraisal committee should be staffed by experts and scholars from institutions and areas that are unrelated to the SOE under evaluation. Local officials can offer advice or suggestions, but they should not be involved in the decisionmaking. Mainland China at this point should learn from Hong Kong, where the government uses high salaries to reduce the risk of corruption (*gaoxin yanglian*); experts and scholars in charge of asset appraisal receive handsome monetary compensation, which serves to reduce the temptation to accept bribes or other material enticements. In fact, mainland China could hire experts from Hong Kong to ensure fair evaluation of the state assets.

In addition, the appraisal committees should be placed under direct leadership of the Bureau of State Property Management (*guoyou zichan guanli ju*), which, in turn, will be controlled by the National People's Congress. It must be made clear that the appraisal of state assets is a legal procedure, not an administrative task. A national assets evaluation committee, which would parallel the Bureau of State Property Management, could be established to better assess the quality of work performed by the local appraisal committees. These procedures may be costly, but compared with the potentially disastrous loss of the SOE capital, which could be uncontrollable and unlimited, they are a wise and worthwhile investment that could generate a great deal of social as well as economic benefit.

Banks also should play a critical role in the process of shareholding reform and management of SOEs. Traditionally, banks and SOEs have been parallel and separate institutions, and banks have little incentive to help the latter make more effective use of capital, or to go after SOEs with bad credit. It is indeed shocking that the average deficit of SOEs at present has reached as high as 80 percent, and most of the bank loans have been uncorrectable and written off.[57] To combat this problem, banks can now become shareholders of SOEs instead of simply creditors. By forming this kind of industrial and financial combination, banks will gain a powerful incentive to become involved in the management and regulation of SOEs. They will automatically and accurately assess the SOEs' total assets value, quality of the management, development potential, and overall credibility before extending significant loans. They will actively monitor how the loan is used, thus effectively curbing, if not eliminating, its misuse or waste.

Furthermore, graduated income taxes and a social security system should be designed to provide special care for underprivileged groups. A study of unemployment shows that while the urban unemployment rate was 7.5 percent, the rural unemployment rate was as high as 34.8 percent by the first quarter of 1997.[58] Unemployment is not only a potentially explosive social issue; it also has serious political implications. U.S. history in the late nineteenth century demonstrated that unregulated competition encouraged both farmer rebellions and labor movements. It resulted in a nationwide Progressive Movement and the New Deal, which promoted the creation of the graduated income tax and social security system partly aimed at diminishing the gaps between rich and poor. Drawing from the American experience, China can implement its own social security and taxation policies. The idea of "unfair" taxes and distribution may have to be applied in formulating a functioning graduated-income welfare system for the poor and a graduated-income tax system for the wealthy in order to provide the necessary relief for poverty.[59]

Currently, the government is attempting to educate people on their responsibility to pay income tax, but there is no effective enforcement of the tax laws. Most people are not familiar with the concept and practice of paying tax, as they had never had to do so before the 1980s when their incomes were extremely low. Tax reform needs to focus on income taxes, although consumer taxes, real estate taxes, business taxes, and sales taxes should not be neglected. With personal income dramatically increasing, a reasonable income tax is not only necessary to provide the state with a stable revenue, but also critical for social stability.

Effective implementation of graduated income taxes needs several steps. First of all, a complete set of legal regulations against tax evasion must be firmly enforced. To do so, a computer network is necessary for the National Bureau of Taxation to conduct regular checking, searching, and auditing. China may need to set up a citizen tax record, which will serve as an important reference when people are applying for jobs, loans, welfare, passports, or identification cards. An effective tax system will also require the provision of better services, including free telephone consultation, free and simplified tax forms, regular seminars, written instructions, and professional accounting services.[60]

Conclusion

The preceding analysis demonstrates that in facing the dilemmas of economic reform, establishment of a new belief system centering on the theme of modernization is crucial for ensuring further economic development. It is also imperative to build a comprehensive and effective legal system to facilitate both ideological reconstruction and economic development, and pave the way for the eventual democratization of politics and society. The ideas of balance, transition, and order are the three critical themes and challenges for the reconstruction of ideology. They are the "blind spots" in both Maoism and Dengism, and constitute the central concerns of today. The process of achieving all three goals provides challenges as China implements its "new deal" in a new era.

Although history once selected the CCP as China's leader, it does not grant the party a permanent "mandate of heaven" and unchangeable legitimacy.[61] At this moment, China faces unprecedented dilemmas as well as precious challenges. Whether or not the country can achieve a theoretical breakthrough and implement creative policies will ultimately determine its destiny.

Notes

1. Jiang Zemin, *Gaoju Deng Xiaoping lilun weida qizhi, ba jianshe you Zhongguo tese shehui zhuyi shiye quanmian tuixiang ershiyi shiji* [*Hold High the Great Banner of Deng Xiaoping's Theory for All-Round Advancement of the Cause of Building Socialism with Chinese Characteristics into the Twenty-First Century: Report Delivered at the Fifteenth National Congress of the Communist Party of China on September 12, 1997*] (Beijing: Renmin chubanshe, 1997). The quotations from this document hereafter will be indicated as "Jiang Zemin, *Report.*"

2. Some scholars describe Deng's China as "de-ideologization." See X. L. Ding, *The Decline of Communism in China, Legitimacy Crisis, 1977–1989* (New York: Cambridge University Press, 1994), p. 114.

3. At the onset of the economic reforms, Deng Xiaoping remarked that "whether it is a white or black cat, the good cat is capable of catching mice." It has since been referred to as the "cat theory" to illustrate Deng's economic pragmatism.

4. Luo Rongqu, *Xiandaihua xinlun xupian—Dongya yu Zhongguo de xiandaihua jincheng* [*Reinterpretations of Modernization—East Asian and China's Process of Modernization*] (Beijing: Beijing daxue chubanshe, 1997), pp. 192–198; Wang Hengfu and Shi Zheng, *Wenhua jingji lungao* [*Theory of Cultural Economy*] (Beijing: Renmin chubanshe, 1995), pp. 118–166; Weng Jieming et al., eds., *Yu zongshuji tanxin* [*Discussion with General Secretary of the CCP*] (Beijing: Zhongguo shehui kexue chubanshe, 1996), pp. 250–281; Xu Ming, ed., *Guanjian shike— Dangdai Zhongguo jidai jiejue de 27 ge wenti* [*The Critical Moment—The 27 Urgent Issues for Contemporary China*] (Beijing: Jinri Zhongguo chubanshe, 1997), pp. 54–85, 452–455, 486–504; Chen Kuide, *Zhujiu lun sichao* [*Discussing Ideology with Wine*] (Taibei, Taiwan: Dongda tushu gongsi, 1997).

5. Jiang Zemin, *Lingdao ganbu yiding yao jiang zhengzhi* [*Leadership Must Emphasize Politics*] (Beijing: Renmin chubanshe, 1996).

6. Some scholars believe that the changing of apostates consists of four stages: (1) belief; (2) doubt; (3) disbelief; and (4) reformulation of belief. See Bill Brugger and David Kelly, *Chinese Marxism in the Post-Mao Era* (Stanford, CA: Stanford University Press, 1990), p. 6.

7. We borrow a concept of "Marxism without Marx" from Bill Brugger and David Kelly, ibid., pp. 171–175.

8. Jiang Zemin, "Shenru xuexi Deng Xiaoping lilun—Jinian Deng Xiaoping tongzhi shishi yi zhounian" ["Promoting Studies of Deng Xiaoping's Theory at the One-Year Anniversary of the Death of Comrade Deng Xiaoping"], *Renmin ribao (People's Daily, Overseas Edition)*, February 18, 1998.

9. Recently, Jiang Zemin proves interesting in his "creative new ideas" (*chuangxin siwei*) to develop both Mao's and Deng's ideas. See Feng Zirui, "Jiang Zemin yiyu xingcheng 'chuangxin siwei'" ["Jiang Zemin Intends to Establish His 'Creative New Ideas'"], *Jingbao (The Mirror)* 256 (November 1998): 24–26. Also see Ruan Ming, "Jiang Zemin de yishi xingtai" ["Jiang Zemin's Ideology"], *Kaifang (Open Magazine)* 134 (February 1998): 39–41.

10. Jiang Zemin, *Report*, p. 21.

11. Ibid., pp. 20–21.

12. X. L. Ding, *The Decline of Communism in China*, p. 166.

13. Yan Sun, *The Chinese Reassessment of Socialism, 1976–1992* (Princeton, NJ: Princeton University Press, 1995), p. 18.

14. Ibid., pp. 16–19.

15. Jiang Zemin, "Promoting Studies of Deng Xiaoping's Theory."

16. Jiang Zemin, *Report,* p. 21.

17. For differences between Mao and Deng, see Zhaohui Hong, "The Subordinate Men and Social Stability in Twentieth-Century China," *Asian Thought and Society* 60 (September–December, 1995): 253–256; and for Deng's duplicity, see Merle Goldman, *Sowing the Seeds of Democracy in China: Political Reform in the Deng Xiaoping Era* (Cambridge, MA: Harvard University Press, 1994), pp. 16–18.

18. Wang Huning, *Mingren riji: Zhengzhi de rensheng [VIP's Diary: Political Life]* (Shanghai: Shanghai renmin chubanshe, 1995), pp. 53, 194.

19. Jiang Zemin, "Guanyu jiang zhengzhi" ["On Stressing Politics"], *Qiu Shi (Searching for Truth)* 13 (1996): 3.

20. See Yuan Hong, "Hong Zhaohui de sanmian yinbi lilun" ["Zhaohui Hong's Theory of the Three-Sided Coin"], *Huaren (Today's Chinese)* (November 1997): 23–25.

21. See Yang Peng, *Dongya xinwenhua de xingqi [The Emergence of East Asia's New Culture]* (Kunming, Yunnan: Yunnan jiaoyu chubanshe, 1997), pp. 140–211.

22. See Lin Zijun, *Chenfu—Zhongguo jingji gaige beiwanglu [The Ups and Downs—The Memorandum of China's Economic Reform]* (Shanghai: Dongfang chuban zhongxin, 1998).

23. For details, see Lin Yusheng, *The Crisis of Chinese Consciousness: Radical Anti-traditionalism in the May Fourth Era* (Madison: University of Wisconsin Press, 1979).

24. Kong Zi (Confucius), *Lun yu [Analects of Confucius]* (Beijing: Hue jiaoxue chubanshe, 1994).

25. Jiang Zemin, *Leadership Must Emphasize Politics,* p. 2.

26. See Hong Zhaohui, "Shehui gaige yu Zhongguo de xiandaihua" ["Social Reform and China's Modernization"], *Zhonggong yanjiu (Studies on Chinese Communism Monthly)* (May 1994): 63–69.

27. Deng Xiaoping, *Deng Xiaoping wenxuan 1975–1982 [Selected Works of Deng Xiaoping, 1975–1982]* (Beijing: Renmin chunbanshe, 1983), p. 347.

28. X. L. Ding, *The Decline of Communism in China,* pp. 162–163.

29. Jiang Zemin, *Report,* p. 42.

30. Ibid., p. 41.

31. Li Yining, "Zhuanxing fazhan lilun" ["The Theory of Transitional Development"], *Xinhua wenzhai (New China Digest)* (July 1997): 50.

32. Zou Dang, "Di erci sixiang jiefang yu zhidu chuangxin xu" ["Preface for the Book Entitled The Second Ideological Liberation and Institutional Reconstruction"], in Cui Zhiyuan, *Di erci sixiang jiefang yu zhidu chuangxin [The Second Ideological Liberation and Institutional Reconstruction]* (Hong Kong: Oxford University Press, 1997), p. x.

33. Li Yining, "The Theory of Transitional Development," p. 24.

34. See Premier Zhu Rongji's Press Conference, *Renmin ribao (People's Daily),* March 19, 1998.

35. Li Zhiping, "Guanyu woguo guoyou qiye gufen zhi gaizao de sikao" ["Review on Reform of SOEs Shareholding System in China: A Case Study on the Maaishan Steel Shareholding Corporation"], *Jingji lilun yu jingji guanli (Economic Theory and Management)* 1 (1997): 1–7.

36. Xu Ming, ed., *The Critical Moment,* pp. 210–211.

37. Zhaohui Hong, "The Shareholding Cooperative System and Property Rights Reform of China's Collective Township-Village Enterprises," *Asian Profile* 23 (October 1995): 359–369.

38. Wang Jue, ed., *Laozhe you qigu: suoyouzhi gaige yu Zhongguo jingji luntan* [*The Share to the Workers: Forum of Reform and Chinese Economy*] (Nanning: Guangxi renmin chubanshe, 1997), pp. 1–3.

39. Li Zhiping, "Review on Reform of SOEs Shareholding System," pp. 1–2.

40. James Meade, "Different Forms of Share Economy," in Susan Howson, ed., *The Collected Papers of James Meade, Volume II: Value, Distribution and Growth* (London: Unwin Hyman, 1988), pp. 212–213.

41. James Meade, *Alternative Systems of Business Organization and of Workers' Remuneration* (London: Allen & Unwin, 1986), pp. 71–113.

42. James Meade, "The Different Forms of Share Economy," p. 221. Meade also designs three other types of sharing arrangements: (1) Employee Share Schemes in which workers share in the fortunes of the firm by owning part of the ordinary shares in the business but do not in fact exercise any decisive control over the firm's operations; (2) Profit-Sharing or Revenue-Sharing arrangements in which labor is paid wholly or in part by a share in the firm's profit or net revenue but does not take part in the control of the firm's operations; (3) A Labor-Capital Partnership in which the workers are not required to own any of the capital invested in the business but in which both workers and capitalists share the firm's revenue and play a part in the control of the firm's operations.

43. Ibid.

44. Jiang Zemin, *Report*, pp. 34, 36.

45. Jiang Zemin, "On Stressing Politics," pp. 3–4.

46. Jiang Zemin, "Geji lingdao ganbu yao nuli xuexi falü zhishi" ["The Various Levels of Leaders Must Study Legal Knowledge"], *Renmin ribao (People's Daily)*, October 10, 1996.

47. Hong Zhaohui, *Shehui jingji bianqian de zuti* [*The Themes of Socio-Economic Transition: Reinterpretation of Modernization*] (Hangzhou, Zhejiang: Hangzhou University Press, 1994).

48. Hong Zhaohui, "Lun Denghou zhongguo de zhixu chongjian yu Jiang Zemin de jiang zhengzhi" ["The Reconstruction of Social Order in Post-Deng China"], *Dangdai Zhongguo yanjiu (Modern China Studies)* (January 1997): 64–65.

49. Merle Goldman, *Sowing the Seeds of Democracy in China*, p. 7.

50. Jiang Zemin, *Report*, p. 34.

51. Li Shenzhi, "Ye yao tuidong zhengzhi gaige" ["Promoting Political Reform Too"], *Dangdai Zhongguo yanjiu (Modern China Studies)* (April 1998): 17–19; Dong Yiyu and Shi Binhai, eds., *Zhengzhi de Zhongguo—Mianxiang xintizhi xuanze de shidai* [*Political China—Facing the Era of New System Selection*] (Beijing: Jinri Zhongguo chubanshe, 1998), pp. 73–82, 233–266.

52. For detailed information about the idea of order and rule of law, see A. V. Dicey, *Introduction to the Study of the Law of the Construction*, 10th ed. (London: Macmillan & Co., Ltd., 1961); F. A. Hayek, *The Constitution of Liberty* (Chicago: Henry Regnery Co., 1960); Lon Fuller, *The Morality of Law* (New Haven: Yale University Press, 1969); John Finnis, *Natural Law and Natural Rights* (Oxford: Clarendon Press, 1980).

53. Dong Yiyu and Shi Binhai, eds., *Political China*, pp. 124–131.

54. For detailed information about China's corruption, see Julia Kwong, *The Political Economy of Corruption in China* (New York: M.E. Sharpe, 1997); Gong Ting, *The Politics of Corruption in Contemporary China* (Westport, CT: Praeger,

1994); Mayfair Mei-hui Yang, *Gifts, Favors, and Banquets: The Art of Social Relationships in China* (Ithaca, NY: Cornell University Press, 1994); Jean Louis Rocca, "Corruption and Its Shadow: An Anthropological View of Corruption in China," *China Quarterly* (June 1992): 402–416; Gordon White, "Corruption and the Transition from Socialism in China," *Journal of Law and Society* (March 1996): 149–169.

55. Jiang Zemin, *Report,* p. 26.

56. Zhao Hui, "Zhongguo dalu zhengfu jigou gaige de yinhuang" ["The Potential Crises of China's Administrative Reform"], *Jing Bao (The Mirror)* 249 (May 1998): 40–41.

57. Hong Zhaohui, "Lun dalu guoyou qiye de zhaiwu weiji" ["The Debt Crisis of Mainland China's State-Owned Enterprises"], *Zhongguo dalu yanjiu (Mainland China Studies)* (August 1996): 58–71.

58. Hu Angang, "Xunqiu xin de ruan zhaolu" ["In Search of the Second Soft Landing: Reducing Unemployment Rate Is the Top Priority of Macro Regulation"], *Liaowang Xinwen Zhoukan (Liaowang Newsweek)* (1998): 12.

59. Zhaohui Hong, "Jiang Zemin's Stressing Politics and Reconstruction of Social Order in China," pp. 95–96.

60. Xu Dianqing and Li Yanjin, eds., *Zhongguo shuizhi gaige (China Tax System Reform)* (Beijing: Zhongguo jingji chubanshe, 1997).

61. Xu Ming, ed., *The Critical Moment,* p. 70.

PART 2

The Political Economy
of Reform

4

Institutional Change and Firm Performance

Shaomin Li

Since the beginning of economic reform in 1978, China's economy has been growing rapidly; the economy increased approximately fivefold from 1978 to 1995.[1] It is generally accepted that the fundamental cause of this remarkable economic performance has been the institutional change precipitated by reform. But how institutions change and how institutions affect performance in this transition have not been adequately examined.

The significance of studying institutional change and performance goes beyond China. Socialist economies (dominated by public ownership) still account for a large share of gross domestic product (GDP) in the world. In no country and at no time have these socialist economies performed well.[2] Thus one of the most important problems of our times is how to reform socialist economies.

This chapter will first review the theoretical relationship between institutions, institutional change, and economic performance. It will then briefly describe the evolution of China's economic transition, followed by the presentation of a theory of endogenous institutional change that examines the driving forces behind institutional change, how institutions change, and the consequences of institutional change on the economic performance of firms. It will next focus on the construction of a theory of the determinants of firm performance that evaluates how much institutional factors account for firm performance, and estimates the role and magnitude of each factor in influencing firm performance in China. Our study finds that while economic factors are the most significant, institutional change is also critical, and government intervention is playing a significant role in firm performance in China's transition. On the basis of these findings, it concludes with a discussion of theoretical contributions to institutional change and firm performance in China's transition, as well as the policy and managerial implications of our studies.

53

Institutions, Institutional Change, and
Organizational Performance

According to Douglass C. North,[3] institutions are the rules of the game in society that govern the interactions among organizations (and individuals), whereas organizations are the players in the game trying to use the opportunities created by the institutions to maximize their welfare. The government is a also a player in the society just like other players. However, there is one important distinction between the government and the other players: the government can set the rules of the game. Institutions include formal and informal constraints that shape human interactions. Informal constraints are conventions and codes of behaviors developed from culture, whereas formal constraints are designed by a society explicitly to regulate social interactions, such as the constitution and other laws. Institutions affect the performance of an economy by their effect on the costs of exchange and production. As they compete and interact, some organizations will perceive opportunities to increase their returns by altering existing institutions and will push for institutional change. However, it is not always the case that those entrepreneurs in the political and economic organizations that initiated change will achieve what they intended. Indeed, many policies have unintended consequences. Institutions explain why a substantial divergence exists among economies, and are thus the underlying determinants of the long-run performance of economies. Western market economies and socialist (or communist) economies provide a stark contrast in terms of institutions, institutional change, and economic performance. According to North, in a social environment where markets are competitive and there are no increasing returns to institutions, institutions do not matter.[4] If markets are incomplete, transaction costs are very high, poor performance will prevail, and institutions do matter. Western market economies come closer to the former description, and socialist economies to the latter description. None of the former socialist economies that are now undergoing reform had competitive markets, and they lacked incentives for efficiency in economic activities. Consequently, they consistently performed poorly. The contemporary reforms aim at establishing institutions that are conducive to strong economic performance.

Janos Kornai's seminal analysis of socialist economies provides a theoretical foundation for the institutional approach to studying economic performance in planned and, later, transition economies.[5] According to Kornai, failure of a planned economy is due to the fundamental institutional arrangement whereby the government is the owner of the enterprises. The government has many important objectives that conflict with maximizing profits. These objectives range from providing full employment and maintaining low-cost or free social services to distributing scarce materials and goods, the shortage of which is characteristic of planned economies. Consequently, firms in planned economies have no incentive to make profits.

Since enterprises are indispensable to the government not because they earn profits, but because they provide employment, secure certain outputs, and shoulder many social services, the government cannot shut them down simply because they are unprofitable. Instead, in order to keep the money-losing firms operating, the government must take funds from profitable firms to subsidize the unprofitable firms—like a father who forces the well-to-do brother to help out his poorer siblings. The government also orders state banks to give loans to these failing firms, knowing full well that the latter will never be able to repay the loans. As a result, the budget constraints of the state-owned enterprises are soft. As the managers of state enterprises are aware of the soft budget constraints, they consistently bargain for more resources and low output goals, and they consistently conceal and hoard resources. The situation is further exacerbated by the inability of the government to run effectively the numerous enterprises it owns due to a lack of information. In summary, socialist economic institutions have failed to provide incentives for economic efficiency.

Thus the increasing returns from institutional change in such economies are not hard to perceive, which is the fundamental reason for the economic transition now taking place in more than twenty former socialist countries. China's transition is particularly interesting; it started as a process of decentralization and is now evolving into a process of rapid privatization.

China's Economic Transition

In December 1978, two years after the death of Mao Zedong, the Communist Party held the historic Third Plenum of the Eleventh Party Congress, which marked the beginning of far-reaching economic reforms. This process evolved into what is now called the economic transition from a planned to a market economy. The ultimate goal of the transition is to move away from central panning and to build a market economy capable of delivering long-term growth and improved living standards.

Essentially, reform has been a two-pronged decentralization process: decentralization from the central government to the local governments, and decentralization from those governments to the basic economic units—that is, enterprises and households.[6] Decentralization from the central to the local governments gave greater incentives to local governments for revenue creation and economic development and allowed many regions to experiment with new and flexible policies, such as the special economic zones.

The transition also decentralized decisionmaking power from the government to enterprises by giving them greater control and residual claim rights.[7] These include the authority to produce, price, and sell extra products after the quota has been met, the authority to hire and fire within state guidelines, and the authority to determine rewards and punishments based on performance.

Associated with decentralization, a second important development has been the diminishing role of central planning and the emergence of markets. Since the early 1980s, China has gradually freed the pricing of goods. Initially, prices of those goods that were deemed vital to the economy and people's livelihood—for example, prices of grain and steel—were controlled. Later, prices of most goods were determined by market demand and supply. Needless to say, the transition is far from complete. On the one hand, there is evidence of the emergence of free markets, competition, and the hardening of budget constraints. On the other hand, institutional factors that are legacies of the planning system still exist, such as high entry barriers erected by the government for some industries, interference in market activities, the imposition of restrictions or the granting of privileges to certain categories of firms, and policies that continue to encourage distorted firm behavior.

The two most important institutional arrangements that affect firm performance in the transition economy are firm ownership and government relationships.

Firm Ownership Structures

Ownership has been recognized as one of the most important institutional arrangements in determining incentive structures, which in turn determine firm performance.[8] There are three types of Chinese enterprises based on the mode through which transactions are coordinated and property rights are embodied.[9] They are state-owned enterprises (SOEs), collectively owned enterprises (COEs), and privately owned enterprises (POEs).[10] Despite the decentralization effort, to a great extent SOEs remain an administrative, not a business, system, with operations planned and controlled by higher-level agencies that provide the necessary inputs and social functions. They still operate under soft rather than hard budget constraints. Consequently, the performance of SOEs continues to deteriorate, but the government cannot simply shut down these poorly performing SOEs because they provide employment and social services on behalf of the government.

COEs carry the ambiguous definition of property rights in socialist economies to the extreme: COEs are the most unclear, fuzzily defined forms of property rights. And yet they have undergone the most dramatic transformation in China's transition economy. COEs first appeared in the first decade of China's socialist economy (the 1950s) as a second-class, less attractive alternative to shoulder the burden of SOEs by employing millions of people whom the SOEs simply could not absorb. By the definition of the time, COEs were "collectively owned by the people," a vague concept without any clear indication of the owner. COEs did not enjoy as many privileges as SOEs in terms of receiving subsidies and scarce resources from the state, but they were subject to all state controls and regulations. Generally, they were poor performers.

The reform granted greater freedoms to COEs, partly because the state could no longer afford to take care of them. Most were "passed down" to be run by local governments. At the same time, fiscal reform gave local governments strong incentives to see that the COEs in their jurisdictions performed well. This newly acquired institutional advantage, namely, operational freedom and local protection, enabled COEs to outperform SOEs and even to some extent POEs.[11]

Unlike SOEs and COEs, private firms follow hard budget constraints, and their survival and operational decisions depend on market performance. Private firms require much stronger entrepreneurial incentives, exacting cost-benefit calculations and greater risk taking and innovation than SOEs.[12] However, private enterprises in a transition economy such as that of China are substantially constrained by the lack of clearly defined property rights.

Government Relationship

All enterprises are directly subordinate to (*lishu*) one of the five levels of government—central, provincial, city, county, or township. The level of government to which an enterprise is subordinate depends on the nature of its operations, location, and scale. SOEs tend to belong to higher levels of government. As one moves down the government hierarchy from state to village,[13] the proportion of SOEs decreases from nearly 100 percent to zero; most public firms at the bottom of the hierarchy are COEs.

Government officials tend to have stronger interests in the public firms as one moves down the hierarchy. Township and village officials are functionally equivalent to a board of directors or shareholders of public firms in the West. Their personal incomes and welfare depend on the performance of the enterprises under their jurisdiction. Decentralization has given strong financial incentives to lower levels of the government hierarchy to ensure that their firms perform well. Thus, in consideration of their own economic benefits, local governments do not tolerate poorly performing enterprises. On the other hand, as one moves higher in the government hierarchy, the fiscal revenue of the government depends less on the revenue from the firms in that jurisdiction and more on taxes. Thus the incentives for higher-level governments to see that their firms perform well remain weak.

Privatization in China[14]

It is generally agreed that institutional change is the driving force behind China's impressive economic performance. Yet little is known about institutional change or the major forces behind such change. Particularly interesting is why China's reforms, which started as a decentralization process, seemingly unintentionally have led to a transition from public to private ownership.

As noted earlier, North's study of institutions and institutional change provides an interpretation of this issue.[15] Montinola, Qian, and Weingast's study of "market-preserving federalism" sheds more light on this issue with particular reference to China.[16] They argued that cross-regional competition has played a central role in the rise of China's economy over the last two decades. However, how cross-regional competition triggers privatization has yet to be addressed formally.

A Theory of Endogenous Institutional Change

This chapter presents a theory of endogenous institutional change in the context of transition economies.[17] The theory uses a mathematical model whereby two firms play a Bertrand-Nash price game in a product market.[18] It demonstrates how decentralization and cross-regional competition force local governments to privatize the SOEs and COEs under their control. The game uses a backward theorizing process, starting from market competition activities. At the market level, in order to increase their market share, firms compete on price. At the firm level, price competition leads to efforts on the part of managers to lower costs, and the results of these efforts evolve into institutional competition to determine which institutional arrangements provide the greatest incentives for managers to lower costs.

To facilitate this discussion, the following terms must be defined. "Ownership of the firm" is defined by residual claims.[19] "Privatization" is a process of shifting residual claims from the government to enterprise managers.[20]

In this game, there are two local governments and two enterprises. The two enterprises were formerly owned by the central government. At the initial stage of the reform, the central government "passed down" the enterprises to the local government, with each local government owning one enterprise. The local governments then obtained the residual claims on after-tax profits and also the right to decide whether or not to shift residual claims to the managers. In other words, the local government now has the autonomy to decide whether or not to privatize the firms. To simplify the analysis, we assume that the manager has complete control of the firm's business, except the rights of taxation and privatization, and that the manager's residual claim rights are well preserved. Thus, when the manager holds all residual outputs of the firm, he becomes the de facto owner of the firm.

At the initial stage of the game, the central government delegates ownership to the local governments. The former still maintains authority to set the tax rate and the latter's share of tax revenue. These parameters are the same for the two localities. At the second stage, the local governments determine the managers' after-tax profit retention rate in an institutional competition, that is, whether or not to privatize to maximize revenue. At the third stage, given the tax rates and the managers' incentives, the two managers choose unobservable efforts in a cost-reduction competition. At stage four, the two firms compete with each other in product markets by choosing prices.

The second through the fourth stages assume that the central government's initial decision to decentralize and the tax rates are made independent of the local governments (or *exogenously* determined). Factors affecting competition include transportation costs, trade barriers, regulation, and other costs. Some of these factors are under the control of the central government, and others are under the control of local governments or are determined by technology. To emphasize how competition triggers privatization, we assume these factors to be exogenously given. It is reasonable to assume that total costs are a function of managerial effort. In a competitive market, in order for firms to survive, they must cut costs as much as possible.

The residual share of the manager gives him an incentive to reduce costs in order to increase market share. Thus the manager's effort increases with his residual share; this means that a firm's market share increases as the manager's residual share increases and decreases as its rival's residual share decreases. This is the fundamental reason why two local governments compete for privatization.

The local government's revenue consists of two parts: the tax revenue and the profit revenue. The trade-off facing the local government is that a higher share of the residual claim for the manager (namely, privatization) generates a higher profit, but reduces its own (relative) share. The first effect (larger absolute size of revenue due to higher total profits) may be labeled the "incentive effect," and the second effect (smaller relative size due to a higher share to the manager as a result of privatization), the "distribution effect."

It is reasonable to assume that the local government cares only for its total revenue, not its share relative to that of the firm.[21] The following propositions are based on the analytical results of the game.

If competition is sufficiently intense, then the local government is motivated to privatize its firm, since the incentive effect dominates the distribution effect. Therefore the local government prefers to obtain the tax revenue since the revenue increase resulting from a bigger profit share to the government is not large enough to offset the tax revenue loss due to weaker managerial incentives.

This implies that a larger share of tax revenue to the local government (as opposed to the share of the central government) promotes a larger private sector. The greater the share of tax revenue to the local government (given the tax rate), the more likely the incentive effect (due to privatization) dominates the distribution effect.

In order for competition to work effectively, regional governments cannot erect trade barriers, and yet they must have autonomy to make other economic decisions to respond to competitive pressure. So far, it has been assumed that regional governments have full autonomy to set after-tax residual shares. When the autonomy of a regional government is restricted by the central government, the privatization process may slow down. Indeed, in the game, if all the rights to set after-tax residual shares are in the hands of the central government, public ownership will prevail; under complete control of the central government, there is simply no need for local governments to motivate their firms to perform.

On the other hand, if two regions perfectly collude, initially there will be no cross-regional competition; each local government will claim one-half of the total profits earned by the two regions and neither government will have any incentives to give any of the residual profits to the managers, and thus the managers will make no effort to reduce costs. However, in general such collusion is not an equilibrium. If one government sets the residual profit of its manager at zero, the other government, in order to beat its rival, will try to give a bit more incentive to its manager. As a result, each local government is tempted to go a little further than its rival toward privatization until equilibrium is restored at full privatization. In other words, when competition in the product market is sufficiently intense, two local governments will compete in terms of the privatization of their firms. They are in a "prisoner's dilemma."

In summary, in a game of price competition by firms owned by local governments, production costs are determined by the managers' efforts. The local government is concerned with its own total revenue, which depends on its market share and profit rate. When competition is sufficiently intense in the product market, the local government will be motivated to shift the residual claim to its manager. As the product market becomes more competitive, the market share and therefore profits are more sensitive to production costs. In order to maintain a minimum market share for survival, the manager must be motivated to work harder to reduce costs. Given that the government cannot directly monitor each manager's efforts, privatization is the only effective means by which the local government can motivate its manager. In contrast, if the central government sets the after-tax residual share, or if the two local governments perfectly collude to maximize their joint revenue, then public ownership may prevail. The game shows that efficiency improves as a consequence of privatization.

Empirical Evidence and Test of the Theory

Empirical evidence from the past two decades supports this theory. In the past two decades and particularly since the early 1990s, both explicit and implicit privatization have been taking place at an increasing pace.[22] In 1978, at the beginning of the reform, 78 percent of the total industrial output came from SOEs. By 1995, the SOEs' share had shrunk to only one-third of the total output.[23] Note that these statistics only account for explicit, not implicit, privatization.

The major players behind the privatization process are local governments at various levels.[24] Although not all local governments are undertaking explicit, wholesale privatization programs, almost all local governments are considering privatization in one way or another.[25] For example, a recent survey estimates that more than 70 percent of small SOEs have been fully or partially privatized in Shandong Province.[26] In November 1997, the Beijing municipal government began to auction off many small SOEs. In early 1998, Dalian city government began to auction off not only the failing SOEs, but also the profitable ones. The aim is to "cut off all SOEs from the government."[27]

This theory was tested using newly available industrial census data from 1993 to 1995. These censuses are conducted by the State Statistical Bureau and cover all manufacturing firms subordinate to the township government (the lowest-level governmental body in China) or above. The censuses include between 400,000 to 500,000 firms. In 1995, the output of these firms accounted for 94 percent of the total industrial sales by all firms with independent accounting systems.[28] Firms not included in the census are the very small, often family-run workshops. The data set contains ownership type, level of government control, geographic location, revenue, and other performance and demographic variables. As mentioned earlier, virtually all firms are subordinate to (*lishu*) governments at different levels (central, provincial, city or prefecture, county, and township). The firms subordinate to a government may be state-, collective-, or privately owned. In general, SOEs are subordinate to county-level governments or above, COEs are subordinate either to county-level governments or above or to township governments and village committees, and private enterprises are primarily subordinate to village committees, or township or county governments.

In this theory, a region's privatization level is determined by the following factors.

1. *Degree of competition from other regions.* The greater the competition from outside, the greater the pressure to privatize. Degree of competition from outside can be measured by two factors: (a) degree of access to transportation measured by road and water route density, and (b) the privatization level of neighboring regions. The

higher the level of privatization in surrounding regions, the higher the intensity of competition, and thus the greater the pressure to privatize.

2. *Degree of control over a region's own public enterprises (SOEs and COEs).* A local government can only privatize the public firms under its control. It has no control over firms located in its jurisdiction but reporting directly to a higher level of government (in fact it may not even have any incentive to do so). Under the pressure of cross-regional competition, the higher the degree of control over its public firms, the more the likelihood that the local government will privatize them.

3. *The existing level (history) of privatization in a region.* A higher degree of privatization in a region implies greater intraregional competition and greater freedom to privatize, thus the greater the likelihood of further privatization.

The theory predicts that all of these factors contribute to privatization by facilitating competition. The proportion of revenue contributed by the private sector to a county in 1995 measures the privatization level. The degree of access to transportation is measured by two variables: one is the ratio of coastline length to land area; and the other is the ratio of railway length to land area; both are at the provincial level. The degree of privatization in the surrounding regions is measured by the proportion of revenue contributed by the private sector to the neighboring counties in 1993. Neighboring counties include all counties in the same prefecture as the county being evaluated (excluding the county being evaluated). The level of control over a region's public firms is measured by the proportion of a county's revenue being contributed by SOEs subordinate to governments at the county level or lower in 1994. The privatization history of a region is the proportion of revenue being contributed by the private sector to the county under evaluation in 1993. The unit of analysis is the county. Information has been aggregated from all firms extant in 1993 (446,265), 1994 (485,052), and 1995 (450,223) at the county level, and the indexes of privatization and level of control for all 2,002 counties has been calculated based on the industrial census. A multiple regression analysis is used to evaluate the hypothesized causal relationship. If the theory is true, then all the factors (1) to (3) will simultaneously exert positive effects on a region's privatization level. Given the comprehensive coverage of our data, the test is rigorous.

The result of the regression analysis shows that factors (1) to (3), as predicted, positively affect a region's privatization in a highly significant way. For example, the regression model shows that a 10 percent higher private share in the neighboring counties triggers a 1.5 percent higher private share in the county under consideration two years later. The statistics show that the chance that the model is wrong is negligible: 0.01 percent. These results provide convincing support for the theory.

The discussion and the test in this section show that the theoretical predictions are consistent with what has actually occurred. The economies of the coastal regions are more privatized than those of the inland regions because the former enjoy not only lower transportation costs (thus facilitating cross-regional competition) but, more importantly, greater autonomy. Similarly, SOEs in the northeast and southwest tend to be less privatized since their high concentration in these regions makes competition less intense. Sectors with simple or standard contracts are more privatized than sectors with complex or specific contracts because the former involve lower enforcement costs and hence face stronger competition than the latter. The former include labor-intensive industries, such as textiles and consumer electronics. The latter generally include capital-intensive and contract-intensive industries, such as machine tools, banking, and insurance. For example, in 1985 the output of SOEs accounted for 17 percent and 64 percent of the total output of the garment and machine tools industries, respectively. By 1995, the SOEs' share of the garment industry had shrunk to 6.9 percent, while the SOEs' share in the machine tools industries was still 40 percent.[29] Privatization of town and village enterprises proceeds more rapidly than that of SOEs because TVEs operate in more competitive markets and their governments (townships) have no leverage to shield them from outside competition.

Institutional Versus Economic Effects[30]

The preceding section attempts to provide an understanding of change in China's transition and the consequences of such institutional change. This section examines the question of how institutional factors affect firm performance. The factors that determine firm performance such as profitability are a central problem both for industrial organizational economics and strategic management research. Scholars in both fields, for example, are concerned with understanding what factors are responsible for persistent unequal returns across industries and firms.[31]

Both fields recognize that there are two groups of factors that explain variations in firm performance: industry-specific factors and firm-specific characteristics. Industry-specific factors include the concentration level of an industry (consolidated versus fragmented); minimum capital requirements (which is a form of entry barrier, e.g., the aircraft industry requires a much higher minimum investment than the garment industry); or product differentiation (also an entry barrier, e.g., if the existing products are highly distinctive, it will be difficult for new producers to attract customers who remain loyal to the existing products). Firm-specific characteristics include firm resources (capital, technology, and human resources), capabilities (marketing, management, or production skills), and strategies.

Industrial organization economists and strategic management scholars differ regarding the roles each set of factors plays in firm performance. Industrial organization economists argue that industry structures, such as concentration and entry barriers, lead to variation in firm performance. They focus on interindustry differences as the main source of varying performance. Firm-specific characteristics are regarded as less important in determining firm performance. Scholars of strategic management, on the other hand, emphasize the choice orientation of a firm's behavior and argue that firm characteristics, such as firm resources, capabilities, and strategies, are essential in determining firm performance. They point out that even in weak industries, there are stars that consistently outperform the others, and in high-profit industries there are failures due to mistakes on the part of firms.

In order to evaluate quantitatively the role of industry- and firm-specific factors on performance variations, scholars in both fields have conducted performance variance decomposition analyses. They find that industry factors explain a relatively small proportion of the variations, 13–19 percent; a much larger proportion of profitability variation, 36–47 percent, is attributed to firm-specific characteristics. The remainder is due to estimation errors.[32]

The above studies of firm performance are all based on Western experiences. To what extent are these studies applicable to firm performance in a transition economy? How much do industry and other economic factors explain performance variance across firms in China? In a transition economy such as China's, are there any determining factors unique to the transition from a planned economy to a market economy?

Studies based on Western economies concentrate on economic factors that determine firm performance. However, in a transition economy such as China's, institutions do matter in terms of economic performance. The institutional legacy of planning hinders an efficient market, and so there are increasing returns to institutions (which is the motivation behind institutional change). Thus, firm performance is jointly determined by both the newly emerging market forces (economic factors) and by the legacy of economic planning (or government interventions—institutional factors).

Decomposing Firm Performance Variance in China

Guided by theoretical arguments, a firm performance variance decomposition analysis can be done. Firm performance is measured by return on assets. In addition to industry and firm factors, two institutional factors were considered: ownership and government relationship, the latter of which should be regarded as the most important (see the above detailed discussion on these two factors). The time period of our analysis was from 1992 to 1995, because China was changing very rapidly during that period. With the time factor (one year) in the analysis, it was possible to evaluate the dynamic effects of institutions, industry, and firms. The results of the analysis show that the dynamic institutional effect accounts for 33 percent of firm performance variance. The dynamic industry effect accounts for only 6 percent, and the dynamic firm-specific factor accounts for 24 percent; the remainder is the variance unexplained by these factors. As expected, performance variance across firms in China's transition is different from that in the West. Institutional factors are most important in explaining variance in firm performance.

Estimating the Effects of Government Interventions and Economic Factors on Firm Performance

The performance variance decomposition analysis demonstrates that institutions matter for firm performance. But it does not reveal the theoretical relationship between each determining factor and firm performance. For example, it does not show whether or not subordination to a lower-level government helps firm performance. Based on the argument that both government intervention and market forces jointly determine firm behavior and performance, and on the general relationship between institutions and firm performance, the theoretical relationships between these factors and firm performance can be developed.

Once the theoretical relationships were developed, an empirical test using China's 1995 industrial census data was conducted. The testing method was multiple regression. From the 1995 census of 450,233 firms, a 10 percent random sample was used to test the hypotheses.

In the empirical test, performance is measured by two variables: sales revenue per employee (a measure of productivity), and returns on assets (a measure of profitability). Using these two performance measures as dependent variables, two multiple regression models were estimated independently.[33]

Government Influences on Firm Performance

The dukedom effect: local protectionism. As part of the economic reform, the central government has delegated much responsibility and authority to lower-level governments. This process provides strong incentives to local governments to help the firms under their jurisdiction.

How does a local government help the firms under its jurisdiction? One obvious measure is local protectionism, or the so-called dukedom economy as it is referred to in China. A good example of the dukedom economy is the automobile industry. By its nature, the automobile industry is highly consolidated because economies of scale are vital for success. Due to high tariffs and other restrictions on imports as well as high demand for automobiles, automobiles are very expensive and highly profitable. Many provinces claim the automobile industry to be a "pillar industry" with a high priority for protection. These provinces set up their own automobile plants and ban the sales and use of automobiles "imported" from other provinces. At present, there are over two hundred assembly plants, some with an annual production as low as a hundred units. One analyst has referred to China's automobile industry as "the most fragmented in the world."[34] Other examples of local protectionism are the tobacco and alcoholic beverage industries.

This local protectionism causes the industry to fragment geographically and the geographic barriers keep profits artificially high. The regression model shows that the lower an industry's geographic concentration, the higher the firm's profit.[35]

Effects due to local support. In China, governments have three sources of revenue: taxes, fees, and the profits of the public firms under their jurisdiction. In general, the higher the level of the government, the greater reliance on taxes for revenue and the less reliance on profits from its firms. The central government relies primarily on taxes for revenue. The central government also receives some profits from the firms it oversees, although these are insignificant compared to the taxes. The main tax sources for local governments are various firm taxes. In addition, local governments rely on the profits of the public firms under their jurisdiction. As one proceeds lower down the government hierarchy, the contribution of firms— in both taxes and profits—becomes more important. As a result, local governments are motivated to ensure that firms under their jurisdiction perform well. In general, the lower the level of government, the more dependent it is on, and the greater its economic interest in, the performance of the firms in its jurisdiction.

Because of their strong financial interest, local governments give preferential treatment to local firms rather than to "nonlocal" firms. Regression analysis finds that because of such local support, firms reporting to the lowest level of government tend to perform best, both in terms of profits and in terms of productivity.

Contribution to the local economy. To ensure revenue, local governments may establish various operation-related fees for firms that operate in the community. These fees are normally set in proportion to the size of the operation. In other words, the more revenue a firm generates, the more the firm will be charged. These charges are key sources of income for many local governments.

In addition, firms contribute to the local community in other ways. They provide jobs for the community and, in many cases, they run social services such as hospitals, schools, and even bus lines—not only for their workers but also for the community at large. (Some local firms even support the daily operation of the local courts!) Given their importance to the local economy, large firms (in proportion to other firms in the same locality) can bargain and receive preferential treatment from the local government. The higher the revenue of a firm in comparison to average firm revenue in the local economy, the better it performs both in terms of profit and of productivity.

Soft budget constraints. Perhaps the best-known government support to firms in planned economies is the "soft budget constraint." This includes loans at reduced interest rates and flexible terms, reduced and ex ante negotiated taxes, and other subsidies.

The practice of soft budget constraints is so common and detrimental in transition economies that many researchers argue that only by reducing such subsidies (a "hardening of the soft budget constraints") will firm performance in transition economies be improved.[36] The rationale is quite simple: if a firm can spend what does not belong to it and is not responsible for its budget constraints, then the firm will not perform well. However, measuring the effects of soft budget constraints on firm performance is not easy,[37] because most subsidies are hidden.

The effect of soft subsidies in taxes on firm performance can be measured by using the variation in county tax rates. Tax rates vary greatly, not only across counties but also across firms within counties, because to a great extent county governments can control tax rates and set different tax rates for different firms; this is a typical form of soft subsidies from governments to firms.

A greater variation in tax rates implies a greater degree of soft budget constraints imposed on firms in a county. This in turn stimulates firms to seek greater tax subsidies, thus providing them with fewer incentives to perform in the market. Rather, they spend their resources on (or under) the negotiation table with government officials. In addition, firms are motivated to reduce their tax exposures by reporting lower performance. As a result, the higher the variation in the tax rate at the county level, the lower a firm's performance (profitability and productivity).

The influence of market forces on firm performance. Based on past studies of firm performance in market economies, the most important factors affecting firm performance are industry concentration, the size of capital investment, product differentiation, and industry risks. These studies have shown that profitability is positively correlated with the above factors.[38]

This study examines the effects of industry concentration, size of capital investment, and industry risk on firm performance. (Due to the lack of relevant data, such as advertising intensity, the effect of product differentiation on firm performance cannot be assessed.) Since the effects of these variables on firm performance are well established in industrial economics literature, these will also apply to China after controlling for the effects of government intervention on firm performance.

Industry concentration. Higher market concentration in an industry reduces competition and encourages collusion in that industry. As a result, firms will enjoy higher profits. On the other hand, reduced competition causes firms to be complacent and they will be less productive. In the regression model, the higher the market concentration in the industry level, the higher the profitability and the lower the productivity of firms in that industry.

Size of capital investment. The scale of capital investment is often seen as a barrier to potential entrants: the higher the capital requirements, the higher the entry barriers. Such barriers in turn ensure that existing firms earn higher profits. In addition, greater investment generally implies large-scale production, which usually correlates with high productivity. As expected, the higher the capital requirement in an industry, the greater the performance of firms in that industry.

In summary, analysis confirms the hypotheses about the effects of government intervention in shaping firm behavior and performance. After two decades of economic reform, the legacy of the planned economy (that is, government intervention) is still felt when firm performance is examined. At the same time, however, market forces also exert an effect on firm performance.

Discussion and Conclusions

This chapter has reviewed a theory of endogenous institutional change and a theory of the determinants of firm performance in the context of transition economies in general and of China in particular. Both theories are strongly supported by empirical tests based on the most comprehensive data sets available: industrial censuses from China.

On Institutional Change and Privatization

Privatization of public enterprises can take place as a consequence of cross-regional competition. Chinese economic reform did not initially intend to privatize public enterprises. But the decentralization policy eventually triggered privatization through cross-regional competition. The recent Fifteenth Party Congress's promotion of joint-stock systems to bail out the vast majority of failing SOEs is widely viewed as implicit privatization. But explicit privatization has thus far not been adopted as central government policy, mostly for ideological reasons. However, competition is far more powerful than ideology. Regardless of whether or not the central government draws up a blueprint for full privatization, both theory and reality reveal that the privatization process will continue and accelerate with its own logic and vigor.

The Chinese experience demonstrates that the "invisible hand" is powerful not only in allocating resources, but also in creating institutions. Once there is decentralization, market competition may precipitate a self-enforcing process of privatization. As a result, decentralization may induce even more privatization than a deliberate privatization policy if the latter is not accompanied by sufficient decentralization. This is a major lesson that other transition and emerging economies may draw from China's experience.

Nevertheless, privatization calls for a sound legal system to protect property rights. In particular, de facto ownership by managers must eventually become de jure ownership. Commercial laws are needed to support contracts between privatized enterprises. Two major problems stand out in the current system of commercial law. First, there are no clear and detailed rules to protect private property. To facilitate efficient private investments, detailed civil codes are needed to protect private property under different contingencies. Second, cross-regional commercial disputes are presently settled in local courts controlled by local governments. To mitigate local protectionism and to facilitate competition, either local courts need to become independent from local government control or major cross-regional commercial disputes should be dealt with in the national courts.

On Determinants of Firm Performance

Analysis in decomposing variance in firm performance shows that in a transition economy such as China's, in addition to economic factors such as industry and firm factors found in market economies, institutional factors measured by ownership structure and government relationship also affect firm performance. Furthermore, these institutional factors exert a larger effect than either the industry effect or the firm effect.

The determinants of firm performance in a transition economy consist of both market factors and government intervention. This chapter establishes the theoretical relationship between industry structure and firm performance, and it identifies and measures the effect of government interventions, especially that of the soft budget constraints. This relationship has been duly tested with empirical data.

Three major findings are worthy of further elaboration. First, in a transition economy such as China's, both government interventions and market forces are powerful in shaping firm behavior. This is important for future theoretical frameworks on transition economies.

The second important finding concerns the complexity of government forces in a transition economy. Local government is very effective in determining firm performance. However, "local governments as industrial firms"[39] is a double-edged sword and ultimately may be a major obstacle to further transition. At best, it is merely an expedient allowing these public firms to operate better than the "iron rice bowl" system of the old planned economy. Theories of political economy have convincingly demonstrated that government should be the "referee" of the economic game in a society, not a player in the game. When government is both the referee and a player, the rules of the game will be unfair and corruption will inevitably occur, in the long run hindering economic growth and firm performance.[40] Fortunately this sentiment is increasingly accepted by reformers in China. At the recent Fifteenth Party Congress, the government explicitly recognized this problem and stressed its determination to solve it.[41] Shunde, a region in China's most affluent province of Guangdong, demonstrates such a shift in government roles. Shunde is known for its investment environment and market institutions. Its evolution from "government as corporation" to "government as government" can be clearly seen from the governing philosophy of its mayor, Feng Runsheng, whose observations follow:

> I used to be a chief representative of all factories in Shunde. You may call me the biggest CEO of all city enterprises . . . Now, the government and enterprises are separate. As a mayor, I have only two responsibilities: to develop the city's infrastructure and services, and to maintain law and order . . . All investors—domestic and foreign—can easily learn and understand our policies and regulations. We welcome everyone to invest, but we will not break the rules for anyone.[42]

The third finding is revealing for the study of institutional change in transition economies. Earlier studies have shown that firm ownership (such as state-owned, privately owned, or foreign-owned enterprises) is very important in determining performance in China's transition.[43] But this study shows that the role of ownership is not very important in and of itself in determining performance, after factoring in government interventions. In view of the heated discussions in all transition economies in general and in China in particular about the role of privatization, this finding is likely to stimulate further debate on the issue. This study suggests that in China, where clearly demarcated property rights are lacking and explicit privatization still faces strong public opposition, the firm—together with the local government—has found a convoluted way to stimulate performance: giving more incentives to the decisionmaker of the firm by making the local government the de facto owner.

Managerial and Policy Implications

For managers operating in or considering entering China, the salience of government interventions on firm performance implies that developing and maintaining a good relationship with the local government (not just the provincial or national government) is of vital importance.

For public policymakers, the relationship between the local government and the firm needs to be restructured so that the former is the referee and the latter the player in the economic game. The government needs to reduce its intervention and to allow the market mechanism to operate freely in order to boost performance. Unless new evidence proves otherwise, thus far both theoretical as well as empirical studies have shown that even with good intentions, most government intervention hinders rather than helps firm performance.

From "isms" to "ownership": Solution to the SOE problem. In the early days of reform, there were heated debates as to whether the reform would lead to capitalism or socialism (*xingshe xingzi*). The conservatives claimed that the introduction of free-market mechanisms represented a "march toward capitalism." Deng Xiaoping declared that it was not important to discuss the "isms"; rather, China needed to focus on whatever route would raise living standards. Deng's political astuteness effectively contained the ideological debate and led to the further development of free markets.

Now the reform has reached a crucial turning point whereby the partial introduction of free-market mechanisms is insufficient; at the foundation of free markets must be a system of clearly defined and well-protected private property rights. However, under Deng, privatization was not possible.[44] The end of the Deng era allowed an opportunity for the restructuring of the property rights system. The current leaders are fully aware of this.[45] The debate today is over "public versus private ownership" (*xinggong xingsi*). The evolution of the debate from "isms" to "ownership" shows that the transition is at a crossroads. The stakes are high: SOEs account for more than one-half of China's total industrial assets, but only produce one-third of its output.[46] Most of the inefficient SOEs are losing money because of ill-defined property rights, mounting debts, and resultant social burdens. The only salvation appears to be privatization.

Notes

1. China National Statistics Bureau, *Zhongguo tongji nianjian, 1996* [*China Statistical Yearbook, 1996*] (Beijing: Zhonggou tongji chubanshe), p. 42.

2. World Bank, *Bureaucrats in Business* (Washington, DC: World Bank, 1997).

3. Douglass C. North, *Institutions, Institutional Change and Economic Performance* (Cambridge: Cambridge University Press, 1990).

4. North, *Institutions, Institutional Change and Economic Performance,* p. 95.

5. Janos Kornai, *Economics of Shortage* (Amsterdam: North-Holland, 1980).

6. Gabriella Montinola, Yingyi Qian, and Barry R. Weingast, "Federalism, Chinese Style: The Political Basis for Economic Success in China," *World Politics* 48 (October 1995): 50–81.

7. Residual claim rights are the rights to claim residual output beyond the agreed-upon quantity. Economists have shown that in order to design an efficient (output maximization) incentive scheme, it is necessary to ensure that the production decisionmaker is the *residual claimant* to output. See Hal R. Varian, *Intermediate Microeconomics* (New York: W. W. Norton, 1996), p. 644.

8. North, *Institutions, Institutional Change and Economic Performance;* Shaomin Li, "Success in China's Industrial Market: An Institutional and Environmental Approach," *Journal of International Marketing* 1 (1998): 56–80.

9. Max Boisot and John Child, "From Fiefs to Clans and Network Capitalism: Explaining China's Emerging Economic Order," *Administrative Science Quarterly* 41 (1996): 600–628; Victor Nee, "Organizational Dynamics of Market Transition: Hybrid Forms, Property Rights and Mixed Economy in China," *Administrative Science Quarterly* 37 (1992): 1–27; Andrew G. Walder, "Local Governments as Industrial Firms: An Organizational Analysis of China's Transitional Economy," *American Journal of Sociology* 101 (1995): 263–301.

10. Private ownership is broadly defined to include all non-SOEs and non-COEs, which are primarily market-driven and have hard budget constraints. They include privately owed companies, joint ventures, limited companies, and joint-stock companies.

11. See Nee, "Organizational Dynamics of Market Transition," and Li, "Success in China's Industrial Market." The advantage of COEs appears to be fading and their performance potential seems to have reached its limit. The reasons for this include: (1) the fuzzy ownership structure (i.e., who is the owner?); and (2) the lack of managerial ability to cope with rapid expansion and market change. See Craig S. Smith, "Factory Towns—Municipal-Run Firms Helped Build China; Now, They're Faltering," *Wall Street Journal,* October 8, 1997, p. A1.

12. Nee, "Organizational Dynamics of Market Transition."

13. Although a village is not a government, it is a public organization that can own COEs.

14. This section summarizes the study by Shaomin Li, Shuhe Li, and Weiying Zhang regarding privatization in China's economic transition. For details, see Shaomin Li, Shuhe Li, and Weiying Zhang, "Competition and Institutional Change: Privatization in China" (Hong Kong: City University of Hong Kong, Working Paper, 1997).

15. North, *Institutions, Institutional Change and Economic Performance.*

16. Montinola, Qian, and Weingast, "Federalism, Chinese Style."

17. By "endogenous" we mean that the institutional change is caused by economic reform.

18. In a Bertrand-Nash price game, the only criterion for buyers' decisions is price; thus sellers compete solely on price. As a result of this competition, the equilibrium price will converge to the cost of the sellers.

19. Traditionally, residual rights have defined ownership. Grossman and Hart define ownership as control rights over assets (see Stanford Grossman and Olive D. Hart, "Cost and Benefits of Ownership: A Theory of Vertical and Lateral Integration," *Journal of Political Economy* 94 [1986]: 691–719). Presently, economists recognize that both residual claims and control rights are indispensable to ownership.

Here we omit control rights, not because they are irrelevant but because of technical intractability. Nevertheless, we suppose that our results apply to control rights as well.

20. Since our model is timeless, "the residual" is best interpreted as the present value of all future residual flows when one applies the theory to reality. That is, privatization should be understood as a permanent transfer of residual claims from government to private hands. A short-term contract between government and management, such as the "contract management responsibility system" practiced in China, can be seen as a partial privatization of state-owned enterprises.

21. One may think that the local government also cares for its market share per se since market share is positively related to local employment levels and often to chances for promotion of local officials in the governmental hierarchy. However, our basic conclusion does not change, but rather is strengthened if market share itself is part of the local government's objective function.

22. Implicit privatization refers to cases in which assets and profits formally belong to governments, but de facto are held by managers and bureaucrats. Typical characteristics of implicit privatization include hiding assets and profits in private accounts, making investments in so-called subsidiary companies with little control by the governments, setting up companies in foreign countries, and transferring state assets to private or quasi-private companies.

23. China National Statistics Bureau, *China Statistical Yearbook, 1996,* p. 403.

24. For instance, in 1992, Quanzhou municipal government of Fujian Province sold all of its SOEs to a Hong Kong businessman, who also bought dozens of other SOEs in other regions and successfully packed them for public offering in the Hong Kong and New York financial markets. From 1992 to 1994, Zhucheng municipal government of Shandong Province privatized all of its 272 government-owned enterprises. A similar process of privatization has been undertaken in many other areas such as in Shunde of Guangdong Province, Yibin and Deyang of Sichuan Province, Shuzhou of Shanxi Province, and Xishui and Xianfan of Hubei Province. See Hu Shuli, "Zhongce xianxiang: guanyu yinzi gaizao de jiexi he sikao" ["The Phenomenon of 'China Strategy': Analysis and Thinking of Restructuring State Enterprises Through Foreign Investors"], *Gaige (Reform Journal)* 3 (1994): 74–85; and see Wang Yanzhong and Xu Heping, *Zhucheng qiye gaige tantao [Studies of Zhucheng's Enterprise Reform]* (Beijing: Jingji guanli chubanshe, 1996).

25. An anecdote among economists is indicative. When an economist told a provincial governor, "I heard that the central government has created regulations forbidding local governments from selling SOEs," the governor responded, "Do you know anyone who wants to buy?"

26. China Reform Foundation, *Xianshi de xuanze [Reality's Choice]* (Shanghai: Shanghai yuandong Chubanshe, 1997), p. 35.

27. "Jingji Banxiaoshi" ["30-Minute Economy"), Zhongyang Dianshitai 2 (China Central Television 2), April 1–2, 1998.

28. China National Statistics Bureau, *Zhongguo gongye renkou tongji, 1995 [Chinese Industrial Census, 1995]* (Beijing: Zhonggou tongji ju, 1995), and *Zhongguo tongji nianjian, 1996 [China Statistical Yearbook, 1996]* (Beijing: Zhonggou tongji ju, 1996), p. 417.

29. China National Statistics Bureau, *Zhongguo tongji nianjian, 1986 [China Statistical Yearbook 1986]* (Beijing: Zhonggou tongji chubanshe), pp. 242–243; *China Statistical Yearbook 1996,* pp. 414, 418.

30. This section summaries findings from the following studies: Shaomin Li and David K. Tse, "Do Market Forces Matter in a Transitional Economy? Effects

of Economic Factors and Government Intervention on Firm Performance in China"
(Hong Kong: City University of Hong Kong, Working Paper, 1997); Shaomin Li,
"Success in China's Industrial Market"; and Seung Ho Park, Shaomin Li, and
David K. Tse, "Determinants of Firm Performance in a Transition Economy: Insti-
tutional vs. Economic Effects in China" (Paper presented at the 1997 Meeting of
the Academy of International Business, Monterrey, Mexico, 1997).

31. Richard Schmalensee, "Do Markets Differ Much?" *American Economic
Review* 75 (1985): 349–365; Richard P. Rumelt, "How Much Does Industry Matter?" *Strategic Management Journal* 12 (1991): 167–185.

32. Schmalensee, "Do Markets Differ Much?"; Gary S. Hansen and Biger
Wernerfelt, "Determinants of Firm Performance: The Relative Importance of Economic and Organizational Factors," *Strategic Management Journal* 10 (1989):
399–411; Rumelt, "How Much Does Industry Matter?"; Thomas C. Powell, "How
Much Does Industry Matter? An Alternative Empirical Test," *Strategic Management Journal* 17 (1996): 653–664; and Anita M. McGahan and Michael E. Porter,
"How Much Does Industry Matter, Really?" *Strategic Management Journal* 18
(1997): 15–30.

33. The profitability regression model is based on the Cobb-Douglas production function. The profitability regression model is estimated by using a linear
model.

34. Michael J. Dunne, "The Race Is On," *Chinese Business Review* (March–
April, 1994): 16-23.

35. A Herfindahl concentration index is used, which is the sum of the ratio of
a location's market share squared. Donald A. Hay and Derek J. Morris, *Industrial
Economics: Theory and Evidence* (Oxford: Oxford University Press, 1986),
p. 104.

36. Justin Y. Lin, Fang Cai, and Zhou Li, "Qiye gaige de hexin shi chuangzao
gongping jingzheng de huanjing" ["Creating an Environment for Fair Competition
Is the Core of Enterprise Reform"], in *Zhongguo guoyou qiye gaige [Reform of
State Owned Enterprises in China]*, ed. Xu Dianqing and Wen Guanzhong (Beijing: Zhongguo jingji chubanshe, 1996), pp 49–89; Orjan Sjoberg and Zhang Gang,
"Soft Budget Constraints in Chinese Township Enterprises" (Stockholm: Stockholm School of Economics, 1996).

37. Sjoberg and Zhang, "Soft Budget Constraints."

38. Schmalensee, "Do Markets Matter Much?"; J. Khalilzadeh-Shirazi, "Market Structure and Price-Cost Margins in U.K. Manufacturing Industries," *Review of
Economics and Statistics* 56 (1974): 67–76; J. L. Bothwell and T. E. Keeler, "Profits, Market Structure and Portfolio Risk," in *Essays on Industrial Organization in
Honor of Joe S. Bain*, ed. R. T. Masson and P. D. Qualls (Cambridge, MA: Ballinger, 1976), pp. 71–88; Hay and Morris, *Industrial Economics.*

39. Walder, "Local Governments as Industrial Firms."

40. Smith, "Factory Towns."

41. Jiang Zemin, *Gaoju Deng Xiaoping lilun weida qizhi, ba jianshe you
Zhongguo tese shehui zhuyi shiye quanmian tuixiang ershiyi shiji [Hold High the
Great Banner of Deng Xiaoping Theory for All-Round Advancement of the Cause
of Building Socialism with Chinese Characteristics into the Twenty-First Century]*
(Beijing: Renmin chuban she, 1997), p. 25.

42. Feng Runsheng, "Wo zhege shizhang xianzai mang xie shenmo?" ["As a
Mayor, What Am I Busy with Now?"] *Juece cankao (Policy References)* 28 (1997):
27–28.

43. For example, see Li, "Success in China's Institutional Market."

44. Deng maintained that public ownership had to remain dominant in China. See *Deng Xiaoping jingji lilun xuexi gangyao* [*Deng Xiaoping's Economic Theory: A Study Outline*] (Beijing: Renmin chuban she, 1997), p. 36.

45. Jiang Zemin, *Hold High the Great Banner*.

46. China National Statistics Bureau, *China Statistical Yearbook 1996,* pp. 403, 409.

5

What Kind of Privatization?

Guoqiang Tian & Hong Liang

The Fifteenth Party Congress of the Chinese Communist Party (CCP) attracted worldwide attention by announcing its adoption of the *zhua da fang xiao* ("control the big, while releasing the small") strategy in reforming its 354,000 state-owned enterprises (SOEs), 240,000 of which are small-sized SOEs. A shareholding system (*gufen zhi*) will be a major instrument for SOE reform. *Zhua da fang xiao* means that the government will effectuate a strategic reorganization of SOEs by tightly managing large enterprises while adopting flexible policies toward small ones. It will establish highly competitive large-enterprise groups with transregional, intertrade, cross-ownership, and transnational operations. At the same time, it will quicken the pace toward relaxing control over small SOEs and invigorating them by way of reorganization, association, merging, leasing, contract operation, shareholding partnerships, or sell-offs. The CCP said that it would encourage merging enterprises, standardizing bankruptcy procedures, diverting laid-off workers, increasing efficiency by downsizing staff, and encouraging reemployment projects. This will form a competitive mechanism that selects the superior and eliminates the inferior.[1]

Due to the special political mobilization efforts of the party congress, this policy guideline led immediately to the implementation of shareholding and cooperative shareholding systems in the SOEs. The shareholding system is held to be a panacea for the success of SOE reform in many regions. The intense interest in a shareholding system in many ways resembles the craze in real estate and special economic zones a few years ago in Mainland China. Some counties or cities, which until a few months ago had taken no action in the SOE reforms, suddenly announced that 80 to 90 percent of the SOEs under their jurisdiction had been transformed into shareholding or cooperative shareholding firms. Some foreign scholars have added to this craze by claiming that the shareholding system is a great theoretical innovation of the socialist market economy, and that the cooperative shareholding system for small- to medium-sized SOEs is superior to the Western shareholding system because it adopts a "one shareholder one vote" rather than "one share one vote" approach.

How should SOE reform and its highly publicized shareholding system be evaluated? What form of shareholding should be adopted: One in which the state or the collective has the dominant share, or one in which individual shareholders as a whole have the dominant share? The latter system seems preferable. This chapter argues that with further marketization reforms and improvement of the market system, the shareholding system with individual shareholders holding the controlling rights will be more efficient than the one with the state or the collective holding the controlling rights. Besides the choice of different forms of shareholding systems, what is the appropriate speed and scale for the shareholding system reform and privatization? What are likely to be the concerns and challenges during the process of SOE reforms?

In addition to addressing these questions, this chapter will discuss an important issue that has until now been largely ignored by scholars: the rapid expansion of government employees. By the end of June 1997, the number of employees in government organs and agencies had increased by 1.35 million compared with the previous year. The first half of 1997 alone accounted for an increase of 1.08 million. The growth rate of employees in this sector was 8 percent, and more than offset the decrease in employees working in the SOEs (which was 1.27 million). This means that the gains from SOE reform in terms of reduced employment in the state sector have been completely consumed by the expansion of government organs and agencies. If this situation persists, it will create serious difficulties for smooth systematic transition. This problem is more serious and pressing than the SOE reform. It will be very difficult to solve and it will involve substantive reform in the political structure.

This chapter is organized as follows: the first section discusses the necessity and urgency of SOE reform, and the next section focuses on the forms of shareholding systems. The speed and pace of SOE reform are analyzed in the following section. The last section discusses the problems posed by the expansion of government organs and agencies in recent years and the challenges this presents to China's transition.

The Necessity and Urgency of SOE Reform

The official announcement of the Fifteenth Party Congress, which launched the systematic reform of SOEs by implementing a shareholding system, is of momentous importance and will have far-reaching historical significance. The CCP now considers the well-executed reform of SOEs as the top national priority and of vital importance in building a socialist market economy. As early as March 1997, the adoption of *zhua da fang xiao* as the means to reform the SOEs and the use of a shareholding system as the reform's major policy tool had been set forth by Premier Li Peng in his report delivered at the Fifth Meeting of the Eighth National People's Congress. Since the CCP holds the ultimate power, the resolution of the Fifteenth Party Congress has significant influence and authority. Without doubt, the implementation of SOE reform and shareholding system is a decisive step forward in the transition toward a market economy. It may be regarded as the beginning of privatization, or, using the official terminology, the "diversification of the ownership structure."

A few years ago, one author of this chapter argued that the smooth transition of the Chinese economy toward the market system would go through three stages:[2] (1) economic liberalization, (2) marketization, and (3) privatization.[3] The first stage began in 1979, when economic reform was initiated in the agricultural sector. The main policy slogan at the time was "untying and relaxing," which meant that the central government would give up some decisionmaking authority. The second stage began in 1992 after Deng Xiaoping gave a major speech during his visit to southern China. The Fourteenth Party Congress in 1993 announced that China would make big strides toward establishing a socialist market economy. The last stage is the nationwide privatization of the SOEs, which for various reasons had been put on hold for a number of years. Experiments with diversified ownership structure in selected SOEs started as early as the mid-1980s, with policy options ranging from leasing, bankruptcy, sell-offs, cooperative shareholding, shareholding, reorganization, and mergers to joint ventures with foreign capital. In various experiments, shareholding increasingly gained momentum. In 1994, there were 25,800 shareholding enterprises, 135,700 cooperative shareholding enterprises, and 2,853,300 township enterprises, the total of which accounted for 10 percent of all SOEs in China.

Why should *zhua da fang xiao* be used to reform the SOEs and transform them into a shareholding system on a large scale? The reasons lie in the early success of marketization reform, the rapid growth in the nonstate sector, and the relative inefficiency of the SOEs compared with non-SOEs. Marketization reform has exposed the SOEs to more competition from the nonstate-owned sector. Although efficiency in many SOEs has improved remarkably, most of them lag behind similar nonstate-owned enterprises. There is a widespread belief that the SOEs are not as profitable as the township enterprises, and the latter are not as profitable as private enterprises. In recent years, the number of money-losing SOEs has increased continuously, and they have created grave challenges to the state budget. The losses incurred by many SOEs were not only caused by low efficiency, but also by mandatory planning and ceiling prices set by the state.

The problems of the SOEs have manifested themselves in the following ways:

1. The number of money-losing SOEs and the amount of the losses have been increasing continuously. About two-thirds of the SOEs are operating with losses. When the SOEs are measured as a whole, the amount of their total losses has exceeded their total profits.

2. The contribution by the SOEs to national industrial growth has decreased. At the present time, SOEs only contribute about 5 percent to the total industrial growth in China, while the non-SOE sector contributes about 95 percent. The SOEs as a whole are so inefficient that they produce about 30 percent of the GDP but use about 70 percent of total capital formation.

3. The SOEs have caused huge deficits in the government budget. It has become increasingly difficult for the government to bear the burden of billions of dollars every year to subsidize the money-losing SOEs, and their number has been rising continuously.

4. The living standard of workers employed by SOEs has been dropping in recent years. Many money-losing SOEs can only pay workers the basic wage with no other benefits, while some are in such bad shape that they cannot even pay the basic wage. This has resulted in many workers living below the poverty level, especially those employed by the SOEs whose production has been idle or semi-idle. After the wage increase for government employees a few years ago, the wage level in money-losing SOEs is the lowest in the economy. It is at about 200 yuan (about US$25) per month and is 50 percent lower than that of government employees.

5. There is widespread erosion of state-owned property. Because the market economy is still in its infancy and government regulations are inadequate, state-owned property has been eroding rapidly. According to some reports, an average of about 100 million yuan (about US$12.5 million) worth of state-owned property has disappeared every day since 1980, which amounts to a total loss of about 1 trillion yuan (US$125 billion) by now.

Ensuring the survival of the SOEs has become an urgent task in the economic transition. Because of the dominant role SOEs play in the economy, their reform will remain at the top of the CCP's agenda in the near future.

Conditions for taking bolder steps in enterprise reform have also improved markedly. Liberalization and marketization reforms have transformed the old planned economy with a dominant state sector to a market-oriented economy with a rapidly growing nonstate sector. The reform policies since the late 1970s have granted individuals limited economic freedom, acknowledged the economic interest of individuals, encouraged decentralization and competition, and allowed diverse ownership forms to develop side by side with the SOEs. These reforms have resulted in the vigorous growth of the nonstate sector (including cooperatives, private enterprises, township enterprises, foreign capital enterprises, and joint ventures) and have profoundly changed the economy.

The share of the state-owned sector in the whole economy is declining continuously. It was about 80 percent in 1979 and had fallen to about 30 percent at the end of 1997. The nonstate sector has become the driving force behind the rapid economic growth. There has also been impressive progress in establishing a market economy. Price reform has resulted in more than 90 percent of all prices being determined by supply and demand in the marketplace, which has greatly enhanced the competition mechanism of the economy. Markets for stock, real estate, and labor have also been set up, though these are still in their early stages. In addition, the economic growth of the past decade has enhanced the state's fiscal capability to handle more bankruptcies of the SOEs.

In summary, both the grave difficulties facing most SOEs and a better-prepared economy now urgently call for large-scale SOE reform. Although some officials and scholars still believe that the SOEs can perform efficiently in a market economy, the government's policy of "controlling the big and releasing the small" is a bold step in the right direction, for it begins to realize that the relative efficiency of SOEs is going to decline further as the market economy develops. Unless privatized, the SOEs have no chance of surviving. The policy of "controlling the big and releasing the small" is going to pave the way for eventual reform of the large-sized SOEs.

The Forms of the Shareholding System

After deciding to implement the shareholding system, the government faces the issue of which form of the shareholding system to choose. Should it encourage the kind of shareholding system in which the state or the collective holds controlling rights, or the one where individual shareholders hold controlling rights? From the report delivered by Jiang Zemin at the Fifteenth Party Congress, the party seems to favor the former. The leadership has not broken entirely with the old ideology. Jiang stated that the government would retain a dominant ownership position and would develop diverse forms of ownership side by side. The dominant position of the state-owned sector is defined as requiring a dominant position in major industries and other key areas that concern the lifeblood of the national economy. Jiang further elaborated on this point by saying, "The public sector includes not only the state- and collectively-owned sectors, but also the state- and collectively-owned elements in the sector of mixed ownership." The dominant position of public ownership should manifest itself as follows: public assets dominate the total assets of society, and the state-owned sector controls the lifeblood of the national economy and plays a leading role in economic development.[4]

Jiang's report at the Fifteenth Party Congress did show some progress on the issue of ownership, but the party is still fettered by the old ideological constraints. This dilemma is best revealed in Jiang's remarks that

> the shareholding system is a form of capital organization of modern enterprises, which is favorable for separating ownership from management and raising the efficiency of the operation of enterprises and capital. It can be used both under capitalism and under socialism. We cannot say in general terms that the shareholding system is public or private, for the key lies in who holds dominant shares. If the state or a collective holds dominant shares, it obviously shows the characteristics of public ownership, which is favorable to expanding the area of control by public capital and enhancing the dominant role of public ownership.[5]

Thus, from Jiang's report, it is obvious that the shareholding system that the Chinese government wants to implement is one in which the state or collective holds controlling rights. Moreover, the CCP seems to hold the belief that it is possible to run a public economy efficiently under market conditions. Neither economic theory nor practice, however, supports such a belief. Of course it might be possible that the wording in Jiang's report is a tactic to avoid being caught in the tangle with the ideological leftists, which would increase domestic resistance to SOE reform. In practice, the CCP may well be much bolder and less constrained by ideology in implementing the reforms. Nevertheless, the ambiguity in such important issues will add difficulty to the privatization of the SOEs. If the state or collective is going to hold a dominant share (and thus have the decisionmaking authority) in the shareholding system, it will inevitably be a detour on the road to real privatization, where individual shareholders have the dominant share. There are several reasons this is true.

First, to avoid unnecessary confusion, private and public ownership must be defined. From modern property rights theory on ownership, the ownership of an enterprise refers to the contractual relationship that distributes the residual claims and residual controlling rights. Different distributions or allocations of the power and responsibility associated with ownership give rise to different ownership structures and arrangements. Private ownership is clearly defined and it grants an individual the exclusive right to claim ownership. On the other hand, nonprivate ownership is not clearly defined since it does not give exclusive right of ownership to any individuals. Compared to private ownership, public ownership (including state and collective ownership, as well as shareholding by the state and collective in mixed ownership) does not clearly set the boundaries of power and responsibility associated with the ownership arrangement. It is worth mentioning here that a private-ownership arrangement does not mean that every right relating to the ownership is concentrated in one person's hands. Some rights can be shared by more than one individual, but with a clear division. For example, shareholders own the means of production, the manager has the right to manage the means of production, and the employees have the right to work with the means of production during the period of their contracts.

What are the benefits of a shareholding system? There are two main benefits. First, it can promote the development of an efficient capital market. Second, it can objectively appraise the economic performance of an enterprise, whereas a supervising government branch usually cannot. Information regarding an enterprise will be more reliably reflected in the price of stocks traded on the stock market. If a firm performs well, its stock price is likely to go up, for more people are willing to buy and hold its stock. Through the trading of stocks, efficient firms will survive, whereas inefficient ones will go out of business. If the state or collective holds the controlling share, the government department responsible for the firm will have the final decisionmaking authority in business management and personnel appointment. Factory directors and managers will be appointed by supervising departments, while smaller shareholders cannot really participate. Since these appointed factory directors and managers do not bear the risks associated with their management, they are less likely to devote all their efforts to increasing the value of their firms. In a market-oriented economy, it is difficult for such businesses to compete with those in which individual shareholders hold the controlling rights and bear the risks of the firms. In other words, because the ownership arrangement is not well defined, firms with the state or collective holding the controlling rights tend to be less efficient than those firms whose ownership is clearly defined. As marketization reform progresses, the relative efficiency of the public-owned sector will continue to fall. Even though the efficiency of some of them may be higher after mergers and acquisitions, their relative efficiency compared with the private sector will be lower as the transition to a full market economy advances.

The evidence is already there. Many SOEs that have been transformed into the so-called shareholding system are examples of "old wine in a new bottle" as they still function in the same old way. Various sources have reported that workers are not very enthusiastic about this kind of shareholding system, especially workers in the money-losing enterprises. Many of them believe that the shareholding system is a way for the government to take their money to pay off the debt accumulated by the money-losing SOEs, because all the debts have been shouldered by the government in the past. Many workers refuse to participate in this type of shareholding system. In response, some firms have threatened to fire those workers who do not want to buy the required amount of stocks. For example, the *Shanghai Interim Procedures for the Shareholding System*, which became effective on June 1, 1997, require that 90 percent of the employees of an SOE must become shareholders when the shareholding system is implemented. As a result, forced participation may emerge when an enterprise wants badly to become a shareholding company and more than 10 percent of its employees do not want to participate.

In many ways, the workers' concerns are justified. Some publicly held companies are big money losers. The mid-year statistical report of Shanghai in 1996 revealed that thirty enterprises listed on the stock market (about 12 percent of the total companies listed) reported losses or earnings of less than one cent per share. The situation seems to be getting worse. According to the newly released report on listed companies in 1996, the money-losing firms increased from eleven in the previous year to seventeen in the Shenzhen stock market, with the loss per share increasing from 0.16 yuan to 0.36 yuan. In the Shanghai stock market, the number increased from six to fourteen, and was 4.49 percent of the total number of firms listed. This represents a 1.4 percent increase over the previous year, and the loss per share grew from 0.29 yuan to 0.49 yuan. The net return on capital, which is a better measure of a firm's performance, has dropped from 12.47 percent in 1995 to 10.15 percent in the two stock markets. It is important to note that all the unprofitable firms were listed on the market before 1996. In addition, it seems that the longer a firm has been listed on the stock market, the worse its losses. For the above two stock markets, the average earnings per share over a five-year period was 0.39 yuan, 0.25 yuan, 0.21 yuan, 0.17 yuan, to 0.15 yuan in Shanghai, and 0.37 yuan, 0.20 yuan, 0.28 yuan, 0.18 yuan, to 0.11 yuan in Shenzhen. In only a few years, many publicly listed companies are facing the possibility of going out of business. Among the two hundred firms newly listed last year, twenty-two had less than 10 percent net return on capital, while others reported very low profits or were on the verge of reporting losses.

Yet most of the listed companies were above-average performers among the SOEs. The original intention of getting these firms listed on the stock market was to attract additional funds and improve managerial efficiency. They were supposed to set examples for other SOEs of how to become modern market enterprises. However, their disappointing performance casts doubt on whether the shareholding system with a dominant public shareholder (be it the state or the collective) can solve China's SOE problem. Such a shareholding system does not provide fundamental changes in the way firms are managed. It only changes the way funds are raised. If the situation continues, inefficiently managed firms will incur losses not only to themselves, but also directly to the general public. This will have far-reaching consequences for SOE reform and the development of the Chinese stock market.

It is apparent that the shareholding system with a dominant public shareholder cannot solve the efficiency problem facing the SOEs. There are two solutions to this problem. The first is to implement a shareholding system where individual shareholders hold a dominant share, which in essence privatizes the SOEs. When individual shareholders bear the costs and benefits of a firm's economic performance, they have an incentive to monitor closely the firm's management. The incentive structure is the main reason modern enterprises are more efficient in market economies. If, because of ideology, the government insists that the public has to hold a dominant share in the shareholding system, there is another solution suggested by one author of this chapter a few years ago: the state or collective can be granted a special kind of shareholding that would give it priority in assigning dividends, but the state or collective would not participate in the election of factory directors, managers, or the board of directors.[6] This is a viable way of solving the dilemma of keeping the public as the biggest shareholder while maintaining enterprise efficiency. There have been some local enterprises and some township enterprises that have implemented shareholding or cooperative shareholding systems along this line, and the results are quite encouraging.

Another important issue relates to the cooperative shareholding system, which refers to the kind of shareholding system in which employees own all the equity of a firm. Outsiders cannot own its stock and shares can only be exchanged internally. The distribution of the firm's earnings is made according to one's contribution as a worker and one's shareholding status. Under current political, economic, and social conditions, the cooperative shareholding system has been well received and is growing rapidly. Although it has the advantages of relatively clearly defined ownership and a flexible structure, it also has serious drawbacks. For example, it prohibits outside capital from coming in and reduces capital mobility. It may be suitable only for small-sized enterprises and various service firms. However, as an enterprise grows bigger in size and scale, capital will become a more important element for the further growth of the firm. The need to attract additional capital will eventually lead many cooperative shareholding firms to become publicly listed on the stock market.

The proposition of "one shareholder one vote" is even more problematic. Besides the drawbacks already mentioned above, the proposition makes it possible for shareholders who control relatively fewer shares to make management and administrative decisions, while the shareholders who have more shares bear a bigger portion of the risk. If the rights of decisionmaking do not depend on how many shares one owns, why would anyone want more shares? It is natural that people with fewer shares at stake are more willing to take bigger risks. But, who is willing to let other people gamble with their money? (Imagine, for example, that you and the authors are going to enter into a partnership. Would you be willing to have equal decisionmaking power with us if you contributed $1 million to the partnership, while we only contributed $100?) On the other hand, if it is required that everybody have an equal amount of shares, the result will be that people who want to invest more cannot do so. This will lead to the inefficient use of capital, as well as a waste of entrepreneurial opportunities.

When discussing the relative merits of various forms of shareholding systems, only the criterion of economic efficiency has been used so far. Reform should be concerned not only with improving economic efficiency, but also with other goals such as social fairness and stability. Economic efficiency and equity are two commonly used criteria for evaluating the consequences of economic activities, although from different angles. They embody two different value concerns of human beings. In general, there is a trade-off between efficient allocation of resources and equal income distribution. Because people are different in their capabilities, in order to improve efficiency and encourage hard work, the amount of income each individual gets will inevitably have to be different. If a person's income does not depend on his efforts or his contribution, he would be unlikely to put in his best effort. Although policies aimed at a more equal income distribution often reduce efficiency in order to maintain social stability and correct social injustice, people are generally willing to trade some economic efficiency for a more equal income distribution.

The economic system before reform overemphasized equal income distribution and basically ignored the efficiency of resource allocation. Many SOEs are in the red and are relatively inefficient compared with similar enterprises in the private sector. Also, since China is still in the early stages of economic development, economic growth is its most pressing challenge. Under these circumstances, the task of transforming the old inefficient SOEs into modern market enterprises with clearly defined rights and responsibilities should emphasize breaking the "iron rice bowl" and enhancing the efficiency of resource allocation. As market reform continues, the importance of a clearly established ownership structure will become increasingly important.

Furthermore, the most suitable ownership structure may be different under different economic conditions. State, collective, and private ownership each has relative advantages in different economic environments. In an article on ownership reforms in the transition economies,[7] Guoqiang Tian argues that when economic freedom is very limited and the market is in its primitive stage, SOEs may have a relative advantage over privately and collectively owned enterprises; when the market economy develops to an interim stage, the collectively owned enterprises may have more advantages than the other two forms of ownership; and when the market economy develops to its mature stage, private ownership may be the best ownership structure.[8]

In recent years, the cooperative shareholding system implemented in many township enterprises has been highly praised. However, the cooperative shareholding system is a transitional form of ownership arrangement.

Although these ownership arrangements in township and other enterprises have advantages at the present time, as the market reform deepens, more of them will be replaced by modern market enterprises with clearly established ownership.

The Pace of Transforming the SOEs

Should China implement large-scale privatization of the SOEs at the present time? Have large-scale bankruptcy and ownership structure reforms become imminent? Does the country possess the necessary conditions for enduring the pains associated with large-scale bankruptcy of the SOEs? According to one report, the government plans to take about three years to clean up the money-losing SOEs. However, this timetable may be too optimistic. Due to the lack of the necessary economic and social infrastructure, the pace of large-scale reform in the SOEs must be deliberate and gradual. The reasons are as follows:

1. The government does not have the required financial resources to support the millions of workers who would be laid off. Restrictions set by the government's financial capabilities will limit the pace of reorganization and bankruptcy of SOEs. Even without reorganization and bankruptcy, the government needs to provide assistance to about 50 million people, which include 13 million workers who are in essence already laid off by unprofitable SOEs, 7 million workers waiting for employment, and 30 million retirees.

2. The output value produced by the state-sector is still about 30 percent of the GDP. If China implements the same type of privatization as in the former Soviet Union and eastern European countries, large-scale bankruptcies may significantly lower the GDP, as well as people's standards of living. Many people will lose their jobs, and the real wages of those still employed may drop, at least temporarily. In the process of transition, it is important to reduce social instability and avoid large-scale unemployment, for hardships of many individual workers may turn them against reform.

3. Since marketization is still an ongoing process, the value system and the way of thinking of many people has not fully adjusted to the workings of a market economy, particularly on issues relating to unemployment and inflation.

4. The social security and unemployment benefit systems are in their primitive stages. If a large number of workers are laid off, their livelihood will be threatened. The frustration and difficulty caused by unemployment, as well as lowered social and economic status, may cause resentment on the part of these workers, and therefore, lead to social unrest. Before social security insurance and labor markets are adequately established, forcing

large numbers of SOEs into bankruptcy would be a serious mistake. At the present time, SOEs serve the role of providing a social safety net to those workers who cannot find other employment opportunities.

5. The labor market has not been fully established, so workers who are idle or waiting for employment cannot effectively find jobs for themselves. Even without SOE bankruptcy, each year China faces the task of providing employment to about 20 million people.

6. There are no effective facilities for training and helping unemployed workers find new jobs.

7. Although the government needs to subsidize an unprofitable SOE, the subsidy may in some cases be far less expensive than the required financial resources to support all its employees if the SOE goes bankrupt.

In light of these constraints to rapid SOE reform, it is of great importance that the enterprise reform be taken with appropriate pace and sequence. In particular, the government should set aside sufficient financial resources for an unemployment fund in order to provide temporary financial assistance to those workers who are going to be laid off by bankrupt SOEs. Policies should be aimed at giving the unemployed workers more freedom in their job search, providing them with more job training, and promoting reemployment projects.

An important area of policy action should be targeted at establishing an efficient labor market so that labor can be more mobile. More freedom in job seeking should be granted to workers in the SOEs. In fact, policy should also be directed toward pressing ahead with all the supporting reforms for establishing a market economy. Many of the current difficulties are the result of immature or incomplete markets. A well-functioning modern market system not only means the absence of restrictions on prices and goods traded, but also includes a market-determined price system, an effective macroeconomic management system, modern market enterprises, an efficient and effective tax (and income distribution) system, a social safety net, rule of law, antitrust (anti–unfair competition) provisions, and open labor and capital markets.

The Issue of Rapid Personnel Expansion in the Government

One important issue that has largely been ignored by scholars and policymakers until very recently is the rapid personnel expansion in government organs and agencies. As market reform continues, the number of employees working in the SOEs has been declining continuously, while the number of government employees has been expanding, and now stands at more than 30 million. That means, on average, there is one government employee for every thirty Chinese people, whereas fifty years ago there was only one for every three hundred people. At the end of June 1997, the total number of industrial employees was about 146.7 million, a reduction of 187,000 compared with the corresponding period of the previous year. On the other hand, government employees increased by 1,352,000. The first half of 1997 alone accounted for an increase of 1.08 million. The growth rate of employees in this sector was 8 percent and more than offset the decrease in employees working in the SOEs (which was 1.27 million). This means that gains from the SOE reform may have been completely absorbed by the expansion of government organs and agencies.

Such an expansion neutralizes the effectiveness of reforms in economic and management systems. One reason for such an expansion is the rapid decline of the SOEs. Many people have realized that the "iron rice bowls" that used to be offered by the SOEs have been taken away and workers in the SOEs face insecurity and lower wages. A government job is viewed as secure and prosperous. In response, many people are trying by every means to secure a government position. The second reason for such rapid expansion is the lack of political reform. There has been little progress in streamlining the government. Much of what has been done is essentially window dressing; many units merely reallocated administrative expenses or changed their names. Some units even took the opportunity of reorganization to expand the unit and the number of employees. This poses a more serious problem involving the reform of political structure and is even more difficult to solve. The reason is obvious: state-owned enterprises still create some value, no matter how inefficient they might be; government organs and agencies, however, are totally consumptive units that do not produce any commodities, or create any output value, or involve any competition, but they spend huge sums of money to support their operations. Even if the government is serious about streamlining its operations and cutting positions, most of the people who are cut from their posts will have difficulty making their way into the enterprises due to their lack of the expertise required by those enterprises. Therefore, reform of the political structure should be conducted as early as possible, starting with simplification of organizational structure and considerable reduction of government positions. As long as the current trend continues, the number of government employees will increase and institutional reform will become more difficult. If this problem is not settled properly, the effort to reform SOEs, to a large extent, will be wasted. Hence, reform of government organs and agencies in a smooth and practical way is an urgent issue yet to be addressed. (It is hoped that this chapter will bring more attention to this issue and attract more research in this area, so that the economic system of China can be transformed into a truly efficient market mechanism with free competition.)

After the first version of this chapter was written in October 1997, the Ninth National People's Congress held in March 1998 carried out a government restructuring program by reducing the number of ministries from forty to twenty-nine. The Chinese government also plans to cut 30 to 50 percent of government administrative employees in the next three years. The government, it seems, has finally realized the importance of this issue and made a remarkable step in reforming the government administrative system. Perhaps the government can reach the proposed goal of reducing the number of government administrative employees by 30 to 50 percent in the next three years, although this goal may be too ambitious. But even if it reaches this goal, the government needs to reduce its number of employees further, and to deepen the reform of the administrative system.

Notes

1. Jiang Zemin, *Gaoju Deng Xiaoping lilun weida qizhi, ba jianshe you Zhongguo tese de shehui zhuyi shiye quanmian tuixiang ershiyi shiji* [*Hold High the Great Banner of Deng Xiaoping Theory for All-Round Advancement of the Cause of Building Socialism with Chinese Characteristics into the Twenty-First Century: Report Delivered at the Fifteenth National Congress of the Communist Party of China, September 12, 1997*] (Beijing: Renmin chubanshe, October 6–12, 1997), p. 20. The quotations from this document hereafter will be indicated as "Jiang's report."

2. Tian Guoqiang, "Zhongguo guoyou qiye de gaige yu jingji tizhi pingwen zhuanggui de fangshi he buzhou" ["The State-Owned Enterprise Reform of China and the Mode—Steps for Transforming Economic System Smoothly"], *Jingji yanjiu* (*Economic Research Journal*) 319 (1994): 3–9. Also see Guoqiang Tian, "State-Owned Enterprise Reform and Smooth Institutional Transition in China—A Three-Stage Economic Reform Method," in *The Reformability of China's State Sector,* ed. G. J. Wen and D. Xu (New York: World Scientific Publisher, 1996), pp. 220–240.

3. "Economic liberalization" is defined here as the loosening or elimination of government restrictions on economic transactions, including freeing prices, trade, and entry of various types of new firms. "Marketization" is defined as the developing and creating of market-supporting institutions such as legal, financial, and social welfare security systems. "Privatization" means the privatization of existing state-owned or collectively owned enterprises, land, and other assets.

4. Jiang's report, p. 1.

5. Ibid., p. 20.

6. Tian Guoqiang, "Zhongguo xiangzhen qiye de chanquan jiegou yu gaige" ["Property Rights Structure and Reform on China's Rural and Township Enterprises"], *Jingji yanjiu* (*Economic Research Journal*) 323 (1995): 35–39.

7. Guoqiang Tian, "Breaking Up Is Hard to Do: The Theory of Property Rights in Transitional Economies," Department of Economics, Working Paper, Texas A&M University, 1995.

8. See "Zhengfu jiguan shiye danwei de xunsu pengzhang" ["Rapid Expansion in the Government Organs and Agencies"], *Guangzhou ribao* (*Guangzhou Daily*), October 19, 1997.

6

The WTO:
What Next for China?

Jason Z. Yin

It has been a long march for China in its quest for World Trade Organization (WTO) membership. China first formally indicated its interest in resuming its original contracting party status with the General Agreement on Tariffs and Trade (GATT), the predecessor to the WTO, in July 1986. A GATT Working Party was appointed in June 1987, and the first meeting of the Working Party took place in February 1988. Since that time, China has met more than two dozen times with the WTO Working Party and has conducted extensive bilateral negotiations on the WTO entry with its main trading partners. The process for China's accession to the GATT/WTO is already the most extensive on record.

GATT/WTO is based on a premise of free trade between member nations. Each member nation should have a free-market economy in which the private sector plays a dominant role. China faces a major challenge in transforming its planned economy to a free-market economy to meet this premise. The quest for WTO membership has been a painful process, but not a process without many gains. In fact, under pressure to comply with the WTO rules and standards, China has achieved remarkable progress in privatization, trade liberalization, and economic integration with the rest of the world. The quest to become a WTO member has been an impetus for China to speed up its ongoing privatization of state-owned enterprises and the establishment of a free-market economy.

Despite the progress China has made in complying with the WTO requirements, at the time of this writing, considerable obstacles remained in the way of the industrialized nations (led by the United States) issuing China an entry ticket to the WTO. It was speculated that a political solution on Beijing's entry to the WTO might be reached in the summit meetings between the presidents of the United States and China. This did not happen during President Jiang Zemin's visit to Washington in October 1997, or during President Bill Clinton's visit to China in June 1998. At the Asian-Pacific Economic Community (APEC) annual summit meeting in November

1998, Vice President Al Gore agreed with President Jiang to make an effort to bring China's WTO negotiation to a closure early the next year. In fact, nobody knows when and under what conditions China will be accepted into the WTO.

At this point, China finds itself in a dilemma. It neither wants to accept the preconditions set by the Western economic powers for instant membership, nor wants to withdraw its application for membership. The WTO bid remains a strategic choice for China. After thirteen years of seeking membership, Chinese policymakers have to reconsider five crucial questions: (1) What are the gaps remaining and what is required for China to close those gaps? (2) What is the likelihood that the United States will say "yes" to China's WTO quest? (3) What are the costs and benefits of membership, and will the benefits it may gain offset the price it has to pay? and (4) What are the strategic options available and what is the best strategy for China? To address these issues, this chapter is organized as follows. The first section assesses the progress China has made in its quest for WTO, followed, in the second section, by an analysis of the gaps remaining. It then discusses the U.S. stance in the third section and the costs/benefits of the WTO membership in the fourth section. Three strategic options are identified in the fifth section, followed by conclusions and recommendations to both China and the Western economic powers.

The Progress China Has Made

During the past thirteen years, along with its open-door policy and economic reforms, China has made sincere efforts to meet the requirements for WTO entry. Its progress can be observed in the following six areas.

Transition to a Private Market Economy

The WTO is premised on the function of a private-market mechanism in the domestic economies of its member countries. The basic idea for WTO is to establish an international economy that is disciplined by the operation of comparative advantage and the "invisible hand" (price), and is governed by the principles of nondiscrimination and reciprocity. Any interference that may distort such free-trade mechanisms should be limited. In other words, it is unlikely that the WTO regulations could impose any effective discipline on the trading sectors of a centrally planned economy such as China's.[1]

China nonetheless has been systematically moving away from its centrally planned economy toward a market-oriented economy. In 1986, the year China applied for WTO entry, state-owned enterprises contributed 62 percent to China's total industrial outputs, whereas nonstate enterprises (including collectively owned, individually owned, and foreign-owned business entities) contributed 38 percent. By 1996, the state-owned enterprises accounted for merely 30 percent of total industrial outputs whereas the nonstate enterprises accounted for 70 percent.[2] The private sector has replaced the public sector as the major driving force in the vitalization of Chinese economy. More and more state-owned enterprises are being privatized through stock sharing, joint ventures, merger and acquisition, and bankruptcy. It is expected that within the next five to ten years, the number of state-owned enterprises will be further reduced from the current more than twelve thousand to about one thousand or less, and the private sector will contribute even more to the total industrial outputs. By then, China can comfortably claim that it has fulfilled its transition from a planned economy to a market economy.[3]

Trade Liberalization

To reduce trade barriers, WTO requires that, among its members, tariff levels be restricted, roughly, to an average of 5 percent for developed countries and 15 percent for developing countries. China has achieved major progress in trade liberalization. In compliance with WTO rules and to give greater access to its market for foreign competition, China has progressively lowered its tariffs. Tariffs were reduced from 36 percent on average in 1993 to 23 percent in 1996, and to 17 percent by October 1997. China is also committed to further cut tariffs to an average rate of 15 percent by the year 2000 and to 10 percent by 2005, the tariff level maintained by most developing countries, as President Jiang promised at the APEC meetings in November 1996 and in November 1997.[4] Furthermore, to encourage foreign investment and international trade, China has developed a scheme of duty exemption for exports and duty concessions for imports. For example, equipment and raw materials imported by foreign-owned enterprises and foreign joint ventures, which constituted about 48 percent of total imports in 1995, were given 50 percent duty concessions. Overall, about 70 percent of total imports enjoyed some kind of tariff exemption or reduction in 1995.[5]

Nontariff Barrier Dismantlement

In addition to tariff reductions to promote free trade, WTO requires its members to dismantle nontariff barriers and make rules, regulations, judicial decisions, and administrative rulings in their domestic trade systems transparent (i.e., open and accessible to the public). China's international trade was originally centrally controlled through a handful of state-owned foreign trade companies. This centrally planned import-export system has been decentralized and put into the hands of local and regional international trading companies. More than eight thousand domestic enterprises and hundreds of enterprises with foreign investment have been authorized to engage in international trade directly. By the end of 1995, 176 nontariff measures, 30 percent of the total import quotas and licensing, had been phased out.[6] Recently, after cutting and scaling down export subsidies for industrial goods, China promised not to provide export subsidies for agricultural products. It has also agreed to phase out import quotas for cars and minibuses in eight years instead of the fifteen years that the Chinese negotiators first offered.[7] The automobile industry is one of the most sensitive industries for which China has insisted on having a relatively longer phase-out period because of the substantial economic costs and political risk for adjusting these industries to international competition.

National Treatment Rule

The "national treatment" rule is the WTO's second manifestation of the nondiscrimination principle. In contrast to the most-favored-nation (MFN) rule, which requires nondiscrimination at a country's border, the national treatment rule requires a country to treat foreign products equally with its domestic products once they are inside the country. China has begun to make major improvements in complying with the national treatment rule.

However, since most of the goods manufactured by enterprises with foreign investment were intended for export, special permission was needed for them to sell their goods in China's domestic market. In addition, foreigners traveling in China were treated differently: they were charged more than Chinese residents for the services they received. For example, airfare was about 50 percent higher for foreigners than for Chinese residents. The tardiness of China in complying with the national treatment rule has drawn many complaints from foreigners traveling or doing business in China. Recently, China has gradually relaxed the restrictions of market entry for enterprises with foreign capital investment. More and more foreign enterprises have been permitted to sell their goods and services in the domestic market. Four foreign banks were recently allowed to enter the financial market and five foreign insurance firms were granted licenses to sell insurance policies to local residents. Many of the discriminatory pricing policies against foreigners have been removed. For example, the double standard in the pricing system for transportation was eliminated in July 1997.[8]

Intellectual Property Rights Protection

Another important aspect of China's bid to join WTO that has resulted in positive policy change is intellectual property rights (IPR) protection. Many multilateral and bilateral negotiations with major trade partners on

IPR protection over the last few years have been difficult.[9] International pressure to protect foreign intellectual property rights has helped China establish its IPR legal systems and set up rules for a market economy. Yet, the record of IPR protection has been quite disappointing. Violations of IPR have been common regardless of whether foreigners or local people owned such rights. Both enterprises and consumers have found themselves the victims of intellectual property piracy, and they are the supposed beneficiaries of the IPR legal system and its tough enforcement. After the serious efforts of the government in the last decade or so, the IPR legal system and IPR protection have significantly improved.

Currency Convertibility

The Chinese currency exchange market was fully under the control of the central government through the control of exchange rates and the control of the availability of foreign currencies. The absence of a freely convertible currency served as the final complicating factor in the quest for WTO membership. To obtain WTO membership, China has committed itself to move faster toward total convertibility of its currency. Starting in 1985, foreign exchange adjustment centers (FEACs) were established on an experimental basis in Shenzhen, Xiamen, and Shanghai in an attempt to set the exchange rate based on market supply and demand. The number and volume of FEACs grew rapidly; they were expanded into all major cities and the volume has reached the multibillion U.S. dollar level annually. In addition to opening its service to institution clients, the foreign exchange market has also been opened for individual clients since 1988. FEACs currently serve as the managed marketplaces for currencies. To further meet WTO requirements, China's central bank, since 1997, has allowed the currency (RMB) to become convertible in current accounts, one step closer to a fully convertible currency. This change has reduced government control over the financial market and international trade, giving more room for the "invisible hand" to function.

Overall, the quest for WTO membership over the past thirteen years has presented a historical opportunity for China to privatize its economy and to liberalize its trading regime. Although it has not yet been accepted as a full member of WTO, China has made extraordinary progress and has benefited from this painful process. The performance of the freer market has been remarkable. With real GNP growing by an average of 9 percent annually, the size of the Chinese economy has quadrupled. International trade has increased from $69 billion in 1986 to $325 billion in 1997.[10] Real income and living standards have been substantially improved. Meanwhile, an animated nonstate sector has emerged as the leading sector. The market distortions of the centrally planned economic system have been reduced and many tariff and nontariff trade barriers have been removed. The economy has also become more open and integrated with the world economy through a growing private sector and increasing foreign trade and investment.

The Gaps Remaining

Recognizing that China is undergoing complex economic reform, Western economic powers still want to arrange a protocol package that will secure solid commitments to provide market access for their goods and services. There are gaps remaining between China's current offers on reducing trade barriers and the preconditions set by the major trading powers from the developed economies. According to a report entitled *Foreign Trade Barriers,* issued in early 1997 by the Office of the United States Trade Representative (USTR), the major barriers remaining in China's foreign trade practice include the following five.[11]

Tariffs and Their Management

Compared with the tariff levels for developed economies and advanced developing economies, China's tariffs are still high, and act in combination with other import restrictions and foreign exchange control to protect domestic industries and restrict imports. Western countries are pushing China to a commitment of lower tariff rates and shorter phase-in periods. The continued poor performance of the state-owned enterprises has been the major concern for tariff protection. The government worries that, with low tariffs, foreign goods would flood in and replace Chinese goods and services in the market. It would threaten the survival of many state-owned enterprises because those enterprises do not have a significant competitive advantage in the international market. In addition to the high average tariff rate, the United States and other Western countries continue to express their concerns about high tariff rates for selected sectors, such as chemicals, in which China is seeking to build its international competitiveness.

In addition to import tariffs, U.S. and other foreign businesses have complained about the lack of uniformity in tariff rate application and in custom valuation practices. Tariffs may vary for the same product, depending on whether the product is eligible for an exemption from the published MFN tariff. This creates difficulties for foreign companies trying to export to the Chinese market. Different ports of entry may charge significantly different duty rates on the same products. Because there is flexibility at the local level in deciding whether to charge the official rate, actual customs duties are often the result of negotiation between businesspeople and customs officers. Allegations of corruption often result. Many foreign businesspeople are frustrated by the lack of market discipline in China in terms of the rights, obligations, and ethics in business conduct.

Nontariff Barriers and Transparency

Nontariff barriers include import licenses, import quotas, and other import controls. Many products are subject to both quota restrictions and import licensing requirements. Central government agencies determine the level of import quotas through evaluation of the particular products needed for an individual project or quantitative restrictions for certain products. Once "demand" is determined, these agencies then allocate quotas that are eventually distributed nationwide to end-users and administrated by local branches of the central government agencies concerned. Western industries complain that China provides little transparency regarding the quantity or value of products to be imported under a quota, although the WTO requires such information.[12] China still maintains strong controls on imports and exports through a nationwide licensing system that is administrated by the Ministry of Foreign Trade and Economic Corporation (MOFTEC). The licensing policy requires enterprises to receive government approval for each of their imports; this may nullify the value of any tariff concession by denying import licenses. China offered in December 1995 to phase out the licensing policy within five years. The United States has pushed for a shorter phase-out and insists that China not discriminate against foreign enterprises in granting trading licenses during the phase-out period.

Import Substitution and Export Subsidies

The United States and other industrial nations are still concerned about the intervention of the government in international trade practices other than tariff and nontariff barriers. Import substitution has been a long-standing trade policy. Despite having agreed in its 1992 Memorandum of Understanding with the United States to eliminate all import substitution regulations, guidance, and policies, China in 1994 announced an automotive-industry policy that includes import substitution requirements. This policy calls for production of domestic automobiles and automobile parts as substitutes for imports. The United States and other industrial nations want to make sure that these policies will be eliminated and any future policies do not contain such provisions in the context of China's WTO accession negotiation.

Although the government claims that direct financial subsidies on all exports ended on January 1, 1991, China continues to use a variety of measures to support and promote exports such as preferential loans and tax policies and preferential energy and raw material supply policies. It remains to be seen that uniformity in the types and amounts of taxes and duties imposed on enterprises can be achieved, particularly with respect to income and other direct taxes imposed on exporters.

Services Barriers

China has promised to liberalize its services markets upon accession to the WTO, but the market for services remains severely restricted. Most of the foreign services, such as banking, financing, insurance, electronic communication, accounting, and legal services, are only allowed to operate on a selective "experimental" basis and are restricted to specific geographic areas or market segments. For example, as early as 1997, eight foreign banks had obtained permission to conduct *renminbi* transactions on a restricted trial basis in Pudong. With regard to insurance services, while China has approved 144 representative offices opened by eighty-five different foreign insurance companies, only six foreign insurance companies have been granted licenses to operate in restricted areas. In other areas, such as retailing, information, and telecommunications services, foreign companies are only permitted to team up with local companies to provide services in restricted areas.[13]

Investment Barriers

Although official policy welcomes foreign investment as critical to China's economic development, the government continues to maintain barriers and controls on foreign investment, channeling it toward certain areas that support government development policies, such as energy production, communications, and transportation. It still prohibits foreign investment for projects with objectives not in line with the national economic development plan. For example, investment in the management and operations of telecommunications as well as in the news media, broadcast, and TV sectors is banned, and investment in insurance, shipping, advertising, education, and travel services is severely restricted. The major reason for the restriction in service industries is to protect these markets and industries from domination by foreign firms.

After thirteen years of negotiation and major concessions, major problems remain, especially restructuring the state-owned industries and dismantling trade barriers to meet WTO standards for developed economies, and opening up the market fully to international competition. The economic costs and political risks for these changes could be very high.

When Will the United States Say "Yes" to China?

China has conducted bilateral negotiations with 35 of WTO's 132 member countries. By the end of 1997, agreements had been reached with seven countries including Japan, New Zealand, Pakistan, South Korea, and three European countries. China expects to reach agreements in the near future with the rest of the member countries except the United States.[14] The United States remains the major barrier to China's membership. However, the United States is also China's most important trade partner.

Trade policy with the United States is the core of China's international trade policy. The U.S. government plays a central role in keeping China out of the WTO. The United States wants to make sure that China pays its dues before its entry. Although the trade between the two countries has grown rapidly, the trade relationship has hardly been smooth.[15] Even though it has announced repeatedly that it is committed to supporting China's accession, the U.S. government continues to delay China's WTO entry.[16] After China's successful bilateral negotiations with the European Union and Japan,[17] the U.S. government is now the only industrialized nation saying "no" to China's WTO quest.

The U.S. position is consistent with its overall trade policy, which has revolved around the concept of "free trade" for the past fifty years. That policy can be characterized as "using threats of trade sanctions and tariffs to force other countries to allow U.S. companies to access their markets (a tactic that has come to be known as 'fair trade')."[18] Reviewing the annual report of *Foreign Trade Barriers,* prepared by the USTR, one finds that its major trade partners have challenged America's dominant position in international trade. The United States had trade deficits with Japan, Canada, the European Union, Mexico, and China, with a total trade deficit of $184 billion in 1995 and $194 billion in 1996.[19] The United States blames these deficits on the market entry barriers of its trade partners. While trade conflicts remain between the United States and its trade partners, the U.S. is taking unilateral actions to force its trade partners to open their markets for U.S. goods and services. Currently, the remaining disagreements between the United States and China are centered on the openness of China's capital market and the market entry for American agricultural goods. Using support for China's WTO accession as a bargaining chip to gain market entry is part of the U.S. "free trade" policy.

In addition, the U.S. stance on this issue reflects the influence of the American politicians opposed to China's entry to WTO. These people insist that China will not get in unless it accepts the terms offered by the United States and other industrialized nations. On the one hand, they recognize that "the WTO can't afford to exclude China," but on the other hand, they insist that China has to be "contained" by demanding that it should reform its economic system and open its market to a far-reaching level as preconditions.[20] Some politicians even want to insert human rights and other political issues into the negotiation agenda. They take China's WTO bid as the last opportunity to discipline China's possible "disruptive behavior" and force it to accept their economic and political terms. Overall, they perceive China's growth and its involvement with the world economic community as a threat.[21]

Nevertheless, the number of American politicians supporting China's accession to WTO is growing. These people view the rise of China in world affairs and its growing power not as a threat, but as an opportunity to establish stable working relations with one-quarter of humanity and to integrate China peacefully and constructively into the norms and institutions of the global community. They believe that a prosperous and stable China is profoundly in America's interests. As Nicholas Lardy argued in a congressional hearing, "China's membership in the WTO will serve the U.S. interests by providing a mechanism for dealing with inevitable trade frictions on multilateral rather than a purely bilateral basis. It would also allow the United States to concentrate in the bilateral diplomatic channel on critical strategic issues." He suggested that "the United States should moderate its demands for reform as a precondition for China's membership in the WTO. In exchange, the United States should expect China to agree to a schedule that would gradually bring the country into compliance with WTO standards."[22]

When the United States will say "yes" to China's WTO membership depends on whether the pro-China policy or the "constructive engagement" policy prevails. It also depends on the growth of U.S. economic interests in China. The rapid growth of U.S. trade and investment will provide more incentives for the United States to say "yes." Jiang's visit to the United States and Clinton's visit to China and the declaration to establish a "constructive strategic partnership" between these two countries as well will give impetus to China's entry into the WTO. It remains to be seen if it will give enough impetus for the United States to say "yes."[23]

The WTO: The Costs and the Benefits to China

Before formulating a strategy for WTO entry negotiation, it is necessary to estimate what kinds of benefits China may receive after its entry into the WTO and what price China will have to pay. This will help determine the leverage that the negotiation provides to China and the industrialized nations as well. It seems that WTO membership will bring great benefits. However, some scholars have pointed out that the benefits of membership are relatively modest.[24] The most important economic benefit associated with membership is the permanent MFN trading status in the market of member countries.[25] All major trading partners except the United States had bestowed this MFN status on China before the WTO was conceived. The United States has provided MFN status for China for the last sixteen years on an annual review basis.[26] It seems unlikely that the United States will revoke China's MFN status in the future given the mutually beneficial nature of the U.S.–China trade relationship.

Another major benefit that WTO offers only to its developing-country members is the General System of Preferences (GSP), which grants the developing country members privileges of a waiver of reciprocity in the negotiation of trade concessions from developed countries. This allows a developing country to obtain tariff concessions from a developed country on a nonreciprocal basis. The purpose of the GSP is to make the developing countries more competitive in the world market and less dependent on the production of raw and primary goods. Currently, China is one of the largest exporters in the world. Manufactured goods have become the major part of its exports, instead of raw and primary goods. It has become clear that China will not be qualified for GSP, according to the officials who participated in the U.S.–China bilateral trade negotiations. Realistically, the best that China can hope for will be a status in between developing and developed nations.

Third, WTO membership may entitle China to benefit from the elimination of Multi-Fiber Arrangement (MFA) quotas. One of the major achievements of developing countries from the Uruguay Round agreement is that the developed countries agreed to eliminate restrictions under the MFA and to return textile and apparel to normal GATT disciplines. According to the Uruguay Round agreement, elimination of the bilateral MFA quotas is designed to take place gradually. It involves increasing the growth rates of MFA quotas under the Agreement on Textiles and Clothing during a ten-year period, and the progressive reintegration of certain export categories under WTO disciplines, followed by the termination of all remaining quotas by the year 2005. Several studies have shown that eliminating MFA quotas accounts for a major part of what China would gain from joining the WTO. Currently, it could not benefit from the elimination of MFA quotas.[27]

The final benefit of WTO membership is to be able to participate in the process of "setting rules for the game" instead of merely being a rule follower. In this situation, one may draw a parallel to China's entry into the United Nations. As a permanent member of the UN Security Council, China is actively involved in setting the rules for international affairs and is able to protect its own interests. However, there is no such Security Council type structure in WTO and China will have no veto power in international trade affairs even if it is accepted as a member. On the other hand, at this point, although China has not been accepted as a WTO member, it has participated in most of the international economic organizations. Also, its interest in international trade can be addressed through bilateral negotiations and regional trade organizations. Furthermore, given the nature of economic competition in the current post–Cold War period, conflicts among WTO members are growing, calling for more unilateral and bilateral actions. The WTO, as a multilateral trade organization, has not yet been very powerful in resolving international trade conflicts.

One price that China is being asked to pay is the dismantling of its remaining tariff and nontariff trade barriers. These barriers are set primarily to protect China's state-owned industries. Because these industries still employ almost two-thirds of urban workers, it would be risky for Chinese political leaders to incur the high level of unemployment that could result if the trade barriers are removed too rapidly. In addition, the wide-open market for foreign goods and a rapid restructuring of the economic and trade regimes may uproot some national industries and weaken the country's ability to export. Consequently, this will lead to trade deficits simply because most Chinese companies have not yet grown to the point where they are competitive in the international market. Trade deficits and the subsequent decline in foreign exchange reserves will have a negative impact on China's ability to repay foreign loans. That, in turn, would make it difficult to attract additional foreign investment. Further, China will not be able to make the currency (*renminbi*) fully convertible before the restructuring of its financial system. This restructuring is a complicated and risky business. The current unfolding financial crisis in several Asian countries will reinforce a more cautious attitude toward opening up its financial market. China is not ready to risk its financial-market stability for quick WTO accession. Finally, China has little experience in opening service industries to foreign competition and it must open that market cautiously.

While WTO membership is strategically important in the long run, the short-term costs of conforming immediately to the preconditions set by the industrialized nations for openness to trade are too high to justify the relatively modest gains from its entry into the international trade club. Especially when the major benefits are already in hand, it is less justifiable for China to open itself to economic and political risks in exchange for WTO membership.

Strategic Options for China

Although China has made significant progress in the last twelve years and Western economic powers have indicated their serious interests in accepting China as a member of the WTO, there is an apparent standoff in the negotiations over membership. After years of negotiation, the true unresolved issue is not whether China should follow WTO rules or should be accepted on "commercially viable terms," but rather concerns the phase-out period of China's remaining trade barriers, that is, the length of time given to meet the terms. The United States insists that dismantling most of the trade barriers is a precondition for China's membership. Under this situation, China has three strategic options:

1. Conforming immediately to the preconditions in exchange for immediate entry
2. Conforming to WTO standards at its own pace
3. Giving up its quest for WTO membership

This situation is like buying a house. In the negotiations, the buyer wants to buy the house at a bargain price and with a low down payment. The rest will be covered by a mortgage from the seller. However, the seller has no interest in either lowering the price or lowering the down payment. If China is the buyer and the WTO is the seller, China can choose to buy the house on the seller's terms, or choose not to buy the house at all. The third choice is to renegotiate the terms by asking the seller either to lower the price to the level the buyer can afford (i.e., granting China GSP status or other concessionary terms) or to accept a longer-term mortgage (i.e., allowing longer phase-out periods for dismantling the trade barriers).

The option "not to buy" is not a good one because China needs to buy the house, that is, China wants to become a member of the international trade organization for its long-term strategic interests. Accepting the seller's terms is not a good option either, because China cannot afford the price and the full payment in the short run. The only remaining choice is to continue the negotiations for granting China developing-country status and/or granting China a sufficient phase-out period. A longer phase-out period would allow China to stretch out the very substantial costs of adjusting its industries to international competition and to reduce the political risk due to radical change in its economic and trade systems. As long as the economic benefits of being a WTO member cannot at least offset the very real costs that would be associated with compliance with WTO standards, China should not accept the preconditions for entry, unless some other important factors come into the bargain.

First, it should be reemphasized that China's membership would serve not only its own long-term interests but also the institutional interest of the WTO. With China excluded, the WTO can hardly claim to be global. The potential disruptive threat of the Chinese economy, the world's third-largest economy behind the United States and Japan, is greater outside the WTO than within it, as many leading economists have pointed out. Second, the size of the Chinese market and the accelerating speed of market access into China by the major trading powers should not be overlooked. For example, trade between the United States and China has grown from $4.8 billion in 1980 to $63.5 billion in 1996. U.S. exports to China, including those sold through Hong Kong companies, have risen from $6 billion in 1990 to about $17 billion in 1996, outpacing the growth of the U.S. exports to any other major foreign market. Many American products, such as Motorola's cellular phone, Microsoft's software, and Coca-Cola and

Pepsi-Cola, already reach millions of Chinese families. Third, the timing of lowering tariff and nontariff barriers has been entirely at China's discretion, not at the discretion of the industrialized nations. Fourth, WTO entry will create a new avenue for China to solve its trade frictions through multilateral negotiation, but will not once and for all solve its trade frictions and disputes with other countries. Conflicts between the United States and China will not disappear after China's entry to the WTO.

Conclusions

The above analysis indicates that WTO entry remains a major trade-off for China. It is clear that China has to take significant costs in the shorter term to gain a long-term strategic benefit as a WTO club member. The costs include further privatization and trade liberalization to the WTO standards. China should realize that privatization is at the core of its economic reform and that trade liberalization is the central piece of its opening policy. The quest for WTO membership can best serve the promotion of its own strategic interests. The right choice for China might be to continue economic privatization and trade liberalization, and to gradually integrate its domestic economy into the world economy based on its own needs and at its own pace. The quest for WTO membership can be and should be used as a vehicle for promoting privatization and free market operations, but the quest by itself is not a substitute for internal reform.

Currently, Western nations have been very firm on the preconditions they have set. It is very unlikely that China will win the WTO bid without making major concessions, especially when political and other nontrade issues increasingly complicate the case. At this point, China should be prepared for major concessions. However, any concessions beyond what its economy can bear in exchange for instant membership might be counterproductive. An important lesson China may have learned from the Asian financial crisis is that an economy may run out of control or even collapse overnight if it rushes into an open-market operation without sufficient infrastructure preparation in place. It may take a long time for China to be sufficiently prepared for the global free-market competition that drives its WTO quest. China has waited for thirteen years. There are no good reasons for China to set a deadline for its accession to the international trade club.

Although many features of China's trade regime are not fully compatible with the WTO system and it is generally agreed that China should make further reforms, membership should not be used as leverage to force far-reaching changes in China's economic system and trade regime. It is good strategy for Western economic powers to tie China's economy into the WTO's regulation structure for the promotion of trade liberalization in

China. However, China's intention to join the WTO and its willingness to comply with the WTO's regulations should not be misinterpreted. One should realize that the most important benefit associated with WTO membership is the permanent MFN trading status in the markets of member countries. All WTO member countries except the United States have bestowed China MFN status, and the United States has done it annually for the past sixteen years. With the most important benefit of WTO membership already granted to China, the leverage of the major trading powers is limited. Insisting that China dismantle most of its trade barriers as a precondition for membership may prove counterproductive. The possibility that China may choose to stay outside the club for as long as it figures that the gains would not offset the costs should not be ruled out.

Notes

1. Paul D. McKenzie, "China's Application to the GATT: State Trading and the Problem of Market Access," *World Trade Journal* 24 (October 1990): 133–158.
2. China National Statistics Bureau, *Zhongguo tongji nianjian, 1997* [*China Statistical Yearbook, 1997*] (Beijing: Zhongguo tongji ju, 1997).
3. Shuanglin Lin, "Resource Distribution Between State-Owned and Non-state-Owned Enterprises in China's Economic Growth" (Working paper, 1997).
4. "Zhongguo jueding jinyibu jiangdi guanshui" ["China Decided to Further Reduce Its Tariff"], *Shijie ribao (World Journal)*, November 26, 1997.
5. Zhang Erzheng, "Qianxi woguo guanshui xiatiao de jingji yingxiang" ["The Economic Impact of the Reduction of Tariff Rates"], *Guoji maoyi wenti (International Trade Issues)* 6 (1996): 25–31.
6. Zhang Jialin, "An Assessment of Chinese Thinking on Trade Liberalization," paper presented at the American Chamber of Commerce Executives International Trade Conference, 1996.
7. *New York Times,* August 4, 1997, A7.
8. David E. Sanger, "U.S. Officials Say China Not Ready for Trade Club," *New York Times,* August 4, 1997, A7; "Zhongguo zai shijie maoyi zuzhi wenti shang zuochu gengduo rangbu" ["More Concessions Made by China to WTO Entry"], *Shije ribao (World Journal),* November 12, 1997.
9. Jason Zunsheng Yin, *Jishu guanli: kaifa he maoyi* [*Technology Management: R&D and Trade*] (Shanghai: Shanghai renmin chubanshe, 1995), pp. 41–46, 256–271.
10. *Renmin ribao (People's Daily, Overseas Edition),* January 10, 1998.
11. The United States Trade Representative (USTR), *National Trade Estimate on Foreign Trade Barriers: People's Republic of China* (1997). See http://www.ustr.gov/reports/nte/1997/china.pdf.
12. Matt Forney and Nigel Holloway, "In Two Minds," *Far Eastern Economic Review* (June 19, 1997): 66–71.
13. *Shijie ribao (World Journal),* November 12, 1997.
14. Chen Weibin and Li Jingchen "The Developing Country Members Have Collectively Declared Their Support for China's WTO Membership," *Renmin ribao (People's Daily),* December 8, 1997.

15. State Council of PRC, "Guanyu Zhong Mei maoyi pingheng wenti" ["On the China–U.S. Trade Balance"], *Renmin ribao (People's Daily),* March 22, 1997; USTR, *Foreign Trade Barriers: People's Republic of China* (1997). See http://www.ustr.gov/reports/net/1997/china.pdf.

16. Sanger, "U.S. Officials Say China Not Ready."

17. *Renmin ribao (People's Daily),* October 15, 1997, and November 12, 1997.

18. Ed Brown, "It's Put Up or Shut Up for U.S. Trade Policy," *Fortune* (October 27, 1997): 34.

19. USTR, "Appendix: U.S. Data for Given Trade Partners in Rank Order of U.S. Export," *Foreign Trade Barriers,* 1997.

20. Robert P. O'Quinn, "How to Bring China and Taiwan to the World Trade Organization," The Heritage Foundation Asian Studies Backgrounder no. 140 (March 22, 1996); Sanger, "U.S. Officials Say China Not Ready."

21. Editorial, "How America Sees China: Friend or Foe?" *Economist* (November 1, 1997): 3.

22. Nicholas R. Lardy, *China and the WTO,* Brookings Policy Brief no. 10, 1997, Washington, DC: The Brookings Institution.

23. Barnathan J. Harbrecht, "Will China Agree to Pay Its Dues?" *Business Week* (December 26, 1994): 34–36.

24. Lardy, *China and the WTO.*

25. The most-favored-nation (MFN) rule requires that each contracting party apply its tariff rules equally to all other parties without discrimination. Article 1, paragraph 1, provides that "any advantage, favor, privilege or immunity granted by any contracting party to any product originating in or destined for any other country shall be accorded immediately and unconditionally to the product originating in or destined for the territories of all other parties" (Ray August, *International Business Law: Text, Cases, and Readings* [Englewood Cliffs, NJ: Prentice Hall, 1993], pp. 315–317).

The MFN rule has been central to the development of international trade in the last half century. However, the MFN rule of nondiscrimination is not without exceptions. The exceptions include the General System of Preferences (GSP), South-South Preferences, and Multi-Fiber Arrangements (MFA).

26. The U.S. government conducts its unilateral review of the trading practices of its trading partners, and the U.S. Congress reserves its right to overwrite the GATT/WTO's rulings.

27. Zhi Wang, "China and Taiwan Access to the World Trade Organization: Implications for the U.S. Agriculture and Trade," *Agricultural Economics* 17 (1997): 239–264; Y. Z. Yang, "China's WTO Membership: What's at Stake?" *World Economy* 19 (1996): 661–682.

7

Breaking the Social Contract

Xiaonong Cheng

At the Fifteenth Congress of the Chinese Communist Party in September 1997, Jiang Zemin consolidated his power and appeared to be the consensual head of a collective leadership.[1] Both inside and outside China, this "third generation of leadership" is seen as weaker and less authoritarian than its predecessor. The current conduct of the leadership, however, seems more courageous and capable than that of Deng Xiaoping, because it has dared to conduct "shock therapy" reform. In the last two decades under Deng's leadership, China achieved striking economic progress in reforming state socialism, but it carried out unbalanced reform, that is, partial marketization under communist political rule. Since the death of Deng, the government has shown its intention of altering the strategy. It has announced a radical reconstruction of the state sector that will lead to the laying off of more than 30 million workers, which even Deng, the iron-fisted leader, declined to adopt. Why does the regime now choose an obviously risky course of action that may immediately lead to social tension and political instability? Has Jiang really become stronger than Deng, or has he obtained new instruments to control the social and political situations? Can China's economic progress under shock therapy help the regime retain its power over the next decade?

Discussion of these questions requires a comprehensive understanding of the reform strategy. China's reform over the past two decades is often considered a good example of putting economic reform ahead of political reform, in contrast to Gorbachev's Soviet Union, which gave priority to political reforms. Supported by the Chinese case, pro-authoritarian theory suggests that market reform can be successfully introduced only under an authoritarian regime and thus economic reform must precede political reform. The argument is that an authoritarian state is less dependent on popular support than a democratic state, enjoys a greater capacity to implement unpopular policies, and can thus behave as *the* universalistic agent to ensure efficient economic performance.[2]

This conventional wisdom ignores the fact that the Chinese communist regime is dependent on performance legitimacy and, therefore, upon a welfare-oriented state-society relationship to sustain it during the period of economic reform. The Chinese strategy of reform is restrained by that state-society relationship. That strategy has not only reduced significantly the capacity of the regime to implement unpopular policies for economic efficiency, but also has exhausted almost all available financial resources and thus shaken the legitimacy and survival of the regime. The shock therapy program is not a well-prepared project with a clear goal for constructing a real market economy, but an urgent response to the failures of Deng's reform strategy.

This chapter employs the concept of a social contract that provides a clue to the relationship between reform politics and the economic situation in the past decades. Unlike an analysis based on power struggles or factionalism at the top, which may help to explain some events, this approach brings society into the analysis of reform politics, focuses on how economic reform is restrained by societal responses, and therefore is able to offer a new explanation of the Chinese road to reform. The discussion focuses on urban reform and the interaction between state and urban society because the decisive part of the state-society relationship in China's polity is the one between those parties.

The chapter begins with a review of economic reform over the past two decades and employs the concept of a social contract to explain how the state-society relationship during this period has changed from "command and obedience" to "feeding and cooperation." Following is an explanation of why this social contract sustains, as well as restrains, economic reform. Relying on the social contract, the more the authoritarian state "buys" societal support and political stability, the weaker the state becomes. Consequently, the present social contract has exhausted its financial resources and necessitates radical reform. The chapter concludes with discussion of the current reform efforts. Any further economic reform has to break the social contract and, in turn, may damage the cooperation between urban people and the regime and undermine political stability. Solving the puzzle seems difficult for the third generation of communist leadership. Very probably, the "honeymoon" between urban society and the regime under the social contract may come to an end, and be replaced by rising social tension. Under the pressure of such tension, it is uncertain whether the government can continue economic reform of the state sector and at the same time maintain political stability.

Reform Under a Social Contract in China

Reform in a socialist country is a process of institutional transformation, which involves redefining the interests of, and the relationship between, state and society. To understand the transformation process, social scientists have tried various methods. Applying the state-centered approach, some scholars emphasize the predominance of the party-state over society, and explain the reform path mainly through the intentions and options of the policymaking elite and negotiations among them. Other scholars, adopting the society-centered approach, see the emerging civil society as an important determinant for the evolution of reform. The former may overlook the possible societal alienation from the state and the influence of popular responses on the direction of state policy, and thus overestimate the state's capacity of realizing its policy goals. By contrast, the latter often give little attention to the structure of state power and decisionmaking, and may have difficulty in explaining when, why, and how reform should take place.

The reform process and the transformation of institutions are not simply manipulated by state, they are also shaped by society.[3] Success or failure of a reform depends upon both the actions of the state and the responses of social groups. One way to better understand the possible evolution and result of the reform movement is to introduce the interaction of state and society into any analysis of reform. The concept of a social contract, borrowed from Soviet studies,[4] can be used to describe the evolution of the state-society relationship in China. It is useful for explaining how the political relationship between state and society helped China achieve progress in the economic reforms of the past two decades, and why the relationship finally undermined the efforts to maintain economic and political stability.

In order to understand the state-society relationship in the reform era, it is necessary to know how societal actors and the state related to each other within the state socialist institutions before reform. The state-society relations of Mao Zedong's era were "command and obedience." Monopolizing all political power and economic resources and building up the people's worship of Mao and his revolutionary ideals, the Communist Party favored loyalists and punished dissidents during continuous political campaigns; thus, the regime secured the loyalty and obedience of much of the populace. The socialist system with a "command and obedience" relationship strangled independent thought and creativity and allowed the rulers to act arbitrarily. Consequently, it brought about great waste and low efficiency in the economy and a low standard of living for the people. Because rulers could not satisfy the people with a better life, they had to suppress the masses by ideology. In maintaining such a state-society relationship, the rulers relied heavily on spiritual instruments, and citizens were inured to expect only the satisfaction of minimum interests. From an economic viewpoint, obedience seemed to be at a low cost for rulers, since people's material demands were suppressed and the rulers did not have to provide a higher standard of living for ordinary people.

Great institutional differences could be observed between Chinese urban and rural societies. While peasants were deprived of almost every opportunity to live and work in cities and had no security at all in the People's Commune system, urban society was dominated by the public sector. That sector included hundreds of thousands of state-owned "units" (*danwei*) of industrial enterprises, stores, schools, and institutes of research and scholarship, formed in a pyramidal structure of primary sociopolitical and economic entities under strict state control. These units not only produced goods and services, but also distributed urban welfare benefits and shaped the political attitudes and the behavior of state employees. They were responsible for a wide range of cradle-to-grave welfare services on which state employees and their families depended. This system did not allow employees to obtain the essentials of life—jobs, food, housing, health care, pensions—from outside the system. Their very survival would be in question were they to reject or even attempt to alter substantially this state of dependency.[5] Through "organized dependency," that is, state employees' economic dependency on their "units" and political dependency on party and management, the Communist Party was able to force the urban populace into subordination to the regime.

The differences between rural and urban areas have contributed much to the patterns of reform and have led to different results in rural and urban reform. Rural reform liberated peasants from the People's Communes, giving them economic freedom at no cost. In this way, the government exchanged economic freedom for political support of the rural reforms with little risk to either the government or peasants.

Urban reform is not such an easy reconstruction project, not only because the hard core of state socialism is located in the urban areas and the majority of the urban population lives in "organized dependency," but also because urban society is politically more sensitive. The urban population receives more education and information and is more influential politically than the rural population. Urban people work in the modern sector, which sustains the daily operations of the system, and are more easily organized and, therefore, carry greater weight in determining political stability. They have been prohibited from any unofficial organized activities, but are usually treated well in terms of welfare provisions. Among the urban population, those who live in the largest cities often get special treatment because of their larger potential influence.

Private businesspeople benefit when retail trade is freed from regulation and peasants benefit from price and land reform, but neither group is politically powerful enough to promote thorough reform of the state sector. Urban reform must confront the vested interests of urban state employees. More than 85 percent of the urban population in the 1980s and the first half of the 1990s worked for the state sector or affiliated organizations. These are people eager to adopt a modern lifestyle but also anxious to protect the benefits they derive from state socialism.

Encouraged by the success of early reforms, the government decided to reform the urban economic system in 1984. The motivation was utilitarian: the government wanted partial reform without undermining the political infrastructure and power of the party. The regime never intended a thorough reform of the socialist economic system, or an abandonment of the basic aspects of the system.

The main thrust of reform was the transfer of management decisions from governmental departments to factories, which was intended to increase industrial efficiency as drastically as the rural reform had done.[6] Decentralization would improve efficiency, but centralized management was only one of the reasons for low efficiency. Without eliminating the "soft constraints" relations between the government and state sector,[7] efficiency might improve slightly though decentralization, while severe inflation might occur.

Government protection of the state sector and the socialist welfare system were considered the "soft constraints." From a purely economic point of view, these constraints should have been abandoned, but for political reasons the government refused to withdraw protection or to reform the welfare system. Economic problems between the regime and state employees could yet become political problems between the state and the people. Protection of the state sector and the welfare system is an important instrument for the government in controlling the populace and in maintaining its legitimacy.

Though the communist regime is an authoritarian one, the imbalance between state and society appears to be increasingly favorable to society. The ability of the state to control has been weakened. Without the personality cult that surrounded Mao, and without terror or political mobilization, the present regime has had to shift its claims to rule from teleological beliefs to an emphasis on economic benefits to the people, that is, seeking performance legitimacy,[8] just as the post-Stalin Soviet regime did.[9] This shift first led to intensive utilization of welfare measures to maintain political rule. These measures turned out to be more and more important as instruments to control and influence urban people, while political intervention became a weapon in reserve, and political repression was used only as a tool to suppress dissidents. The shift also led people's evaluation of the regime to focus on the role of government in providing social and economic benefits for its citizens, thus shifting unconditional societal obedience into a conditional pattern.

While the reform regime relied upon performance legitimacy and, therefore, carried out only partial reform, this reform strategy was actually welcomed by urban society. Urban residents are mainly employees of the state sector, and they have motives for reform quite different from those of the peasantry. Rural reform was stimulated chiefly by peasants pursuing economic freedom, whereas urban reform has been largely motivated by consumer materialism. Urban state employees, however, have two motives for urban reform. On the one hand, they want to continue their vested interests in relaxed work disciplines, frequent promotion to redundant positions, and an unemployment-free life in the state sector, all of which could only come from the old socialist system. On the other hand, they are eager to embrace new interests, for example, higher living standards and more opportunities to make extra money, which are only available from the developing market system.

These two expectations are not compatible, but such expectations are politically useful to the regime. The government's intentions and the people's expectations are related. While the people worry about the risks of reform, the regime worries about how its legitimacy might be shaken by thorough reform and the possibility of unrest when people lose their vested interests. Wanting to exchange economic benefits for political support, the government has avoided talking about the losses and risks, and instead promised more benefits to console the people, and, in this way, encouraged their high expectations and gained their confidence. Expecting the reform benefits promised by the government, the urban population has kept a positive attitude toward economic reform and has become accustomed to having benefits delivered by the government.

To carry out economic reform, the regime needs not only people's obedience, but also their cooperation. First of all, reform requires the creativeness of state employees in implementing the policies of the government, as decentralization has provided them more independence and power in decisionmaking. Second, when labor discipline is tightened and productivity targets are increased, workers' cooperation is necessary. Third, and most important, the government has to expect the forbearance of state employees once the reform damages their vested interests. Traditional psychological instruments such as worship of the supreme leader and propaganda about the necessity of the policies no longer work, and the goals of economic reform and modernization may never produce enough incentives to make people work harder or sacrifice for the ruling party and the state. The regime therefore has had to appeal to economic interests to elicit people's enthusiasm for reform and to secure their cooperation.

Since the end of the 1970s, the state-society relationship of "command and obedience" has been replaced by a new pattern of "feeding and cooperation." In the new pattern, the state must offer people more and more economic benefits and compensate for any losses produced by the reform. Thus the government seeks public cooperation and confidence in the reform, instead of simply showing severity, and must hope that the people accept and support the economic and political requests of the state through cooperation, in return for obtaining economic favors from the state. The urban reform path is thus constrained by the state-society relationship.

The state-society relationship in the "feeding and cooperation" era may be defined by the same concept of a social contract as that used in Soviet studies. Early in the 1970s, a concept was developed to explain the stability of the Soviet political system, and the perspective has been developed further recently. The basic idea is derived from a distinctive feature of the state-society relationship in the Soviet Union. The state-society relationship is based on exchange: both the regime and the population contribute something the other needs for its survival. Thus a social contract relationship between the state and society is maintained when rulers provide benefits and security, and the people agree to acknowledge the legitimacy of the government, and to support, at least passively, the established political order.[10]

Application of the social contract concept to China can aid in understanding not only the recent state-society relationship, but also its reform strategy. In pursuing economic modernization, post-Mao leaders have adopted new political and economic policies, and these policies have led to a reconstruction of state-society relations. A key question for the social contract is how the populace in the social contract can prevail upon the state to grant economic interests in a nondemocratic country. Obviously, the state-society relationship cannot be defined as a social contract if the government bestows favors on the people but the people cannot influence decisionmaking. The Chinese have had no opportunities to choose their leaders by democratic elections. A strict vertical social control system still works, and officials appointed by the party are both the supervisors of the people and, at least nominally, the political representatives for the people. In such a political system, people cannot influence decisions of the state by political participation. Only the government's aversion to social disaffection restrains decisionmaking.

In the 1980s, such a state-society relationship had never been fully and officially planned, promised, or claimed, but was actually institutionalized as operating principles guiding not only economic and social policy, but also political policy. After the Tiananmen demonstration of 1989, the implicit social contract was openly admitted by the government. For example, in his meeting with the mayor and other local officials in the early 1990s at Shanghai, Jiang Zemin, then general secretary of the Communist Party, suggested that "buying political stability with money" was a key policy that local officials should understand.[11] After the early 1990s, one can also find expression in the official mass media about "loans for political stability" (*anding tuanjie daikuan*), implying that local governments ordered local branches of the state banking system to make loans to state enterprises as part of the social contract.

The usual manner of making concessions to the people's economic demands may take two forms. When top decisionmakers become aware of serious dissatisfaction, those most eager to stem dissatisfaction can prevail by making concessions, which generally means offering people more benefits or taking fewer vested interests from them. Also, the central government may tacitly consent to local governments making concessions to the people by abandoning some aspect of the reform policy, so that the policy loses its efficacy. Almost every official, even a factory manager at the lowest level, understands and plays the game of politics quite well. In such a way, public attitudes have gained greater influence on decisionmaking than ever before.

In the post-Mao era, a significant difference from previous times is the weakened state capability to control social disaffection, while more and more disaffection appears in the course of reform. From the beginning of the 1980s, the ruling party has gradually changed its old social control method, and the state's ability to satisfy people's material needs has become a self-imposed standard of the party's legitimacy.[12] The nature of "organized dependence" has seemingly changed from Andrew Walder's original definition to a new type of dependence on the social contract. In the past, state employees were dependent on the workplace for lack of any alternative; now, they are dependent as a result of the high opportunity costs of working elsewhere. When consumer markets appeared and control of labor mobility was loosened, employees of the state sector were able to get necessities and services outside of their workplace and could shift to other workplaces. In the social contract era, however, almost every state-owned work unit delivers a great deal of welfare benefits, from luxury goods to free travel, which are not available from private firms. The high welfare benefits have rapidly raised the opportunity costs of shifting to the nonpublic sector, and thus maintained the economic dependence of state employees on the state sector.

This state-society relation creates a self-reacting process for both the government and the people. Though the "exchange relationship" of the government offering economic interests and the people offering cooperation has never been presented in any official document, both parties to the "exchange" know their own obligations clearly from the behaviors and responses of the other party. Once the sociopolitical relationship of "feeding and cooperation" has been formed and stabilized, both parties are inclined not to destroy it. Today many state employees firmly support the official claim about keeping the current system stable because this means to them a stabilization of their socioeconomic status under the social contract. The longer the government maintains authority in this way, the more difficult it is for them to find another strategy that would be more effective in preserving its political power and achieving its goal of economic development as well.

The social contract has limited the goals of reform. Under the social contract, the very nature of urban economic reform strategy has become an effort to straddle two systems: a gradually developing market system and a remaining core socialist system. Some aspects of reform, such as trade reform and tax reform, are relatively easy, since these reforms need an effective central authority and the authority is well maintained in the social contract. Other aspects, such as price reform, can be handled as long as people's real income keeps growing, as is required by the social contract. But some aspects of reform, such as bankruptcy of the state enterprises or reform of the state banking system, are completely constrained by the social contract and have made little progress because these reforms may undermine the institutional foundation of the social contract.

The government has recognized the necessity and urgency of enterprise and employment reforms, and made decisions in support of these reforms several times, but each time it has silently withdrawn them. In 1986, when the Bankruptcy Law, pushed by some reformers, was discussed in the National People's Congress and met resistance from both local governments and the official labor unions, the central government agreed to add some restrictions to the law so that it would not operate over the next six to eight years, except in a few designated cases. In 1991, Deputy Prime Minister Zhu Rongji, who was in charge of economic policy, supported a local reform experiment to lay off redundant workers in the state-owned mining enterprises of Jiangsu Province and urged the entire state sector to follow the model. His instructions were implemented by some managers, but soon several managers were threatened by angry workers and one was actually killed. Zhu, frightened by the workers' responses, simply gave up.

Can the Social Contract Continue?

Maintaining the social contract has had both positive and negative effects. Reform has created opportunities for the nonpublic sector and has stabilized the polity and economy for a certain period, permitting economic growth and foreign trade. But, reform remained partial: it has protected the institutional legacies of the past, allowed corruption, and, most important, exhausted resources for the social contract. Diminishing resources, a result of the social contract, makes it more and more difficult for the government to keep the social contract working.

Reform usually requires a strong state as well as societal support. In a politically and economically centralized system, reform implies reducing the original state capacity. If societal support or cooperation with the state is not available, the state may have to "buy" societal support with economic benefits. An authoritarian communist state is strong in promoting some economic reforms within the state apparatus and strong in implementing political control or repression over dissidents, but is weak in carrying out thorough reform within the state sector and is feeble as well in protecting its remaining resources. A dilemma may then appear: the more the state "buys" societal support, the weaker the state capacity becomes; the weaker the state capacity, the more the state relies upon "buying" societal support for reform. This is exactly the situation today.

The country has received advantages from partial urban reform protected by a welfare-oriented social contract. The reform has been "sweet" for most state employees, since all their losses due to the reform were compensated by other welfare measures, and, furthermore, their total real income and consumption level have maintained annual increases of more than 5 percent since 1985. Their standard of living rose, not because of any rise in their productivity or any rise in the profit rate of the state sector, but because the state was able to pay the costs of welfare. Reform convinced the government that the more benefits offered in a reform program under a social contract, the more stable the reform process would be. The social contract and partial reform thus coexisted and were mutually supportive.

The social contract produced the effects of political and economic stability, which in turn led to confidence among the domestic population and foreign investors, and, therefore, encouraged more domestic savings and foreign investment, which were critical to economic growth. The social contract thus sustained not only the reform effort, but also political and economic stability and a good growth record. This may also explain why the transformational recession, which Janos Kornai suggests would be inevitable in any transition,[13] has not been seen in China, even in the state sector.

The institutions of the dominant state sector experienced only gradual change, as evidenced by the following. First, workers were able to influence wage raises and promotions, and the distribution of bonuses and welfare.[14] Second, decentralization gave firms greater control over their revenues and incentive payments, and factories sought to increase their services and benefits for employees, which actually increased the employees' dependence on the state sector. Third, the state budget continued to provide subsidies, not only serving old welfare aims, but also compensating for losses due to reform. Fourth, the goods and services in the new market economy were much more expensive, raising the opportunity costs for state employees to make the decision to switch from the state sector.[15] As the state offered more benefits, such as jobs, housing, health care, consumer and durable goods, and free travel for vacations, in exchange for the citizens' cooperation with the communist regime, the social contract not only strengthened people's dependence on the state, but also shaped people's expectations and behavior. This social contract worked for performance legitimacy, but was unfavorable for marketization and economic efficiency.

With that social contract, Deng appeared to have found a balance between political stability and partial economic reform, but balance was achieved at a cost to the state and the public sector. Providing social benefits proved more expensive than the cost of ruling before the reform. Once the government had complied with demands for better living conditions, it had no choice but to offer more economic benefits to the people.

A welfare-oriented social contract may buy stability, but cannot buy efficiency or productivity. The social contract leaves workers with limited incentives to work hard and has actually encouraged economic inefficiency. Using material incentives in the social contract is not an effective stimulation for working, but is the government's way of securing public support. Under the social contract and in the reform effort, the government plays a dual role: it is the "boss" of the state enterprises in managing their business, and the "father" of state employees responsible for their well-being. The two roles are contradictory. To play the role of the "father," the government should guarantee people shared wealth. At the same time, in its role as "boss," it ought to distribute income according to people's differing abilities.

As solving this dilemma has proved impossible, the government then chose to emphasize its role as "father," distributing income relatively equally. Because people usually thought of the new benefits they managed to obtain as "welfare" or "free lunch," not as rewards for hard work, they were not motivated to work harder. In most situations, rising wages did not increase productivity, but reduced wages would definitely decrease it; the "material incentive," therefore, had actually become a way to prevent productivity from falling, rather than to improve it.

The social contract thus ties political stability to the state's capacity to deliver welfare. Since the state sector has been unable to provide the welfare alone, the high economic cost of maintaining the social contract has to be covered by other resources. The ability of the regime to finance the social contract is a precondition for the maintenance of the social contract. Whether the social contract can be maintained in the long term depends on the balance between the available resources and those the social contract consumes.

The first and the easiest source of funding is the state budget. Before reform, the government carried out most investment in the planned economy, financed by transferring state enterprise revenues to the state budget.[16] The government therefore directly controlled about one-third of the gross national product (GNP).[17] Reform has reduced the share of the state budget of the GNP by decreasing the transferred revenues from state enterprises and leaving those enterprises to deliver welfare provisions.

Another possible source of funds is the banking system. All banks are state-owned and centrally controlled by the party-state as a machine to collect savings and distribute financial resources. Individuals can only put their savings into the state banks, but usually cannot borrow from these same banks for their own businesses. The banks operate on instructions from the government and make loans primarily to the state sector. As all bank directors are appointed by the Communist Party, the banking system is actually an extension of the state, and the banks function as a "second state budget." In considering the state's financial capacity, one should never ignore the portion built on the banking system. The financial resources of the banking system are greater than that of the state budget.

Before 1988, the government relied mainly on the state budget to cover the expenses of the social contract. Economic reform changed this as more financial control was given to the enterprises. The state reduced its expenditures in line with reductions in its revenues. The state's share of national income steadily declined from 35 percent in 1978 to 20 percent in 1988.[18] Since then, the state budget has been unable to finance the social contract and the government has had to find an alternative way to cover the welfare expenditures of the social contract.

Because financial liberalization was excluded from the reform effort and the banking system remained a government monopoly, it was quite easy for the government to make the switch from budgetary resources to banking resources to finance the social contract. As the household share of national income increased 10 to 15 percent in the 1980s, the ratio of household savings to national income jumped from 4 percent in 1978 to 15 percent in 1990.[19] The government is now able to use those bank savings to fund the state sector.

Performance of the state sector has experienced little improvement since reform started, but state enterprises, fulfilling the social contract, have increased wages, bonuses, and welfare provisions, even when the enterprises themselves could not afford these expenditures. As a result, the operating costs of state industries have soared while profits have declined from 15 percent in 1985 to 2 percent in 1993 and have remained low.[20] This sector employs 45 million people, but half of its enterprises have been money losers since 1995.[21] As these enterprises made little or no money but had to provide more wages and welfare to "buy" political compliance, they became increasingly dependent on bank loans. The state banking system was thus under constant pressure from the state enterprises backed by the government to provide a steady stream of credit.[22] The state sector now gets 79 percent of national financial resources, while the share of its output in GNP fell to 43 percent in 1994.[23]

Financing higher wages and welfare benefits through borrowing, many managers of the state sector recognized that their priority was to make their employees happy rather than to make or keep their enterprises profitable. As loans were necessary to maintain the social contract, many managers had no plans for paying back these loans. Some of the poorest state enterprises were even unable to pay the interest, and the loans became "donations" from the state banks. The government used personal savings for political purposes, and the state banking system was required to play a "cashierlike" role for the government and the state sector. Thus, the social contract reinforced the "soft budget constraint," a well-known feature of a socialist system as defined by Janos Kornai.[24]

Using the state banking system as the financial resource for the social contract has had two major consequences. First, the huge loans the state sector owed have become a heavy debt burden that has led many state enterprises into bankruptcy. Formerly, the state sector had very few external liabilities; in 1979, for instance, the sector only owed banks a sum equal to 26 percent of their book value (depreciated fixed capital plus the value of all inventories). This ratio doubled during the period from 1980 to 1989, and rose to 83 percent by 1994.[25] This rapidly increasing equity rate indicates that if debts are subtracted from gross assets, the total net assets of the sector shrank during the reform period, and the heavy external liabilities have resulted in risks of more bankruptcies.[26]

Second, as two-thirds of the state enterprises were struggling to survive and could not repay the loans, by 1994 about 60 percent of bank loans had turned out to be bad or "dead" loans.[27] In a market economy, once a bank is found to have such a high dead-loan rate, the bank is considered bankrupt. According to international standards, technically the Chinese banking system is already bankrupt, but, as it is the only banking system in China and protected by the government, the state banking system will not be closed, but may be shaken by possible financial crisis. To support the social contract, the banking system has almost depleted its financial resources. In this situation, the state sector can no longer depend upon the banking system to obtain financial resources.

While political stability is a significant outcome of the social contract, the contract has created several economic problems. For example, as the decentralization gave local governments incentives to build more new factories, it reinforced the typical socialist "investment thirst," and led to a waste of funds. Overinvestment can be found in almost every industry, and many new factories built in the past decade have been unprofitable since the day they opened. This is why China's industrial-structural distortion has worsened.

Another example is the growing urban-rural income gap, which has had an unexpected negative impact on the state sector. Since 1986 most financial resources have been put into the state sector concentrated in the cities. Consequently, the urban-rural income gap, after a temporary reduction from 1979 to 1985, grew again after 1986. The difference is now even larger than in the prereform era, though the government promises almost every year to reverse this trend.[28] While low rural purchasing power reduces the potential rural demand for the low-quality products of the state sector, the fast-growing urban consumption level stimulates demand for imported goods and reduces the demand for goods from the state sector. The state sector has received most of the country's financial resources, but has seen diminished domestic demand for its products as well, and therefore hurt itself.

Maintenance of the social contract is expensive. The financial resources from the state budget and banking system were available only in the early decades of the reform period. While the government continuously raised urban living standards, as promised by performance legitimacy, the high costs of the social contract have resulted in an imbalance between the available resources and the required resources. Once the resources from the state budget and banking system have been exhausted, maintenance of the welfare-oriented social contract will become more difficult economically, and then the "feeding and cooperation" relationship may have to be altered.

Will the "Honeymoon" Between State and Society End?

The social contract has sustained political stability and a partial economic reform for almost two decades. To maintain the social contract, available financial resources have almost been exhausted, and further economic reform now appears to be inevitable. Any further economic reform will have to break the social contract, and, in turn, may damage cooperation between the urban population and the regime and undermine political stability. Solving the puzzle will be very difficult for the third generation of communist leadership. Very probably, the "honeymoon" between the urban society and the regime under the social contract may come to an end, to be replaced by rising social tensions. Under pressure of possible social tension, it is uncertain whether the government will be able to continue economic reform of the state sector and maintain political stability as well.

Since the beginning of the urban economic reform program, reform of the state-owned enterprises (SOEs) has fallen far behind other reforms such as price reform and liberalization, and little progress has been made in improving the efficiency of the state sector. Some Chinese economists have appealed to the government for a thorough reform of the state sector and also have warned many times of the danger of exhausting the state's financial resources, but their voices were ignored for as long as decision-making was restrained by the social contract. It was only when the dead loans of the state banks exceeded the security line of the banking system in 1995 and a looming financial crisis threatened economic and political stability that the government finally took action to protect the banking system from collapse. To reduce loans for wages and welfare expenditures of those nearly bankrupted SOEs, the government quietly changed its employment policy and allowed the SOEs to lay off some redundant workers. Recent statistics indicate that from 1995 to 1997 about 12 million employees were laid off, about 7 million of whom are now still unemployed.[29]

A consensus was reached in the Fifteenth Party Congress that in order to save the banking system from bankruptcy, the state sector must be reconstructed by laying off more workers and closing those SOEs that are losing money. If this reform is implemented, there will be at least 24 million employees laid off in the next few years,[30] and about 25 percent of state employees may lose their jobs at almost the same time. The government is acutely aware of the political risks of this program, but it must exclude a large portion of the population from the social contract in order to reduce that cost of the contract and thus save the banking system and stabilize the rule of the Communist Party.

According to an estimate by a former deputy director of the State Commission on Restructuring Economic Systems, to carry out the program, the government needs at least 2,000 billion yuan to repay part of the bad loans to the banks. It needs yet another 730 billion yuan to build a safety net for unemployed people, whereas only about 40 to 50 billion yuan each year is available.[31] Without sufficient financial resources, the "shock therapy" may cause more severe social consequences than have occurred in the former Soviet bloc.

Politically, the reconstruction program implies that the government intends to rescue the banking system at the cost of breaking the social contract. While this will reduce the risk of economic instability, it may undermine political stability. If the "feeding and cooperation" relationship ceases to work, the state-society relationship will be destabilized, and the performance legitimacy the regime relies upon will be shaken.

At the end of the 1970s, the bankrupt orthodox ideology and personality cult of Mao had seriously damaged the traditional legitimacy and authority of the communist regime. People's loyalty to the regime was gradually transferred in a pragmatic direction, that is, to expectations that the regime could solve various economic and social problems. The regime gradually changed its social-control method from political and ideological mobilization to a loosened political control with material incentives. Since then, both the state and urban societies have experienced a honeymoon period in their interaction. Both parties thought that the social contract satisfied their own interests and preferred to maintain it. Such a honeymoon, however, is conditional; it depends on the degree of realization of popular expectations and the promises the regime has made. Once the state is unable to meet society's rising expectations, the social contract will necessarily be broken and the honeymoon will be over.

During the honeymoon, people were encouraged to turn their concern to the improvements in their living standards, and they became sensitive to changes regarding their new or vested interests. As soon as people find themselves worse off due to economic reform, extensive social dissatisfaction may appear. The reconstruction program of the SOEs will withdraw most welfare provisions from millions of employees and leave them unemployed without economic or political compensation. Although the program is justified by the rationale of economic efficiency, SOE employees will find that they are required to make sacrifices. In such a situation, the regime can no longer expect political compliance of these people, and must find an alternative for the social contract to maintain political stability and regain people's cooperation.

It could be argued that under threat of repression and strict control, the Chinese people are atomized and depoliticized, and are socially and economically dependent on and manipulated by the state or work units. Therefore, they are unable to organize effective collective action in behalf of their own interests and are not a viable party in any bargaining with the government. So far, workers' protests against pay cuts and possible unemployment have been small enough in scale not to constitute a social movement, though some strikes and collective bargaining occurred in 1989. What does make the state nervous is the structured homogeneity of individuals' opinions, which means that a spark might produce an extensive societal response. The state responds neither to public opinion nor to organized interest groups, but to spontaneous societal reactions, which are often initiated by those in an unfavorable situation in the reform. Under Deng, almost every time the leaders confronted significant social costs in response to reform policies, they retreated.

Society under an authoritarian regime lacks organized bargaining power, and has no independent leadership; however, discontent shaped by structured dependence upon the state sector may produce massive unorganized collective action, even without an organized power emerging.[32] State employees enjoying the socialist welfare system share the same opinion in opposing reductions in welfare benefits or reforming the socialist employment system. On other matters, such as wage system reform, workers in the public sector, party officials, and intellectuals may have different opinions, but relatively homogenous ideas exist within each group. Individual dissatisfactions can be quickly transformed into institutionalized homogenous public disaffection.

Expression of popular disaffection has four stages. First, complaints begin in private among relatives, friends, and others, but not with superiors. Second, as more and more express the same sense of dissatisfaction, they dare to talk about it in public places and criticism of the government arouses a sympathetic response in the populace, so that the dissatisfaction spreads rapidly. Third, if the regime fails to solve problems, social discontent accumulates, and people may begin work slowdowns as a means of protest. Fourth, when people's dissatisfaction is ignored by the government for a long time, they may doubt the regime's capability and there will be a "crisis of confidence" in the regime, party, and system. People may keep their distance from authority and refuse to obey orders from the regime, and finally may withdraw their loyalty if there is a chance to do so. Anger may rise, leading to public protests. This may take the form of nonpolitical, unorganized collective action, such as panic purchasing, withdrawal of bank deposits, and even demonstrations for economic demands.

The regime will find it difficult to deal with such disaffection. First, institutional barriers to the transmission of pubic opinion make it hard to discover and respond to social disaffection in its early stages. Once information about social disaffection reaches the central government, disaffection may already have spread. Second, having relied on the social contract for two decades, the regime has become unable to control social disaffection by the old instruments such as Maoist ideology or extensive political persecution. When official propaganda convinces fewer people and political mobilization no longer works, the government actually lacks any instruments to deal with dissatisfaction effectively. Third, the regime cannot simply employ despotic power to repress social discontent. Seeking legitimacy, the government can hardly reject the economic demands of the populace or respond with political persecution. Severe political persecution may also seriously damage the reform efforts.

Throughout the reform era, decisionmakers at various levels often have been motivated to make economic concessions. In addition to the reasons already cited, social unrest can be used as a weapon to attack those in decisionmaking positions in the power struggle within the party. Worrying about people's passive withdrawal of support may also interfere with economic performance and, in turn, produce more social dissatisfaction. Chinese politicians usually try to evade responsibility for any social unrest or economic instability, and compromise economically with those most disaffected people.

Today's leaders are weaker than Deng and need more societal support to carry out their policies. The critical financial situation, however, forces them to carry out a radical reconstruction program of the state sector, though they lack the necessary financial resources and political instruments. More likely, they dare not break the social contract completely, but reduce only the range of welfare provisions and decrease the number of people the social contract protects. Even so, the social foundation of the Communist Party will rapidly shrink and social conflict intensify. Under social pressure the regime may vacillate in implementing the reconstruction program and economic growth may gradually slow down. Yet hesitation in the reform program can only make the financial situation worse and lead to more tension, which may, in turn, call for political reform.

The social contract has helped the communist regime insulate itself from pressure for democracy but will ultimately undermine its rule. Radical reform can save China from a collapse of the banking system, but cannot help the regime retain its power. The looming financial crisis probably signifies a turning point on the road to reform. The gradual and peaceful reform process under the social contract may come to an end, and a swifter and more profound transition may occur, propelled not only by the goodwill of policy designers, but also by the conflicts in the current political and economic system.

Notes

1. Andrew J. Nathan, "Even Our Caution Must Be Hedged," *Journal of Democracy* 9 (January 1998): 62–63.
2. Jose Maria Maravall, "The Myth of the Authoritarian Advantage," in *Economic Reform and Democracy,* ed. Larry Diamond and Marc F. Plattner (Baltimore: The Johns Hopkins University Press, 1995), pp. 13–14.
3. Victor Nee and David Stark, "Toward an Institutional Analysis of State Socialism," in *Remaking the Economic Institutions of Socialism: China and Eastern Europe,* ed. Nee and Stark (Stanford, CA: Stanford University Press, 1989), pp. 1–31.
4. Janine Ludlam, "Reform and the Redefinition of the Social Contract Under Gorbachev," *World Politics* 43 (January 1991): 284–312; Linda J. Cook, *The Soviet Social Contract and Why It Failed: Welfare Policy and Workers' Politics from Brezhnev to Yeltsin* (Cambridge, MA: Harvard University Press, 1993), pp. 1–8.
5. Andrew Walder, *Communist Neo-Traditionalism: Work and Authority in Chinese Industry* (Berkeley: University of California Press, 1986), pp. 14–17; Kenneth Lieberthal, *Governing China: From Revolution Through Reform* (New York: W. W. Norton & Co., Inc., 1995), pp. 109, 168.
6. Central Committee of the Chinese Communist Party, "Zhonggong zhongyang guanyu jingji tizhi gaige de jueding" ["Decision of the Central Committee of Chinese Communist Party on Reform of Economic System"], *Renmin ribao (People's Daily)*, October 21, 1984.
7. Janos Kornai, *The Socialist System: The Political Economy of Communism* (Princeton, NJ: Princeton University Press, 1980), pp. 140–145.
8. Samuel P. Huntington, *The Third Wave: Democratization in the Late Twentieth Century* (Norman: University of Oklahoma Press, 1991), pp. 50–51.
9. Stephen White, "Economic Performance and Communist Legitimacy," *World Politics* 38 (April 1986): 462–482.
10. Ludlam, "Reform and the Redefinition," pp. 284–312.
11. This information is drawn from an interview the author had with a former official of the city government of Shanghai in 1997.
12. Walder, *Communist Neo-Traditionalism*, p. 224.
13. Janos Kornai, "Transformational Recession: A General Phenomenon Examined Through the Example of Hungary's Development," *Economie Appliquée* XLVI, no. 2 (1993): 181–227.
14. Barry Naughton, *Growing out of the Plan: Chinese Economic Reform, 1978–1993* (New York: Cambridge University Press, 1995), pp. 104–105.
15. Walder, *Communist Neo-Traditionalism*, pp. 237–240.
16. Naughton, *Growing out of the Plan*, p. 31.
17. Cheng Xiaonong, "Gaige zhong guomin jingji shouru liucheng de bianhua" ["Changes in Distribution of National Income in the Process of Reform"], *Zhongguo: Fazhan yu gaige (China: Development and Reform)* 8 (August 1987): 17–24; "Gaige zhong de hongguan jingji: Guomin shouru de fenpei yu shiyong" ["The Macroeconomic in the Process of Reform: Distribution and Use of National Income"], *Jingji Yanjiu (Economic Research)* 8 (August 1987): 16–28.

18. Xiaonong Cheng, "Distribution of National Income During Economic Reform," Working Paper (San Francisco: 1990 Institute, June 1991); Naughton, *Growing out of the Plan*, p. 85.

19. Cheng, "Changes in Distribution" and "Distribution of National Income."

20. Cheng Xiaonong, "Weichi wending yu shenhua gaige: Zhongguo mianlin de jueze" ["Transition Versus Stability: China's Dilemma"], *Dangdai Zhongguo yanjiu (Modern China Studies)* 1–2 (March 1995): 95.

21. Niu Wenwen, "Jianshao guoyou qiye de kuisun: jinhou de jianju renwu" ["Reduce Losses of the State Sector: A Tough Task in the Next Year"], *Jingji ribao (Economic Daily)*, December 11, 1997.

22. Naughton, *Growing out of the Plan*, p. 205.

23. Cheng Xiaonong, "Fanrong cong he er lai?—Zhongguo jingji xianzhuang he qushi de fenxi" ["The Puzzle of China's Economic Prosperity: Problems and Perspectives"], *Dangdai zhongguo yanjiu (Modern China Studies)* 3 (October 1996): 31–36.

24. Kornai, *The Socialist System*, p. 144.

25. Cheng, "Transition Versus Stability," p. 97; Gao Shangquan, "Guoyou qiye de zhidu chuangxin he fazhan ziben shichang" ["Institutional Innovation of State Enterprises and Development of Capital Market"], *Jingji cankao bao (Economic Information Daily)*, September 30, 1997.

26. Cheng, "Transition Versus Stability," pp. 97–98.

27. Cheng, "The Puzzle of China's Economic Prosperity," p. 51.

28. Survey Department of Household Income, State Bureau of Statistics, "Woguo cheng xiang shouru chaju wenti yanjiu" ["On Urban-Rural Income Gap in China"], *Jingji Yanjiu (Economic Research)* 12 (December 1994): 34–35.

29. *Zhongguo gaige bao (China Reform News)*, January 21, 1998.

30. Gao Shangquan, "Institutional Innovation of State Enterprises."

31. Ibid.

32. Xueguang Zhou, "Unorganized Interests and Collective Action in Communist China," *American Sociological Review* 58 (February 1993): 54–73.

8

Financing Unemployment and Pension Insurance

Wei Yu

Since 1978 when economic reform began, China's economy has been growing rapidly. From 1981 through 1990, the annual average increase in gross domestic product (GDP) was 10.1 percent; from 1991 through 1995, the average increase was 11.6 percent.[1] Although reform has improved considerably the average standard of living, it also has profoundly changed the country's industrial structure. State-owned enterprises (SOEs) have declined in productivity while other types of enterprises (private, collective, and foreign investment) have grown dramatically. Among the enterprises registered at township or higher government levels, SOEs accounted for 72 percent of total output in 1985, but only 47 percent in 1995. During the same period, the total share of output by enterprises with foreign investment, including investment from Hong Kong and Taiwan, jumped from almost zero to 16.5 percent.[2]

Implications of such a sharp change in economic structure go far beyond the boundary of economic reform. As Guoguang Wu pointed out in Chapter 2, "political legitimacy is shifting from the communist revolution and revolutionary ideology to the regime's economic performance." The welfare system discussed in this chapter reflects one of many aspects affected by the change of political legitimacy. Under the old socialist regime, financing welfare programs was built into the central planned economy. The principle was very clear: everyone contributes to the society based on the state's economic plan, and the state, in turn, should take care of the elderly and arrange full employment. When the political legitimacy shifted, financing policy for the welfare system changed completely, which resulted in a substantial loss for the middle-aged and older generations.

It is clear that many problems in the current welfare system are rooted in the old planned economy. On the one hand, SOEs complain that they cannot compete with other enterprises because they must shoulder the heavy burden of social programs. Hence, SOEs cannot reform their basic structure without an effective social system to take over their responsibility.

On the other hand, an effective social-safety system cannot be established because of the high cost of setting up such a system. This paradox is a typical phenomenon when the financing policy is no longer consistent with the communist ideology. According to *Xinhua News,* in Shanghai, for every 100 yuan paid to an employee by SOEs, the SOEs must pay 46 yuan for fringe benefits, including pension contributions, unemployment insurance, health insurance, housing-fund contributions, and public transportation restructuring.[3] Management of the government and SOEs in Shanghai is the most efficient in the nation. If SOEs in Shanghai can barely support the social programs, other SOEs across China may not be able to afford such a system at all.

There is no simple solution for reforming social-safety programs. SOEs can afford neither the old system, which is the financial responsibility of each individual enterprise, nor the new system, which is managed by pooling resources at the level of the city or province. After investigating China's current pension policy, a World Bank team concluded that the current pension system is not viable in the long run. The system's dependency ratio will rise to 76 percent by 2050, while the sustainable contribution rate is 45.9 percent.[4] In most developed countries, the employers' contribution to a pension is less than 20 percent of total wages and salaries. In the United States, employers' total contributions to all social security programs was 13.35 percent in 1995.[5] In comparison, the cost of maintaining the current level of social programs would bankrupt the SOEs.

China's social programs consist of four major components: pensions, unemployment insurance, health care insurance, and welfare programs. Because each program has its own characteristics, it must be separately analyzed. This chapter discusses the basic problems of financing unemployment and pension insurance in China's urban areas. It focuses on three aspects of each program: (1) its social nature and reasons for the government's interference, (2) the impact of the economic transition from a planned to a market economy, and (3) the trade-off among different financing policies and the nature of income redistribution.

Unemployment Insurance

SOE layoffs are the result of economic reform that replaces a planned economy with a free-market system. The planned economy was based on the theory of Karl Marx, which maintains that, in an uncontrolled capitalist system, workers are exploited because they cannot earn enough to purchase and/or maintain the tools and raw materials for their livelihood. As a result, they depend on financial support from the wealthy and must accept payment that is less than their own contribution to their products. In theory, the socialist state provides all citizens with an equal opportunity of working (universal employment), and thus provides everyone with social insurance through universal employment. The theoretical basis of a socialist planned economy is to let the state plan resource allocation, including human resources. Hence, in theory, unemployment does not exist in a planned economy. But since planned economies cannot compete with market economies, most socialist countries have begun economic reform and introduced market mechanisms. As a result of market adjustment, unemployment appears.

Establishing an unemployment insurance program cannot solve the unemployment problem in major industrial cities. In many such cities, SOEs are laying off thousands of employees (10 percent to 30 percent of the total SOE labor force).[6] Because SOE layoffs are so extensive, simply pooling SOEs with other enterprises to finance unemployment insurance is equivalent to asking other enterprises to rescue the SOEs. Also, in the planned economy, much of the profits of SOEs have been disbursed to other parts of the country via the central government. Now, these SOEs are facing market pressure and need significant adjustment to survive. Should the entire country share the cost of such adjustment?

Current Financing Plan to Assist SOE Layoffs

Current government policy calls for local unemployment insurance programs to assist the unemployed in urban areas. According to the State Council, in 1994 employers paid 0.6 percent of their total wages for unemployment insurance. The local government decides the pooling level. If a fund has a surplus or shortage, a local government has the power to adjust the premium. The maximum rate, however, cannot exceed 1 percent of total wages.[7] The redistribution effect of this financing policy is to ask sound firms (both SOEs and non-SOEs) to subsidize weak SOEs. The level of the subsidy depends on the proportion of SOE layoffs in the local area. The higher the proportion of SOE layoffs, the heavier the burden to local business firms.

This financing policy can create unfair competition between enterprises with different levels of unemployment insurance payments. For example, a firm in Shenyang (an old industrial center dominated by SOEs) cannot compete with a similar firm located in Shenzhen (a newly developed coastal industrial region with almost no SOEs), even if the former is more efficient, because it has to pay more to support the large number of SOE layoffs.

Using local insurance in response to SOE layoffs also increases the gap among regional economies. If economic development in a city is slow, the proportion of SOE layoffs will be higher and the burden to local business heavier. Because firms located in regions with little economic growth will have greater financial burdens than firms in other regions, they cannot compete. This will further slow economic growth and lead to higher levels of unemployment. In addition, heavy taxation will wash out the advantage of low labor costs and discourage investment from other regions and foreign countries.

The current financing policy for unemployment insurance has at least two practical problems in major inland industrial cities where SOE layoffs are extensive. First, the current premium is not nearly enough to cover unemployment benefits. If insurance pays 60 percent of average local wages to the unemployed and employers pay the maximum amount of premium (1 percent of their total wage), this only covers 1.7 percent of all employees. According to the newspaper *Zhongguo gongshang shibao*, SOE layoffs in Shanghai, Shenyang, Fujian, Zhengzhou, and Chengdu account for 14 percent, 23 percent, 27.5 percent, 14.8 percent, and 20–30 percent of total employees, respectively.[8] Second, compliance rates in these cities are low. Many SOEs have no money to pay for unemployment insurance at all. Based on statistics provided by the Labor Bureau, the national average compliance rate in 1994 was only 88.7 percent.[9] In fact, SOEs that must lay off a large number of employees are also the ones that cannot afford unemployment insurance, which makes the insurance program more like a rescue program.

Some Chinese scholars have suggested using some of the funds obtained from selling the assets of SOEs to assist the unemployed.[10] The rationale behind this suggestion is that profits created by SOEs during earlier years include contributions for various social benefit programs. Therefore, workers laid off by SOEs should obtain some money from state-owned assets. In 1994, the State Council decided that assets of bankrupt SOEs should be used to assist workers prior to paying any debt. This financing method can reduce the burden of local firms in those major inland industrial cities, but government revenue from state assets will decline accordingly. Government revenue comes from two major sources: taxes and the return on state assets. When state assets shrink, government revenue will decline unless taxes are increased. The redistribution effect of this financing method depends on who gets the money from selling state assets and how the revenue decline is covered. Usually, funds raised from selling state assets do not go to local governments. When the funds are used for unemployment, government banks are more likely to be the losers because most bankrupt SOEs have a considerable amount of debt accrued from government banks. Therefore, financing assistance for laid-off employees of the SOEs by selling state assets will indirectly spread the burden to other areas through government banks or other channels.

Policy Considerations

The current unemployment insurance program will be viable and its financial status sound only if the laid-off employees receive financial assistance from the central government. As discussed earlier, SOE layoffs are the result of structural adjustment due to the transition from a planned economy to a market system. It is very hard for local governments to handle such large-scale economic adjustment. The key question is whether all local provinces can agree to the establishment of a national program to assist SOE layoffs. A program financed through the central government may have negative effects if it is not properly managed. Sending money to cities with large numbers of laid-off workers may encourage local governments to do nothing but wait for financial aid from the central government, and the number of layoffs may increase when more funds flow in. In addition to other factors, management efficiency and the financial capability of local governments are major determinants of economic development. Hence, a multidimensional program is needed to assist the large number of laid-off workers during the economic transition.

Many believe that the lack of a functional social insurance program is a major obstacle to SOE reform. It seems that if SOEs do not lay off large numbers of workers, reform cannot proceed. This impression is enhanced by many newspaper reports. For instance, Zhong Jianqin and Luo Jun[11] reported statistics from the Ministry of Labor showing that during the Ninth Five-Year Plan, 15 million state employees will be laid off. When this is added to the current SOE layoffs (estimated at 15 million), the total number of workers laid off during the Ninth Five-Year Plan will be 30 million. This number ignores the possibility that the number of workers laid off may be reduced if the structure of SOE management is successfully reformed. A typical example is the well-known Wang Yitang incident reported by *Zhongguo qingnian bao.*[12] A county-owned cement factory replaced twelve directors and still lost money. Finally, the county contracted with an entrepreneur, Wang Yitang, who was once a farmer, and gave him complete control of the factory's management. The factory made a profit of 700,000 yuan in the first year and 2.5 million yuan the next year. He did not lay off any workers and did not even change regulations. He just fired the previous director and eight associate directors and strictly enforced existing regulations. Of the 415 factory employees, only about 20 left the company. They had been previously paid without actually doing any work. This example suggests that if reform is successful in SOEs, layoffs may be minimal.

Many believe that people laid off are "extra" employees of the firm. Based on economic theory, if the marginal return of a worker is less than his or her marginal cost, the worker is an extra employee because the firm's cost will be reduced or its profit will be maximized if this worker is laid off. Because most SOEs are inefficiently operated, reform may improve their efficiency, increase workers' productivity (marginal return), and reduce the number of laid-off workers. It should also be kept in mind that those laid off might not be those whose marginal return is less than their marginal cost. It has been observed that the relationship between the worker and the manager is an important determinant of being laid off. If reform goes in the right direction, economic considerations will be used to decide which employees are laid off.

Another factor that should be considered when reducing the number of SOE employees is the overall cost to society. When a worker is laid off, the government has to assist the worker and his family. In this case, even if the worker's marginal return is less than his marginal cost, it is better for both the state and the worker if he can continue to work as long as the money being lost is less than the cost of government assistance. Of course, in the long run, resources are better allocated if layoffs lead workers to be more productive. In many situations, however, workers laid off by SOEs have difficulty transferring into more productive careers.

The problem of layoffs is closely related to China's history. Layoffs affect a generation that grew up under the planned economy. Most of them have been assigned to the same job since they started working. When they suddenly lose their jobs, they do not know where to go, what to do, and how to find another job. Industrial workers used to be treated as the leading class. Because losing a job means losing social status, many laid-off workers are deeply depressed. Therefore, the government should provide various assistance programs to help them, such as job training, market information, and psychological consulting.

SOE layoffs and slow economic growth often go together in large industrial cities. Without financial capability, none of the present social programs will be available. It is true that SOEs are not efficiently organized and cannot compete with other types of enterprises, but SOE employees have worked very hard to follow each economic plan and contributed a great deal to the nation's economy before the economic reform. During that period, economic planning, including resource allocation and income distribution, was controlled by the central government. Therefore, SOE layoffs are the cost of national economic reform, rather than a local problem. Should the entire country share the cost? Market factors cannot be allowed to answer this question. It must be answered by society.

Pension Insurance

The Dynamics of Pension Finance

To understand the problems of pension reform, an understanding of the dynamics of pension finance is necessary. There are two basic principles for financing pension programs: individual accumulation and pay-as-you-go. Individual accumulation takes the form of mandated personal savings. All citizens are required to put aside a certain amount of money while they are able to work. In the early years of such a program, one's contribution depends on the number of years left before retirement. To obtain the same level of benefits, people who are closer to their retirement have to contribute more. Therefore, a pension completely financed by individual accumulation is feasible only for young people who can gradually increase their accumulation as time goes by.

The pay-as-you-go system is a quick-fix method to initiate a pension program. Unlike individual accumulation, pay-as-you-go does not require accumulation; it simply pays the retired by taxing the working population. Therefore, it can immediately cover the entire retired population. A special feature of pay-as-you-go financing is that almost all adults would benefit from the new program, especially those who are close to age sixty-five or older, and no one is worse off. The system would reach its stable status after the cohorts who entered it at age twenty-one die. Then, the new system financed by the pay-as-you-go method would become the same as the one financed by individual accumulations. Because most adults are better off and no one is worse off, a pay-as-you-go pension plan is easily accepted in a democratic country.

However, if a government wants to change from a pay-as-you-go pension plan to one financed by individual accumulation, the redistribution pattern would be just the opposite. During the transition to individual accumulation, all adults, especially older people, will lose and no one will benefit. Older people do not have enough personal savings and would have to reduce consumption considerably. The aggregate impact on the economy would be that consumption decreases and saving increases. When the entire working generation dies, the system would reach stable status. The implication of changing from pay-as-you-go to individual accumulation is that the public debt owed by the next generation to the current generation would not be honored.

Reform and Policy Consideration

The financing method used for the previous pension program in the SOEs is equivalent to the pay-as-you-go plan outlined above. The principle of the current reform of pension finance is to transfer from that system to individual accumulation. As pointed out in the previous section, this change involves the problem of public debt. The currently retired and employees in middle age or older have contributed a great deal of their lifetime income to support the people who retired before them. Now they will have to take care of themselves. To ease this problem, the current reform includes a social-pooling plan to pay the currently retired with savings acquired from the young.

There are three basic problems under the previous pension system in the SOEs. First, unlike other pay-as-you-go systems, the previous pension finance system does not have a clear accounting of the contributions, distributions, and balances. Pensions are distributed through the payroll account and retired persons receive their pensions from the company they last worked for before retirement. When SOEs accept financial self-responsibility, they also have to pay the pensions of people who retired from them. As a result of the financial self-responsibility principle and the old payment method, the previous pension finance becomes, after the economic reform, a company-based pay-as-you-go system. If a company loses money, it cannot pay any pensions. If a company is very old and has a large number of retired employees, the working employees in that company will have very heavy burdens funding their pension program.

The second problem with this system is the rapid growth of nonstate-owned enterprises. Before economic reform, SOEs accounted for 99 percent of industrial production. From 1985 through 1995, the production of foreign- and joint-owned enterprises grew from 0 percent to 16.5 percent.[13] Most foreign- and joint-owned enterprises are new and hire young people. As the ratio of retired to working employees in SOEs increases, along with this shrinkage of SOE production, the burden on SOE employees is incrementally heavier than before.

The third problem is the increasing proportion of the aging population. Due to family planning and an increase in life expectancy, the ratio of the retired to the working is rising significantly. Pay-as-you-go financing will place a heavy burden on future generations as the population grows older.

Of these three problems, only the last one is related to the pay-as-you-go financing method. It is caused by the aging population rather than by economic reform. Even the aging problem can be solved by gradually increasing accumulations in the pension fund. For instance, the U.S. pension system is financed by pay-as-you-go. Realizing the problem caused by an aging population, the U.S. Congress passed a law in 1983 that increased pension taxes and extended the retirement age from sixty-five to sixty-seven. Its financing method is still pay-as-you-go and no dramatic change is needed. Because China's pension program only exists in SOEs and government agencies, however, more than 80 percent of the population still depends on family to support the elderly. Therefore, the problem of the aging population will not be as serious as in a country with a universal pension program.

To solve the first two problems of the previous pension program, retired employees will have to be separated from enterprises. If the pension-financing pool is based on a community such as a city, the entire working population should be included to finance the system. A program such as that can be financed by a community-based pay-as-you-go method. However, the current policy, expressed in State Council Document 6 of March 1995, provides two basic plans for local authorities to choose from. Both plans involve individual accounts and social pooling, although they are organized in different ways.

The first plan, designed by the State Commission for Economic Restructuring of Economic Systems, emphasizes individual accounts. All new workers will use individual accounts for their pension and a social pool would be responsible for pensions for those already retired and current workers not fully covered by individual accounts. Contributions into individual accounts would be approximately 16 percent of total wages and would consist of three parts: (1) an individual contribution of 3 percent of total wages; (2) an enterprise contribution of 8 percent of each worker's wages; and (3) an enterprise contribution of 5 percent of the average local wage.[14]

The second plan is based on the previous model developed by the Ministry of Labor, which focuses more on social pooling than on individual accounts. The basic pension insurance premium would be paid by both enterprises and workers, according to a proportion to be decided by local governments. Part of the pension funds will be contributed to individual accounts. For those whose payment period is longer than ten years, the pension will be granted as follows: (1) a social pension, which equals 20–25 percent of the local average wage; (2) a premium pension, which is about 1.0–1.4 percent of basic wage figures; and (3) all money in individual accounts.[15]

In principle, both plans combine social pooling with individual accounts so that the pension finance will be eventually transferred into individual accounts. Rather than reducing the burden on SOEs, this policy, in fact, doubled the SOEs' financial responsibilities. In addition to providing pensions for retired workers, SOEs now have to contribute to individual accounts. In most industrial cities, enterprises contribute from 20 to 30 percent of total wages and workers contribute 3 to 5 percent of their own wage.[16] If 16 percent of total wages is deposited into individual accounts, the social pooling will not be enough. In this case, many local insurance programs use the money in individual accounts to pay those currently retired. Individual accounts thus soon become empty accounts.

The major advantage of individual accounts disappears when they are empty. First, there will be no return from individual accounts. The promised interest from individual accounts will have to be paid by future contributions. Moreover, individual accounts will reduce personal savings because workers feel that they already have their pension saved. Also, there will be less savings flowing into investment, which in turn may slow economic growth and increase the burden on future generations. With empty individual accounts, the financing method of pension insurance is equivalent to a pay-as-you-go system.

The World Bank has made feasible suggestions for reforming the pension system.[17] In 1996, a World Bank investigation team suggested that the pension system should consist of three pillars. The first pillar is completely financed by employers and controlled by the government. Its benefit is equal to the poverty level. Since many nonstate-owned enterprises do not have retired employees, the World Bank team estimates that this part of the pension system would cost about 9 percent of total wages. The second pillar is mandated individual accounts jointly financed by employers and workers at 8 percent of an individual's wage. This is only half of the current contribution to individual accounts. Because the contribution to the social pooling is less than before, enterprises should be able to afford it. The most important feature for individual accounts is full accumulation. The entire fund in individual accounts should be fully invested in holdings with sound returns. Individual accounts can smooth the financial problem caused by the aging population. With good returns, 8 percent of a worker's wage can be a considerable amount of money for retirement in forty years. The third pillar is any complementary program provided by employers.

The World Bank plan has two important features. First, the first two pillars include all workers in the plan so that contributions to the basic plan (the first pillar) from enterprises with large numbers of retired workers are considerably reduced and become affordable to them. The second feature is that the benefit of the basic plan is reduced to poverty level, which also reduces the burden to all employers. The World Bank plan, however, does not consider how SOEs with serious financial problems will pay for the pension. Many SOEs are close to bankruptcy and have no money to pay any pensions. In many inland industrial cities, about 20 percent of SOE employees have been laid off and receive no pension from their enterprises. According to the World Bank report in 1996, the compliance rate in Beijing and Tianjin is 95 percent, Shanghai is 90 percent, and Shenyang and Changchun are 80 percent and 76.9 percent, respectively; Chongqing is the lowest, with only 70.2 percent compliance.[18] Therefore, even following the World Bank plan, local governments must subsidize the basic plan for some employees so that they can obtain at least poverty-level financial assistance when they retire.

Conclusion

This chapter has discussed the relationship between financing methods and two common social-safety programs: unemployment and pension insurance. Almost every social-safety plan contains two features: welfare and insurance. If a plan is more like welfare, its collecting principle is often based on income, reflecting redistribution from the rich to the poor. If a plan is more like insurance, its premiums should follow the risk levels of individual workers. The riskier the person, the higher the premium. Many economic disasters are insured through the market and carried out by private insurance companies. Some events, however, cannot be insured through the market because charging insurance premiums according to personal risk level conflicts with the moral standards of society. A person with chronic medical problems is riskier than a healthy person. If, following the insurance principle, sick people pay a higher premium, this creates a situation that is unacceptable in many societies. Hence, many governments either provide a national health insurance program, or strictly regulate private health insurance so that sick people are not excluded. As society's moral standard is closely related to a country's cultural and historical background, so is the financing principle of social-safety programs.

The difficulty with China's social-safety programs comes from its special historical background, which is the thirty-year experience of trying to establish a socialist country. From 1949 through 1978, China had a series of political movements and disasters, about one every three to five years. A majority of the people who need help now are those in middle age or older, the same people who survived the thirty-year political storm. The currently retired generation has dedicated its entire life to the country's economic development. Most retired people have little savings for their retirement. All they can rely on is the socialist state and the enterprises for which they worked. Most middle-aged employees not only have no savings but also have no training for today's job market. What they do have is family responsibility, including children to raise and parents to support. When the political legitimacy is shifted from the communist ideology to a regime of economic performance, its impact on people who have followed the old regime for most of their lives is much deeper and longer. The society is challenged to keep balance between smoothing the intergenerational transfer due to policy change and establishing a more efficient economic system.

The limitations to this discussion are as follows: first, this chapter only discusses urban social-safety programs. But this does not mean that rural problems are less important. In fact, compared with urban residents, rural people have almost no social-safety programs at all. However, the financing method in rural areas is quite different. There are no employers in rural areas to subsidize the social-safety system. Second, the financial issues discussed in this article may not be problems in many coastal and developed cities because these cities either do not have a large proportion of SOE employees (such as Shenzhen), or do have a fast-growing economy to support a social-safety system. Because of differences in the economies among urban areas, financial strategies for a social-safety system should be different.

Notes

1. China National Statistics Bureau, *Zhongguo tongji nianjian, 1996* [*China Annual Statistics, 1996*] (Beijing: Zhongguo tongji chubanshe, 1997), p. 30, table 2–3.
2. Ibid.

3. Zhong Jianqin and Luo Jun, "Zaijiuye yali jiujing you duoda?" ["How High Is the Pressure of Reemployment?"], *Jingjixue xiaoxibao* (*Economics Highlights*) (Chengdu: Jingjixue xiaoxibao chubanshe), March 21, 1997, p. 1.

4. World Bank, *China: Pension System Reform, The World Bank Country Report, Report No. 15121-CHA* (Washington, DC: World Bank, 1996), pp. 36–39.

5. U.S. Social Security Administration, *Social Security Programs Throughout the World—1995* (Washington, DC: GPO, 1996).

6. Zhong Jianqin and Luo Jun, "How High Is the Pressure?" p. 1.

7. Deng Dasong, Zhu Shifan, and Song Shunfeng, "Lun Zhongguo shehui baozhang shuishou zhidu jiqi gaige wanshan de silu yu duice" ["Concepts and Policies of China's Social Safety Tax Structure and Its Reform"], in *Zhongguo shuizhi gaige* [*China's Tax System Reform*], ed. Xu Dianqing and Li Yanjin (Beijing: Zhongguo jingji chubanshe, 1997), pp. 250–264.

8. Zhong Jianqin and Luo Jun, "How High Is the Pressure?" p. 1.

9. World Bank, *China: Pension System Reform.*

10. Hu Yicheng, "Zouchu chengzhen pinkun yu yanglao kunjing" ["Get out of Urban Poverty and Pension Problems"], *Jingjixue xiaoxi bao* (*Economics Highlights*), March 21, 1997.

11. Zhong Jianqin and Luo Jun, "How High Is the Pressure?" p. 1.

12. Wang Yitang's surprising success was reported by *Zhongguo qingnian bao* (*China Youth Daily*) in 1997.

13. China National Statistics Bureau, *China Annual Statistics, 1996*, p. 30, table 2–3.

14. World Bank, *China: Pension System Reform (Appendix)*, pp. 96–99.

15. Ibid., pp. 100–102.

16. Ibid., pp. 9–10.

17. Ibid., pp. 43–55.

18. Ibid., p. 11.

9

A Survey of Beijing Residents

Yang Zhong, Jie Chen & John M. Scheb II

With the death of Deng Xiaoping, discussion about the future political development of China is once again in the spotlight. In fact, debate over the
viability of the current political regime in China started immediately after
the 1989 Tiananmen Square crackdown. The prospects for reform in the
People's Republic of China (PRC) and the fate of the Chinese Communist
Party (CCP) projected by China watchers were then overwhelmingly pessimistic.[1] Seven years after the Tiananmen Square events, the survival of
the CCP against all odds (including the aftermath of the collapse of communist regimes in eastern Europe and the Soviet Union) is in itself no
small miracle. The post-Tiananmen political regime in China has been, by
and large, stable. Not only has the CCP survived, it has also made impressive economic progress in the past seven years. This new development has
caused a major reassessment of the situation in the PRC among China
watchers. The *New York Times* called the phenomenon of China's rapid
economic growth in an authoritarian environment the "riddle of China."[2]
One China specialist even posed the question whether China is where
Samuel Huntington's "third wave" stopped and whether the PRC would be
an exception to the fall of communism worldwide.[3]

The most often-cited factors to account for the political tranquillity in
the PRC are the remarkable economic growth and political oppression.[4]
These two factors are certainly indispensable in understanding developments in China after 1989. However, they alone fall short of providing us
with a satisfactory and convincing explanation of the "China exception."

This chapter is taken from Yang Zhong, Jie Chen, and John M. Scheb II, "Political Views from Below: A Survey of Beijing Residents," *PS: Political Science &
Politics* XXX, no. 3 (Sept. 1997): 474–482. Reprinted by permission of the editor.

Support for this project was provided by the Social Science Research Institute
of the University of Tennessee at Knoxville, the University of Wisconsin at River
Falls, and the Public Opinion Research Institute of the People's University in Beijing.

Economic growth in and by itself does not directly contribute to political stability. In fact, it has been argued that economic development and modernization lead to political instability.[5] Also, it is simplistic to argue that the survival of the current communist leadership in the PRC is mainly due to political repression such as arrests and terror. A heavy-handed approach to controlling the population was adopted during the immediate aftermath of the June Fourth crackdown in some urban centers. Since then, tight political control has been replaced by a more relaxed approach by the government in dealing with the discontent among the masses, even though the high-profiled dissidents are still either imprisoned or under constant police harassment. It is a fact that criticisms of or even cursing the CCP and its leaders are not uncommon in China today.[6]

This study, which is based on a survey of permanent residents of Beijing or residents with Beijing *hukou* ("residential registration"), intends to tap the mood and feelings of ordinary people in China regarding levels of political interest and democratic values, attitudes toward economic reform, evaluations of government performance in different policy areas, and levels of satisfaction and confidence generally. The survey had two purposes. The first purpose was fact-finding. Simply put, it was to find out what ordinary Beijing residents thought about political issues. The second purpose was to see where China was heading with regard to its political future, for public opinion does affect public policy. In a recent book, Allen Liu argues that post-Mao economic and political reforms should be considered as a result more of public opinions—which had grown too strong for the Communist Party leaders to ignore after the death of Mao Zedong—and less of the political motivations of any individual leaders.[7] The fact that the government has made noticeable efforts to control inflation and combat official corruption is evidence that the leaders and their policies are constrained to a certain degree by public opinion.

The Survey

Our survey of Beijing residents was conducted in December 1995 in cooperation with the Public Opinion Research Institute of People's University in Beijing.[8] A total of seven hundred permanent Beijing residents eighteen years old or older were sampled using the multistage random sampling procedure.[9] The questionnaire was taken by the interviewer to the randomly chosen individual respondent to be filled out, and was brought by the interviewer back to the survey center. As a result of this survey measure, the response rate was 97 percent, considerably higher than surveys done in other fashions. The sample includes equal numbers of females and males. All age groups (from eighteen years old to over sixty-six years old) and occupation sectors are represented in the sample. Over

75 percent of the respondents have either middle school or high school diplomas. Nearly 80 percent of the respondents live in the urban areas of the city. Based upon a comparison between this sample and the 1990 Beijing census, the sampling error is less than 2 percent for gender and less than 3 percent for age.

Since the population of the sample was the permanent residents of Beijing, the survey results are not applicable to the rest of the country. The survey of Beijing residents can be regarded as a crucial case study for the special status of Beijing in Chinese politics and history. As the capital of many dynasties as well as the People's Republic of China, Beijing has a special place in the history of contemporary China, not paralleled by any other city. Significant historical events, such as the May Fourth Movement of 1919, the Cultural Revolution of 1966, the April Fifth Incident of 1976, and the Tiananmen Square democracy movement of 1989, all started in Beijing. The mood of Beijingers is often looked at as the barometer of the mood of the country. The mood among Beijing residents six years after the dramatic events of 1989 should be especially interesting.[10]

Findings

Level of Political Interest and Democratic Values

A conventional view is that nowadays people in China are too much consumed with making money and pay little attention to political and public affairs. With the influence of market economic reforms and the disillusion with democratic reforms, people are said to have become increasingly apolitical and pragmatic.[11] However, the survey shows that this perception of a low level of political interest may be incorrect or exaggerated. As Table 9.1 shows, about two-thirds of the respondents are still interested in national affairs. An even larger number of people are interested in Beijing local affairs. Another indication of the level of political interest is the frequency of discussion of politics. Our survey shows that many people do talk about politics with their family members, relatives, friends, and colleagues. Specifically, about 40 percent of our respondents said that they engage in political discussion with others very often, while about 50 percent said they talk about politics occasionally (see Table 9.1). Apparently, while they do not often share their thoughts with others, many people are interested in national affairs or Beijing affairs. These findings are not surprising, given the concerns about the leadership succession at the top and the high-profile cases of official corruption, particularly the case of former Beijing mayor Chen Xitong, in the last two years.

Demographic factors affect the level of political interest. We found that residency, education, age, and income seem to be the factors affecting the

Table 9.1   Level of Political Interest

	Very interested	Interested	Somewhat interested	Not interested	N
National affairs	13.8%	56.9%	27.3%	2.1%	682
Beijing affairs	22.6	58.5	17.6	1.3	682

	Whenever we see each other	Very often	Not often	Never	Can't tell	N
Discussion of politics with others	2.5%	40.9%	50.6%	3.4%	2.5%	670

Note: N denotes total number of responses.

respondents' interest in politics. Our findings are very similar to those studies on mass political behavior in other countries. Specifically, the level of political interest is higher among urban residents, the more educated, older people, and people with higher incomes. Table 9.2 clearly shows this pattern when it comes to people's level of interest in national affairs. The sharpest contrasts are between urban residents and rural residents and between low-income people and middle/high-income people (see Table 9.2).

Table 9.3 illustrates the complexity in the political attitude toward democracy and civil liberties among Beijing residents. Over 85 percent of the respondents seem to be tolerant of people with different political views; the majority favors wider press freedom; and an overwhelming majority voice support for a more democratic way of choosing local government officials (see Table 9.3). However, findings from the next three questions indicate a low level of political efficacy among Beijingers. Seventy percent of the respondents lack confidence in themselves. Most of the respondents are reluctant to challenge the authorities, and an overwhelming majority of the people surveyed prefer stability and order to a freer society. The two sets of results seem to be contradictory. Apparently, Beijingers are in favor of the general and abstract principles of civil liberties and democracy, yet their cultural and behavioral pattern is still marked by elitist orientation, deference to authority, and preference for order. We suspect that the contradiction results from the gap between the two levels of political culture: the cognitive level and the behavioral level. On the cognitive level, buzzwords such as "democracy," "freedom," and "liberty" are quite acceptable to the general public. Indeed, even the Chinese constitution is filled with those terms and concepts. Yet, on a deeper level, a much longer term of socialization and experience is needed to change people's behavior in this regard.

Attitudes Toward Economic Reform

Economic reforms that Deng Xiaoping started in the late 1970s have changed the face of China and have made it one of the fastest-growing economies in the world. Economic reforms in general have improved the

Table 9.2   **Interest in National Politics by Residence, Education, Age, and Income**

	Very interested	Interested	Somewhat interested	Not interested	N
Residence					
Urban[a]	15.7%	61.7%	21.0%	1.4%	
Rural	5.0	42.9	47.1	5.0	668
Education					
Primary school					
or below	9.9	53.1	32.1	4.9	
Middle school	11.2	53.7	31.8	3.3	
High school	15.6	58.3	25.7	0.4	
College	19.0	65.8	13.9	1.3	678
Age					
Young (18–35)	10.0	53.2	34.4	2.3	
Middle (36–55)	14.3	55.7	27.2	2.4	
Old (over 55)	18.0	65.1	15.7	1.1	682
Monthly income					
Lower (below 250 yuan)	4.8	37.1	56.5	1.6	
Middle (250–800 yuan)	14.6	58.4	24.8	2.1	
Upper (over 800 yuan)	20.1	64.5	15.3	0.0	643

Note: N denotes total number of replies.

a. Urban residents here include both residents of urban districts of Beijing and residents of urban county towns in Beijing.

Table 9.3 **General Political Attitudes**

	Strongly agree	Agree	Disagree	Strongly disagree	N
Regardless of one's political beliefs, he or she is entitled to the same legal rights and protections as is anyone else.	39.8%	47.5%	11.2%	1.5%	676
The press should be given more freedom to expose wrongdoings such as corruption.	68.5	25.8	5.2	0.4	677
Elections to local government positions should be conducted in such a way that there is more than one candidate for each post.	49.8	43.8	5.1	1.3	671
The well-being of the country is mainly dependent upon state leaders, not the masses.	37.0	34.4	21.8	6.8	675
In general, I don't think I should argue with the authority even though I believe my idea is correct.	22.5	41.0	28.7	7.8	676
I would rather live in an orderly society than live in a freer society that is prone to disruptions	61.8	33.0	3.6	1.6	673

Note: N denotes total number of replies.

people's standard of living. Yet economic reforms have also had their downside effects. Specifically, economic reforms have brought about corruption, inflation, job insecurity, declining welfare programs, and income inequality. What is the impact of the negative drawbacks on people's views on economic reform? This survey shows the opinions about the economic and ownership system and attitudes toward economic reform in general. Figure

9.1 and Figure 9.2 show an interesting pattern of preferences for economic system and ownership structure. With regard to economic system, very few prefer a total central planning economy (CPE). Less than 16 percent are fond of a predominantly CPE. Nearly a quarter of Beijing residents seem to favor a truly mixed economy, namely, half planning and half market economy, indicating they want to have the benefits of both systems. One-third of the respondents favor a predominantly market economy. Another 20 percent of the people are not sure which system works better for them. These findings indicate that even though many Chinese people have embraced the concept of the market economy, most are still uncertain about the adoption of a complete or predominant market economy. It should be pointed out that the official goal of the economic reforms since the early 1990s has been the introduction of a full market economy. With more than one-third of state enterprises in the red, fear of losing one's job due to competition in a full-fledged market economy is a real fear for workers in the public sector.

The survey shows that socialist values are still very strong among Beijing residents when it comes to forms of ownership and means of production.

Figure 9.1 Preference of Economic System (N=680)

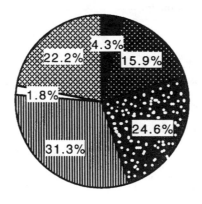

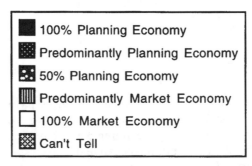

Figure 9.2   Preference of Economic Ownership System (N=680)

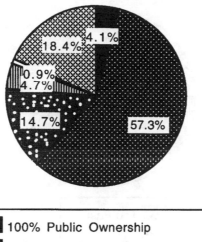

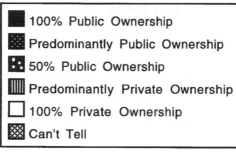

- ■ 100% Public Ownership
- ▨ Predominantly Public Ownership
- ▨ 50% Public Ownership
- ▥ Predominantly Private Ownership
- ☐ 100% Private Ownership
- ▨ Can't Tell

Over 60 percent of Beijing residents still prefer predominantly public ownership (see Figure 9.2). Even a true mixed-ownership system gets little support. This finding means that CCP's official policy of maintaining a by-and-large public ownership (i.e., the so-called socialist market economy) has wide popular support.

When asked about the speed of economic reforms, about 40 percent of the respondents seemed to be satisfied with the current pace of economic reforms (see Figure 9.3). However, nearly one-third of the people we surveyed think the economic reforms are happening "too fast" or "fast." Very few think the reforms are either "slow" or "too slow." Once again, nearly a quarter of the respondents could not answer the question. These findings show that the public is quite divided on the speed of economic reforms. Many people have been negatively affected by the market-oriented economic reforms and have suffered from the "pains" in the economic transition, even though the economic reforms have been perceived to be gradual and less radical than the economic reforms in the newly democratized eastern European countries and the former Soviet Union.

Figure 9.3   Attitude Toward the Speed of Economic Reforms (N=682)

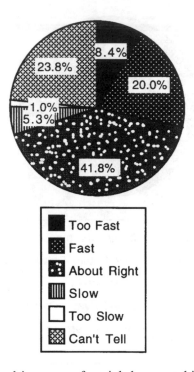

When analyzed in terms of social-demographic characteristics, support for particular economic systems varies among different societal groups (see Table 9.4). Urban and rural residents do not seem to differ in support of different economic systems. But it is telling that a very high percentage of rural residents have no opinion on this issue. It also seems that the more educated a person is, the more likely he or she is to support a market-oriented economy. The support of a predominantly market economy is highest among college graduates. This is probably due to the fact that the better educated are better equipped to compete in a market-driven economy. It is also clear in Table 9.4 that people between eighteen and thirty-five give the strongest support to a predominantly market economy. This is primarily because people in this age group tend to be better educated, more energetic, and mobility-oriented, and are less afraid of new challenges. These qualities make them more competitive and marketable. Not surprisingly, more people in the upper-income bracket are supportive of a market economy, presumably because they have benefited the most from the market-oriented economic reforms. It is also quite noticeable from Table 9.4 that rural residents and people with primary education or below and in the low-income bracket have the lowest efficacy in choosing what kind of economic system they prefer.

Table 9.4 Preference of Economic System by Residence, Education, Age, and Income

	100% CPE[a]	Pre-CPE[b]	50% CPE	Pre-ME[c]	100% ME	Can't tell
Residence (N=666)						
Urban	3.8%	17.5%	26.0%	33.1%	1.9%	17.7%
Rural	6.4	10.0	17.1	27.1	0.7	38.6
Education (N=676)						
Primary school						
or below	11.1	12.3	18.5	19.9	2.5	35.8
Middle school	4.2	17.5	2.9	25.0	1.3	29.2
High school	2.9	15.9	27.9	35.1	1.8	16.3
College	2.5	15.2	24.1	49.4	2.5	6.3
Age (N=680)						
Young (18–35)	4.0	10.9	20.8	41.6	1.8	20.8
Middle (36–55)	2.0	15.4	27.2	27.9	1.8	24.6
Old (over 55)	6.4	22.5	25.1	29.4	1.6	20.3
Monthly income (N=641)						
Lower (below 250 yuan)	11.3	9.7	9.7	25.8	1.6	41.9
Middle (250–800 yuan)	4.3	17.3	26.8	29.3	1.6	20.6
Upper (over 800 yuan)	0.0	16.0	22.3	44.7	2.1	15.0

Notes: a. CPE = Centrally planned economy
b. Pre = Predominantly
c. ME = Market economy

Evaluation of Government Performance

How do the people of Beijing evaluate the performance of the government? Their evaluation reflects their level of satisfaction and can be used as one of the predictors of stability in the country. Respondents were asked to rate the performance of the government in ten policy areas using a scale of 1 to 5 points (1–very poor, 2–poor, 3–fair, 4–good, and 5–very good). The grades given are presented in Table 9.5. The overall evaluation of government performance by Beijingers in all ten policy areas is close to fair, or at 3-point level, which is barely a passing grade. The respondents give the lowest score to government performance in narrowing the income gap. The widening income gap (partly due to official corruption) is becoming a major sociopolitical problem. The government's effectiveness in controlling inflation was also given a low grade. A substantial number of people are not happy with the government's efforts in improving housing conditions, maintaining societal order, and combating pollution. The highest marks were given to the government's performance in implementing family planning and national defense, indicating the effectiveness of government policies in these two areas.

Do people of different demographic and socioeconomic groups differ in their evaluation of government performance? To address this question, the statistical analysis of variance was used to detect any such differences. This analysis is designed to examine the variability in the sample in order

Table 9.5   Evaluation of Government Performance

	1 Very poor	2 Poor	3 Fair	4 Good	5 Very good	Average grade	N
Controlling inflation	11.3%	36.9%	38.4%	9.4%	3.4%	2.6	681
Providing job security	5.7	26.7	53.3	10.4	3.4	2.8	671
Minimize rich-poor gap	16.5	43.7	28.5	6.2	4.3	2.4	677
Improving housing conditions	8.17	29.7	42.2	13.6	4.9	2.7	677
Maintaining societal order	8.7	29.3	39.9	13.5	8.2	2.8	679
Providing adequate medical care	5.7	24.9	45.0	18.3	5.7	2.9	678
Implementing family planning	0.9	3.1	18.3	40.4	36.8	4.1	678
Providing welfare to the needy	3.7	18.5	48.1	20.4	7.7	2.9	671
Combating pollution	11.0	35.8	31.5	14.1	7.3	2.7	679
Ensuring a strong national defense	1.3	3.4	30.8	33.7	30.6	3.9	679

Note: N denotes total number of replies.

to determine whether the population means are not equal. The results, presented in Table 9.6, show that the means between rural residents and urban residents are indeed different. The rural residents tend to give the government higher marks for its performance in the ten policy areas than do urban residents. Also, as indicated in Table 9.6, people with middle and upper incomes are more likely to rate the government highly than are people with lower incomes. Even though the non–college graduates rate government performance slightly higher than the college graduates, the difference is not statistically significant. Evaluation of government performance remains constant with all age groups.

Satisfaction and Confidence

The findings shown in Table 9.7 illustrate the mood of Beijingers and, perhaps, the Chinese people as a whole. On the one hand, it seems that people are extremely dissatisfied with several specific economic and political factors. An overwhelming majority of respondents expressed serious discontent with the growing gap in incomes. Over 90 percent "strongly agree" or "agree" that the income differentials are becoming too big. A majority of the people are not happy with the responsiveness of the government to their concerns. Over 70 percent of the respondents indicate that suggestions and complaints made to the government were often ignored. The majority are not satisfied with the speed of political reform. Over 80 percent believe that economic reforms far outpace political reforms in the country.

On the other hand, people seem to be satisfied with the improvements made in their standard of living and social status since the reforms began in the late 1970s. Nine out of ten "agree" or "strongly agree" with the statement that since 1978 their standard of living has noticeably improved,

Table 9.6 Evaluation of Government Performance (Index) by Residence, Education, Age, and Income

	Mean	F Ratio	Significance
Residence			
Urban	28.04		
Rural	31.05	23.33	.0000
Education			
Non-college	28.80		
College	27.32	3.59	.0584
Age			
Young (18–35)	28.64		
Middle (36–55)	28.60		
Old (over 55)	28.67	0.01	.9943
Income			
Lower	27.66		
Middle	29.39		
Upper	28.71	5.34	.0050

Table 9.7 Level of Satisfaction and Confidence

	Strongly agree	Agree	Disagree	Strongly disagree	N
The gap between rich and poor is getting too big.	56.0%	37.4%	5.9%	0.6%	673
Suggestions and complaints made by the public to the government are often ignored.	25.8	46.5	26.4	1.3	675
Economic reforms in China far outpace political reforms.	22.6	57.6	18.4	1.3	668
Since the reforms in 1978, my living conditions have noticeably improved.	39.3	52.1	7.3	0.4	682
Since the reforms in 1978, my social status has noticeably improved.	19.9	49.7	25.3	5.0	672
It is unlikely that China will experience political and social turmoil in the next ten years.	29.1	55.2	14.1	1.6	676
I am confident that China will become an economic power in the 21st century.	38.0	52.3	8.2	0.9	674

Note: N denotes number of replies.

and seven out of ten "agree" or "strongly agree" that their social status has improved (see Table 9.7). These findings are consistent with other survey results.[12] This is one indication that economic reforms have achieved considerable success. The general satisfaction with the improvement in the standard of living and social status in part provides the basis for overall confidence and an optimistic view of development in the future. Nearly 85 percent do not believe that China will experience major sociopolitical turmoil in the next ten years, and 90 percent of them are confident that China will become a world-class economic power in the twenty-first century (see Table 9.7).

Do demographic factors play a role in the level of life satisfaction and confidence about the future? An analysis of variance shows that residence, education, and age do not make any difference in people's satisfaction level and confidence level. The only relevant factor is income level. As indicated in Table 9.8, the population means are significantly different among three income groups, particularly between the lower income group on the one hand and the middle and upper income groups on the other. This means that people of higher income are more satisfied with the improvement in their living standards and their social status. In addition, the more money people make, the more optimistic they are about the prospect of future development (see Table 9.8).

Implications

The results of the survey support the following tentative implications. First, the political culture still tends to be conservative. On the economic

Table 9.8   Satisfaction and Confidence by Income

	Mean	F Ratio	Significance
1. Since the reforms in 1978, my living conditions have noticeably improved.			
Lower income	3.15		
Middle income	3.41		
Upper income	3.45	15.62	.0000
2. Since the reforms in 1978, my social status has noticeably improved.			
Lower income	2.65		
Middle income	2.93		
Upper income	3.21	16.88	.0000
3. It is unlikely that China will experience political and social turmoil in the next ten years.			
Lower income	3.02		
Middle income	3.17		
Upper income	3.23	4.76	.0088
4. I am confident that China will become an economic power in the 21st century.			
Lower income	3.16		
Middle income	3.33		
Upper income	3.51	9.46	.0001

front, even though most people in the survey admit that their lives have noticeably improved in the reform era, still the majority of them hesitate to endorse the adoption of a predominantly market economy and very few prefer a predominantly private ownership system. Apparently, people are still wary of the repercussions of the ongoing economic transformation. There does not seem to be a public consensus on the government's goal of eventually adopting a "socialist market economy." Therefore, the government should be careful in handling the transition from the central planning economy to a market economy. Dissatisfaction with the negative results of the economic reforms partially contributed to the outbreak of the Tiananmen events in 1989.

On the political front, the majority still seems to be elitist and authority-oriented. What is striking is that the overwhelming majority (over 90 percent) prefer an orderly society to a freer society that is prone to disruptions. It seems that the public has been buying the "stability first" argument advocated by the government, partly because people are aware of the breakdown of order in many former Soviet republics after the collapse of communism. Relentless efforts by Chinese leaders to stress the need for stability for continued economic growth and development have struck a chord in the psyche, which is stigmatized by *luan* after more than a century of upheaval, revolution, and instability. The chaotic Cultural Revolution is still fresh in the minds of many people. This stability and order-oriented mentality explain, in part, the relative success of the post-Tiananmen regime in controlling the country since 1989.

Second, the strategy of eudaemonism, namely, making people happy by providing them with material benefits, adopted by the government to boost its political legitimacy since 1989 has partially worked in Beijing. It is apparent from the survey that a majority have experienced improvement in their living standard and social status. This high level of life satisfaction leads to a relatively high level of confidence in further economic development. Yet, the survey shows that people in Beijing only gave passing grades to government performance in a variety of policy areas. Consistently, people with higher income expressed more satisfaction with government performance, more satisfaction with their lives, and more optimism about the future. This provides part of the answer to the puzzle of the survival of the current political regime and the relative political stability since the 1989 Tiananmen Square crackdown. As the government continues to raise the standard of living, it will probably increase its political legitimacy. However, what we have also found is that materialism, partially encouraged by the leadership, has not reduced people's attention to political issues. A majority of the respondents in the survey are interested in national affairs, and more than 40 percent of them discuss politics with someone else "very often." Obviously, since Beijing is the political center of the country, figures concerning the level of political interest for the rest of the country may be lower.

Third, the findings also indicate that the most likely supporters of the current government are not in Beijing. The support for the CCP most likely comes from rural areas and people of higher income. As the survey results show, rural residents tend to have a lower level of political interest and efficacy. Hence, they are more susceptible to government control. Furthermore, rural respondents gave markedly better grades for government performance than their counterparts in the urban areas. It should be noted here that peasants in the suburbs of Beijing are generally wealthier and more urban than peasants elsewhere in China. Another likely support group for the regime in Beijing is the people who are better off and have gained materially in the reform era. Conversely, it seems likely that challenges to the CCP may come from the urban areas and people of lower income. The urban poor (many of them are workers and employees of the near-bankrupt state-owned enterprises) may be a major source of instability in the future.

The overall picture portrayed in this survey is certainly not all rosy, but it is far from gloomy. If the major findings from our survey of Beijing residents hold true for the rest of China, it is hard to imagine that the CCP will encounter major problems and challenges from below in the period of post-Deng power transition.

Notes

1. See, for example, Lowell Dittmer, "The Tiananmen Massacre," *Problems of Communism* (September–October 1989): 14–15. Also see Michael D. Swaine, "China Faces the 1990s," *Problems of Communism* (September–October 1989): 20–35.

2. Nicholas D. Kristof, "The Riddle of China: Repression as Standard of Living Soars," *New York Times,* September 7, 1993, pp. A1 and A6.

3. Andrew J. Nathan, "China's Path from Communism," *Journal of Democracy* 4, no. 2 (April 1993): 30.

4. Ibid.

5. See, for example, Charles Tilly, "Does Modernization Breed Revolution?" *Comparative Politics* 5, no. 3 (April 1973): 425–447.

6. In two trips to China in the summer of 1994 and 1995, Yang Zhong, one of the authors of this chapter, personally witnessed people cursing Jiang Zemin and Li Peng at bus stops on several occasions.

7. See Allen P. L. Liu, *Mass Politics in the People's Republic: State and Society in Contemporary China* (Boulder, CO: Westview Press, 1996).

8. Doing a good survey in China depends heavily on having a reliable Chinese partner. Public Opinion Research Institute of the People's University in Beijing, which was set up in 1986, was the first of its kind established in the PRC and has done numerous surveys for both Chinese as well as foreign organizations.

9. Seven urban districts and rural counties were randomly chosen after the first stage of sampling. Five residential neighborhoods (*juweihui*) or villages (*cunmin weiyuanhui*) were randomly chosen after the second stage of sampling. The third stage of random sampling produced a sample of twenty households from each

of the five residential neighborhoods or villages of the seven urban districts or rural counties. One individual was chosen randomly from each household as the respondent at the final stage of sampling in our survey.

10. Two of our papers from this survey, "The Level and Sources of Popular Support for China's Current Authoritarian Regime" and "Assessing Political Support in China: Citizens' Evaluations of Governmental Effectiveness and Legitimacy," are forthcoming in *Communist and Post-Communist Studies* and *The Journal of Contemporary China.*

11. Even the former participants of the Tiananmen Square democracy movement have become pragmatic and materialistic. See "Tiananmen and China's Future: The View Five Years Later," *Current History* 93, no. 584 (September 1994): 248.

12. For example, according to one survey conducted in the city of Qingdao, Shandong Province, at the end of 1993, 90 percent of the respondents were satisfied with the supply of goods in the market, and 75 percent of them felt their life was improved. See *Renmin ribao (People's Daily,* Overseas Edition), May 13, 1994, p. 2. A Gallop nationwide poll conducted from May 20 to September 15, 1994, found that more than half of those surveyed expressed satisfaction with their lives, among other things, as reported by Li Jianmin and Chuck Lin in "China: A Tough Market, U.S. Survey Says," *Chinese News Digest* (an electronic news magazine), February 19, 1995.

PART 3

Economic Strategies
for the Future

10

Macroeconomic Issues and Policies

Gene Hsin Chang

Western scholars have long wondered if there would be a major change, or even a setback in Chinese economic policies after the death of Deng Xiaoping. Such speculation has gradually faded as reform became more evidently irreversible. Indeed, the death of Deng on February 19, 1997, changed nothing in the current economy and economic policies. It is now widely expected that the economic reform will continue into the twenty-first century.

While few believe that China will return to central planning, most scholars agree that the road to a free-market economy will be bumpy. China has enjoyed rapid economic growth since 1978, when reform started, but it has also experienced high inflation, rising unemployment, deterioration in income distribution, failures in restructuring state-owned enterprises, and other problems. Whether China can continue its rapid growth in the long run is still uncertain; it depends on many factors, including the government's skill in handling emerging difficulties. One of the most important requirements for growth is macroeconomic stability.

This chapter focuses on macroeconomic issues and policies in the post-Deng era. It first reviews economic events in the "soft-landing" period. This was the time when the current leadership started to play the dominant role in economic policymaking. Their practice in the period was an important preview of their current policies and the likely policy orientation in the future. Then the chapter examines the current debate among Chinese scholars over macroeconomic policies. Mainstream macroeconomic thought has shifted from the pro-growth ideology that was dominant during Mao's Great Leap Forward period to the current emphasis on maintaining macroeconomic stability for sustained growth. A new bureaucratic and academic elite has matured, and its thinking is in line with official policy, both echoing and influencing official policies. Finally, the chapter discusses policy options. China's future macroeconomic policies have particular significance as China's neighbors are currently experiencing monetary and financial crises.

The Macroeconomic Policies in the "Soft-Landing" Period

The leadership responsible for the current and future economic policies was formed long before Deng's death. Deng's speech on acceleration of the reform and liberalization of the economy during his 1992 visit to Shenzhen, a special economic zone in southern China, was the last episode of his direct influence on economic policy. After that, he was seriously ill with Parkinson's disease and unable to supervise daily decisionmaking. Economic policies hence were made by Vice Premier Zhu Rongji and his associates, the same people who constitute the current leadership. Their philosophy of macroeconomics has dominated economic affairs for the past five years and will continue to dominate macroeconomic affairs in the future.

The current philosophy of macroeconomics can be seen in practice during the five years from 1992 to 1997, which was known as the "soft-landing" period. This was a period in which the government exercised macroeconomic contraction but avoided a drastic decline in the GDP growth rate. The new leadership has distinguished themselves from the old generations of Deng and Mao in their training and knowledge of modern macroeconomics and in their skill in handling a market-oriented economy. The new leadership has emphasized macroeconomic stability for sustained growth. They are not as zealous as Mao or Deng about a high growth rate; they are more concerned with inflation and macroeconomic stability. Unlike Mao and his associates, the current leadership knows that macroeconomic stability is essential for sustained growth. Yet they pursue a cautious macroeconomic policy probably for a more important reason—they cannot afford any risk that would jeopardize political and social stability. For the same reason they are also afraid of a slowdown in the economy, which could cause widespread unemployment. That is why they adopted a "soft-landing" strategy to allow the economy to cool down during 1992–1995.

The Chinese economy became overheated shortly after Deng's visit to special economic zones in Southern China in 1992. During this trip, Deng called for an acceleration of both economic growth and liberalization. Deng's message spurred rapid economic growth and reform; nevertheless, at the same time, it loosened macroeconomic discipline. More than ten thousand new construction projects were launched. Money supply surged. The growth rates of currency in circulation (denoted by M0), currency and demand deposits (denoted by M1), and "broad money" (which includes M1 and quasi-money, denoted by M2) accelerated to 36.4 percent, 35.9 percent, and 31.3 percent, respectively (see Table 10.1). Fixed capital investment grew 44.4 percent from the previous year.[1] In July, observing that the economy was overheating, the central bank attempted to tighten credit but failed, largely due to pressure from local governments and the inability of the central banks to control local commercial banks, and other investment

trust corporations. Overexpansion created shortages of construction materials, including steel, cement, and lumber. Accordingly, their prices rose
dramatically: steel prices rose 80 percent and cement prices doubled.[2]

Deng and Mao differed in their attitudes toward a modern, market-
oriented, and open economic system. Deng accepted the modern market-
oriented system because of his pragmatic philosophy, while Mao had re-
jected the modern economic system due to dogmatism. However, the two
strongmen were similar in one aspect: their zeal for rapid growth. This was
probably due to their strong aspiration to catch up to the West as well as
their lack of economics training. They did not understand that an overheated

Table 10.1 Growth Rates of Money and Fixed Assets

	M0	M1	M2	Fixed Assets
1991	20.2	24.2	26.5	23.9
1992	36.4	35.9	31.3	44.4
1993	35.3	38.8	37.3	61.8
1994	24.3	26.2	34.5	30.4
1995	8.2	16.8	29.5	17.5
1996	11.6	18.9	25.3	14.8
1997	15.6	22.1	19.6	10.2

Source: From State Information Center, China Economic Information Network,
www.cei.gov.cn.
   Note: M0 refers to currency in circulation.
      M1 includes M0 and demand deposits.
      M2 includes M1 and quasi-moncy.

Table 10.2 Macroeconomic Indicators of the Chinese Economy

	1995	1996	1997
GDP (billion yuan)	5,848	6,789	7,345
GDP growth rate (%)	10.5	9.6	8.8
Inflation rate (CPI, %)	17.3	8.3	2.8
Inflation rate (Retail Price Index, %)	14.8	6.1	0.8
Urban unemployment rate (%)	2.9	3.0	3.1
Money growth rate (currency, M0) (%)	8.2	11.6	15.6
Money growth rate (M1) (%)	16.8	18.9	22.1
Money growth rate (M2) (%)	29.5	25.3	19.6
Fixed asset investment growth rate (%)	17.5	14.8	10.2
Central government budget deficit (billion yuan)	−58.2	−52.9	−58.2
Trade balance (billion U.S. dollars)	16.7	12.3	46.2
Current account balance (billion U.S. dollars)	1.6	7.2	29.7
External debt service ratio (%)	7.3	6.7	7.3
External debt/GDP ratio (%)	15.5	14.3	14.8
Foreign reserve (billion U.S. dollars)	73.6	105	140

Source: All data are from the most recent issues of the *China Statistical Yearbook,* except the
money growth rates are from the State Information Center, China Economic Information
Network, www.cei.gov.cn.

economy is detrimental to long-term growth. The unbalanced growth from overinvestment could not be sustained in the long run. It would induce inflation and macroeconomic instability, thus eventually resulting in economic stagnation and decline. Mao's Great Leap Forward movement in 1958 is an example of a short-run economic overexpansion that turned into an economic catastrophe.

It is now widely recognized that macroeconomic stability is indispensable for sustained growth. The new leadership is maturer than the older generations in this respect. As the inflation rate rose to 10.2 percent (the two-digit psychological barrier) in March 1993, the central government was alarmed. By mid-1993, the Politburo dismissed Li Guixian, the chairman of the central bank, for his failure to contain overinvestment and inflation, and appointed First Vice Premier Zhu to supervise macroeconomic policy.

Zhu immediately ordered a series of stabilizing measures. The first was monetary contraction, including contracting the money supply, increasing interest rates on loans, tightening credit and loans, and attracting savings by paying consumer price index (CPI) interest rates on saving deposits. The second measure was controlling the scale of investment, including reducing fixed asset investment, restricting construction investment, and scrapping new construction projects. The third measure was monetary and financial discipline. This included imposing strict regulations on local and regional capital fund-raising, reexamining and suspending various new financial institutions, and controlling the capital and cash holdings of all financial organizations. Most of these macroeconomic stabilizing measures were as conventional as those used by other countries in dealing with similar problems. Controlling the investment scale was somewhat indigenous because this involved the soft budget constraint behavior of state-owned businesses.

The macro contraction seemed to have had positive effects at the beginning of 1994. The inflation rate decelerated in February and this continued into May. Prices of construction materials and consumer durables even began to fall. In June, the government thought inflation was already under control and decided to raise the grain procurement price, a long-delayed step of price reform. Unexpectedly, inflation resumed as prices of grain and other food products rose quickly. The inflation rate surged to a record 27.7 percent in October. In August, the Politburo convened a special meeting, declaring fighting inflation to be the number-one task of the government.

The 1994 inflation was different in nature from that of 1992–1993. While the 1992–1993 inflation was due to monetary overexpansion, the 1994 inflation was due to restructuring from a previously existing price distortion.[3] In 1994, there was a macroeconomic contraction rather than expansion. The growth rates of money (measured by M1 in Table 10.1) and fixed asset investment fell by 12.6 and 31.4 percentage points, respectively, from those of 1993. Prices of construction material and consumer durables fell. Inflation in 1994 was due mainly to increasing food prices.

The leadership recognized the structural nature of the 1994 inflation. In addition to maintaining a tight money supply, the August meeting of the Politburo added other measures to control food prices. These policies included accelerating structural adjustment by increasing investment and other inputs in agriculture to raise food production, and accelerating industrial restructuring to increase productivity. In addition, the government also adopted administrative measures to control inflation. Price reforms were suspended and state enterprises and food stores increased supplies while holding prices steady. Food prices in free markets would be monitored and anyone guilty of price gouging would be penalized.

Under these measures, the inflation rate, based on the CPI, fell to 17.3 percent in 1995 and further dropped to 8.3 percent in 1996 (Table 10.2). The CPI and retail price index in September 1997 rose only 3.4 percent and 1.3 percent, respectively, from a year before. Meanwhile, the annual growth rate of the GDP was kept above 9 percent each year during the disinflation period. Hence, the government called it "a successful soft landing."

During macroeconomic stabilization and the soft landing, the bureaucratic elite responsible for macroeconomic policy was also formed. These people are now making macroeconomic policies. In addition to Zhu, the chief figure, the group includes Dai Xianglong, who succeeded Zhu as president of the People's Bank of China (PBC); Chen Yuan, vice president of the PBC; Zhu Xiaohua, vice president of the PBC; Zhou Xiaochuan, vice president of the Bank of China, and now the chief of the State Foreign Exchange Administration; and Lou Jiwei, director of the Macroeconomic Balance Bureau of the State Committee of Reform and Restructuring. Compared with the older generation of leaders and economists, these new figures are more professional and mature in their understanding and handling of a modern economy. They have modern macroeconomics backgrounds, understand the importance of macroeconomic stability, and are knowledgeable about the market system and international financial institutions. They can effectively communicate with officials and economists from the World Bank and International Monetary Fund (IMF). They advocate a cautious macroeconomic and monetary policy, which has become the mainstream not only among the bureaucratic elite but also among academic economists. This is a noticeable contrast to the situation under Mao and Deng.

During the soft-landing period, the central bank adopted a "moderately tight" monetary policy. Dai Xianglong, chairman of the People's Bank, has emphasized that the central bank will continue this policy in the near future.[4] Other mainstream economists support his position. They have set a long-term goal of a GDP growth rate of around 8–9 percent and an inflation rate of 6 percent or lower.[5] Most Western economists would think that a growth rate of 8–9 percent would be too high and lead to inflation, yet many Chinese economists believe this high growth rate can be sustained with stable prices, since the GDP growth rate remained above 9 percent during the disinflation period. The World Bank's view was just slightly different from that of the Chinese. The World Bank and IMF believed that a growth rate around 7–8 percent is more likely to be compatible with monetary stability. Despite the slight disagreement, the World Bank and IMF are cooperating quite well with Chinese bureaucrats and economists over the issues of maintaining macroeconomic stability and cautious monetary policy.

The Current Debate over the Economic Situation

The macroeconomic thought that dominated policy during the soft-landing period has recently been challenged. With an inflation rate close to zero, an increasing number of economists are suggesting that the central bank relax monetary supply to stimulate the economy in order to create more jobs.[6] Their arguments are based on signs of an economic slowdown, and they cite the following facts.

First, statistics show that the factory capacity utilization rate continues to slide. Two-thirds of factories report considerable idle capacity. An increasing number of factories have virtually no orders for their products. A survey of ninety-four major industrial products in 1995 showed that 65 percent have excess supply and only 35 percent have adequate demand. The products having adequate demand were mostly energy and chemicals. The situation worsened in 1996 and 1997. Shortages have been replaced by surpluses in the markets. These economists describe the situation as "insufficient effective demand."

Second, the financial situation of the state-owned enterprises (SOEs) is deteriorating. At the end of 1996, 44 percent of the SOEs reported losses. The situation could be even worse because many enterprises misstated their condition so they could continue to apply for bank loans. Operation profits also declined in 1996 by 55 percent from the previous year.

Third, bad loans and nonperforming loans are estimated to be more than 20 percent of receivables in bank accounts. Arrears among enterprises are continuously increasing. An extensive survey of 380,000 enterprise entities in November 1996 found that unreasonable arrears exceeded more than 300 billion yuan. Excessive inventory amounted to more than 150 billion yuan.

Fourth, layoffs and unemployment rose. In September 1997, there were more than 80 million unemployed workers. Among them, 60 million were laid off by their companies. The official unemployment figure was 4 percent, higher than the previous level. However, if the underemployment and rural surplus labor were included, the unemployment rate was estimated to be 17 percent.

Finally, while disinflation is continuing, prices of some products have fallen. For instance, the price index of machinery and electric goods fell by 3.3 percent in March 1997.

Li Yining of Beijing University and others believe that these facts signal an economic recession. They argued that the recession will cause high unemployment and slow down the improvement of living standards.[7] They indicated that money supply (in M2) in the first half of 1997 rose only 19 percent from a year before, which was not only the lowest growth rate in the last five years but also lower than the planned target of 23 percent. The growth rate of fixed asset investment in the same period was 13.5 percent, which was also low compared with other years. Fan Gang, a prominent economist, said that these indicators imply that the macroeconomic policy is too tight, leading to insufficient effective demand.[8] These economists advocate increasing the money supply and capital investment scale.[9]

In response to the challenges, PBC Chairman Dai, in a speech on August 25, reiterated that the central bank will continue the "moderately tight" monetary policy. He said that the central bank would control the overall scale of loans and credit. However, he left room for flexibility. He said that the bank would support structural adjustment and reform, and that banks should issue loans to profitable enterprises, including nonstate enterprises. The state banks should particularly support the key enterprises that are selected by the government for modern enterprise experiment.

Dai's speech represents the official view of the macroeconomic policy. Qiu Xiaohua, chief economist of the State Statistical Bureau, holds the same view,[10] saying that macroeconomic policies in the coming years should not change substantially. The government's general macroeconomic policy should still be "moving with stability, moderately tight, and tight but with certain flexibility."[11] Like Dai, Qiu believes that macroeconomic policy should support structural adjustment and reform. Although the overall amount of investment should be controlled, the government should give preference to selected areas for investment projects. For instance, the government should allocate more funds for urban infrastructure and high technology.

The macroeconomic policy views of most mainstream economists are similar to those of government economists. Liu Guoguang, adviser to the Chinese Social Science Academy, objected to the pessimistic view represented by Li Yining. Liu said that the current economy is not "too cool" because the growth rate is still the highest in the world. The growth rate in 1997 exceeded the original target of 8 percent. M0, M1, and M2 in 1997 rose by 15.6 percent, 22.1 percent, and 19.6 percent respectively. None of these were low by international standards. So the general money supply is not as tight as Li and others have suggested. The current state of the buyer's market and the excess supply of some products in the market are normal in a healthy market economy. Such indicators are good for restructuring and reform. The rise in unemployment was not simply caused by a "tight" money supply, but by institutional factors such as historical inefficiency, longtime overstaffing in SOEs, and existing structural distortion. Hence a loose monetary policy would only do harm to the economy. Liu thinks that the most urgent task of economic policies in the near future is accelerating institutional reform and structural adjustment.[12]

Other mainstream economists, including many younger experts, support Liu's argument. They contend that the current money supply is adequate and the investment scale should be controlled. They attribute the current economic difficulty to structural problems rather than macroeconomic contraction.[13]

This debate over macroeconomic strategy has important implications about future policies and the prospect of the economy and should be watched carefully by Sinologists for the following reasons.

First, the debate is over macroeconomic expansion versus contraction. While this has been debated for decades, the current debate is fundamentally different from those of the past. During Mao's era, the debate was of a political nature. Those who disagreed with Mao's progrowth line were politically persecuted. During Deng's era, the debate was of an academic nature and nonmainstream opinions were politically tolerated, but the mainstream was still generally progrowth.[14]

Because growth was often placed above macroeconomic stability, the economy in Deng's era was like a roller coaster, swinging up and down drastically. Now that debate over macroeconomic policy has been encouraged, the mainstream has shifted to the pro-stability school, which is consistent with the official line. Yet disagreement with the official line has been allowed. One example was that in 1994, Li Yining openly criticized Zhu's macroeconomic contraction in a Hong Kong newspaper. Zhu was very angry with Li, but Li was still able to continue to voice his opinion.

Second, the nature of the debate has changed considerably. Both sides consist of professional economists who have good training in modern macroeconomics, use concepts based on theories commonly accepted by economists all over the world, and are knowledgeable about empirical experience in other countries. They all agree on the importance of macroeconomic stability. All are concerned with the consequences of unemployment due to economic slowdown. The key difference between them lies in how the economy may change and what the best strategy is. Mainstream opinion has preferred continuing a cautious policy to accelerate economic restructuring, while the minority view has preferred some macroeconomic expansion to fine-tune the economy in order to alleviate the pain of the rise in unemployment. The debate is much like that among alternative economic schools in the United States.

Third, although the debate takes place in academic circles, it is not isolated from the bureaucrats. In fact, the debate likely will influence the policies to be adopted by the government. Although the official line favors cautious policies, there are signs that the government is moving in an expansionary direction. For instance, although the central bank originally said that it planned no interest cut at the beginning of 1997, shortly after the news about the slowdown in economic growth in the third quarter was released, it cut the interest rate on October 23. The government is also accelerating approval of new projects. More money is being pumped into large state enterprises at a faster speed. The government also announced that it would lift the cap on loans made by the state-owned commercial banks, starting on January 1, 1998.[15] All these changes signaled that the leadership is accepting some points advocated by the minority side in the debate and is now moving in an expansionary direction.

Fourth, as leadership becomes more technocratic, there is no clear personnel line between academic economists and bureaucrats. There are frequent personnel exchanges between the two circles. For instance, influential economic officials Lou Jiwei and Wang Zhan were prominent academic economists before they took government posts. Disagreements in academic circles likely are the same among government economists. Contact between the two groups is more frequent than in Japan, where academic discussion has little influence on government economic decisions.

Therefore, debate among economists over macroeconomic policy will largely reflect the likely policies and should be followed closely.

The Effects of the Current Financial Crisis in Asia

The Asian financial crisis was the top economic event of 1997 and alerted the Chinese leadership to the potential for monetary and financial danger. The crisis began with the sharp devaluation of the Thai *baht* under speculators' attacks in the foreign exchange market. Shortly after Thailand, the "Fifth Asian dragon," experienced financial trouble, the crisis spread to other Asian countries, including Japan. It eventually led to the dramatic event of the near bankruptcy of South Korea, the eleventh largest economy in the world. The crisis was rather unexpected because it occurred in a region that had experienced continuous rapid growth for decades.

The only currencies that did not depreciate in the region during the crisis were the Hong Kong dollar and Chinese yuan. The yuan stood firmly for several reasons. The first is that the yuan is not fully convertible. The government restricts exchange conversion in the capital account. Second, China has a formidable foreign reserve of US$140 billion, the second largest in the world. The third reason is that China has low debt ratios in all categories according to international standards. However, the stability of the yuan does not mean that the Chinese financial system is risk-free. Certainly, the financial crises in South Korea and Japan have had a profound impact on the thinking of the Chinese leadership. South Korea did not open its financial market to foreign investors, and Japan had even larger foreign reserves and lower foreign-debt ratios. If these two Asian countries were not immune from financial crises, China cannot be either.

Indeed, a financial crisis in China is very likely if the government does not take precautions. A crisis would more likely be indigenously produced rather than the result of an attack from speculators in the foreign exchange market. Three serious problems exist in the Chinese financial market.

First, the current monetary and financial system is underdeveloped and deficient. Transactions lack efficient supervision and monitoring. Formal and informal financial institutions exist that conduct banking transactions but are not monitored by the authorities. Several cases have occurred recently in which officials illegally used bank reserves to speculate in the stock and forward markets.[16]

Second, it is estimated that nonperforming and bad loans accounted for about 20 percent of the total outstanding loans of state-owned banks. Considering that the percentage in the South Korean banks is only about 17 percent, Chinese banks, according to Western standards, are virtually insolvent. These bad or nonperforming loans mainly consist of delinquent loans from SOEs and unsold real estate projects.

Third, the rapid increase in money supply has resulted in a large amount of "hot money" in the economy. The ratio of M2 to GDP exceeded 1.1 to 1, which is much larger than that in other comparable economies. The magnitude of this indicator implies that much of the "hot money on deposit" is in the hands of a volatile public. Financial difficulty could easily lead to a crisis of confidence and therefore to a bank rush and panic purchasing.

The government is very much aware of the danger. In November 1997, the Central Committee of the Communist Party and the State Council convened a three-day conference on preventing financial crises. The main focus was said to be "to make concrete arrangements for resolving major issues in financial reform and development."[17]

The conference claimed that "as China continues to develop a market economy, financial activities penetrate every part of society, and the economy and the financial sector play an increasingly important role in macro-control. . . . Safe, highly-efficient and stable financial operations are essential for the sustained and healthy development of the national economy."[18] It acknowledged problems such as the inability of the financial system to meet the needs of economic reform and development under the new situation, imperfections in the legal system, weak financial supervision, and relative confusion in the financial sector.

The proposed solutions for the financial problems and for speeding up the financial reform include the following:[19]

a. Banks must become real banks in keeping with the requirements of the socialist market economy.
b. The supervisory function of the central bank should be intensified. The pace of commercialization of state-owned commercial banks should be accelerated. A multi-tier system of financial institutions should also be established.
c. The financial sector must be ruled by law. Financial order must be safeguarded and financial controls consolidated. The government must deal sternly with criminal activities in the financial sector.
d. The transformation of the economic system should be speeded up to create a favorable environment for financial operations, especially reforms of state-owned enterprises
e. The financial sector must improve its service to better serve the reforms and development. Financial reforms and solving financial problems should be accelerated in the current good macroeconomic situation.
f. Financial laws and policies should be publicized and society made aware of financial risks. More qualified people should be trained to meet the financial reform and development needs.

These decisions show how the Asian financial crisis has influenced future macroeconomic policy in two directions. Reform in the domestic financial and banking system and in state-owned enterprises will be accelerated. Also, the government will be more cautious in its monetary and foreign exchange policies, slowing down the openness of the capital market to match that of the rest of the world.

The government recently announced its macroeconomic policies at the annual Central Economic Conference by the Central Committee and the State Council in December 1997.[20] The policies specified in the platform are consistent with this analysis. The polices include the following:

- The government will adhere "to a moderately tight monetary policy to achieve financial growth and stability, and to promote sustained, rapid and healthy national economic development";
- "Based on the premise of structural optimization, China should maintain moderately rapid overall economic growth and an appropriate rate of growth in investment, exports and consumption, and avoid major fluctuations in economic development";
- The government should avoid "any factors which could spark inflation and the use of economic and legal means to establish a price regulation system to maintain a relatively low inflation rate";
- "The relationship of foreign exchange, trade, investment and debt must be properly handled to maintain an appropriate level of foreign exchange reserves and ensure the balance of international payments";

- "The conference voiced great concern about the financial sector, and urged a speeding up of the financial reform needed to establish a modern financial system. The supervisory role of the central bank must be strengthened, while existing State-owned commercial banks should be transformed into true commercial banks."[21]

The first three points are consistent with what was practiced during the soft-landing period and what is being done now. The last two points reflect new concerns arising from the Asian financial crisis. The platform largely summarized the likely policies of the near future.

Outlook for Macroeconomic Policy and Concluding Remarks

The above discussion has summarized the background and philosophy of the economic policymakers. Macroeconomic policies and actions in the future will shift from previous practice, as the leadership develops policies consistent with practices in other countries, taking into account the special circumstances of China.

But the new leadership and the academic elite, although being more familiar with modern economics concepts than the older generation, will not simply follow the Western textbook on economics. They face concrete and practical problems and must consider unique institutional circumstances and devise practical, indigenous solutions. For instance, they have to incorporate the structural problems in formulating macroeconomic policy. From time to time, they may have to resort to administrative measures for solving problems rather than relying on market means. These measures may not be justified by Western standards, but may be functional in China, a transitional economy moving from the old planning system to a market system.

Monetary policy will continue to be "moderately tight," which means that it will be cautious. Overexpansion such as occurred in 1992 will not be allowed. Macroeconomic policies will be fine-tuned according to the rates of inflation and unemployment. Structural adjustment and job creation will be priorities in the allocation of loans and credits. Financial and banking reform will be accelerated. In 1998, money supply and capital investment will be more expansionary than in 1997 in order to stop further deceleration of growth and to create more jobs.

Economic performance will determine macroeconomic policies. Economists have set a goal of a GDP growth rate of 8–9 percent with an inflation rate of 4–6 percent. Economists will closely monitor the unemployment rate, hoping that it will not further climb above the 4 percent level. They expect economic growth to create enough jobs to absorb the majority of laid-off workers in urban areas and to reduce the surplus labor in rural areas. A growth rate of 9 percent may not be acceptable from the point of view of the central banks in developed countries. For instance, Alan Greenspan, chairman of the Federal Reserve Board in the United States, would think that a growth rate of 9 percent would inevitably cause inflation. But, based on their own experience, Chinese leaders think a 10 percent growth rate with price stability is feasible, although they do not like to live with a growth rate of below 7 percent.

However, if the GDP growth rate falls below 7 percent, unless there is high inflation, the government will seek stimulus measures. This can be surmised from the recent changes in the central bank's attitude toward expansion, as previously discussed. Macroeconomic stimulus measures will include increases in money supply and fixed asset investment. These are equivalent to the expansionary monetary and fiscal policies practiced in the West, although the implementation methods will be adapted to the Chinese situation. The role of the Open Market Operation will increase because of the immaturity of the securities market in China. Allocation of credit and loans will be heavily influenced by the government, though the leadership has reiterated that it will rely more on market means. Loans and credits will be channeled, by market or other means, to selected areas such as infrastructure, environmental protection, agriculture, and key state-owned enterprises.

In sum, the bureaucratic and academic economists are reform-minded and pragmatic. Reform in the monetary and financial system will continue and accelerate. The new leadership has consistently adopted cautious macroeconomic policies with flexibility and will continue to do so.

Notes

1. China National Statistics Bureau, *Zhongguo tongji nianjian, 1993 and 1994* [*The China Statistical Yearbook, 1993 and 1994*] (Beijing: Zhongguo tongji chubanshe, 1993 and 1994).

2. Gene Hsin Chang and Jack Hou, "Structural Inflation and the 1994 'Monetary' Crisis in China," *Contemporary Economic Policy,* July 1997, pp. 73–81. Also see Gene Hsin Chang, "What Caused Hyperinflation at Big Bang: Monetary Overhang or Structural Distortion?" *China Economic Review* 6 (1995): 137–147.

3. Chang and Hou, "Structural Inflation," pp. 73–81.

4. Speech on August 15, reported by the State Information Center, August 25, 1997.

5. State Information Center, "Dui jingji 'ruan zhaolu' de fenxi he sikao" ["Analysis and Reflection of the Economic Soft-Landing"], *Jingji redian fenxi (Economic Hotspot Analysis)*, October 20, 1997.

6. Li Yining, "Braking Is Easy but Starting Is Difficult." Reported by the State Information Center, China, available at Webpage: *www.cei.gov.cn,* August 18, 1997.

7. Ibid.

8. Beijing National Economic Research Institute and China Economic Reform Research Foundation, "Zhongguo hongguan jingji fenxi" ["Analysis of the Chinese Macroeconomy"] (Beijing: available at webpage, www.cei.gov.cn, October 1997).

9. Yang Qixian, "Shidang zengjia touzi guimo" ["Properly Increasing Investment Scale"], *Jingji redian fenxi* (*Economic Hotspot Analysis*), August 18, 1997.

10. *Jingji redian fenxi* (*Economic Hotspot Analysis*), September 15, 1997.

11. Ibid.

12. Liu Guoguang, "Muqian jingji bing bu taileng" ["The Current Economic Status Is Not Too Cool"], *Jingji redian fenxi* (*Economic Hotspot Analysis*), September 8, 1997.

13. See Yang Zaiping, "Baochi ruan zhaolu de hao shiduo" ["Keeping the Good Momentum of 'Soft-Landing'"], *Jingji redian fenxi* (*Economic Hotspot Analysis*), October 20, 1997; Ji Hong, "Jixu kongzhi touzi guimo" ["Continue to Control Investment Scale"], *Jingji redian fenxi* (*Economic Hotspot Analysis*), September 8, 1997.

14. Strictly speaking, progrowth thinking dominated during the period from 1978 through 1992, but Deng was the paramount leader of China from 1980 to 1997. In the final four-year period of Deng from 1993 to 1997, however, policy was made by Zhu. As discussed previously, Zhu adopted a cautious policy.

15. News Release, CCTV (China Central TV Station), December 25, 1997.

16. China's State Information Center, *Meiri baodao* (*Daily Report*), December 11, 1997. In February 1995, the largest security company, Shanghai Wanguo Securities Company, went bankrupt in an illegal government security speculation.

17. *China Daily,* November 21, 1997, p. 1.

18. Ibid.

19. Ibid.

20. See *China Daily,* December 12, 1997, p. 1.

21. Ibid.

11

China's Economic Prospects in the New Century[1]

C. W. Kenneth Keng

Perhaps the most striking development that economic history has so far experienced is the rapid growth of the Chinese economy that has extended over almost two decades in a country where more than one-fifth of the world's population resides. A sustainable growing economy is a necessity for China's future stability. The growth sustainability of the Chinese economy depends essentially on its continued commitments to institutional reform and economic deregulation. China's relaxation of government intervention in economic activities has led and will be leading China to decentralize its central governmental authority over economic planning and control. This will consequently stimulate the emergence of regional economies in Mainland China. In the next two decades, there will likely be ten regional economies with relatively independent industrial structures emerging in Greater China as a result of economic decentralization.[2] In this chapter, we present our analysis of and predictions on China's economic future in the new century. We believe that regionalization is not only an emerging trend of China's economic development, but also a controllable process that may be accelerated by proper development policies. Regionalization is indeed the best strategy for China's economic future.

If the Chinese central authority follows the laws of the free market and leaves the regional economy intact, the Chinese regional economies are likely to generate robust and endurable productivity advancement, which will prolong China's current rapid growth into the first two decades of the next century. China's neighbor economies, Taiwan, Hong Kong, and Macao, may also contribute to and benefit from this anticipated trend of economic regionalization if they integrate their industrial structures and economic markets with the mainland's economic regions. Should this happen, there will likely emerge four new regional economies—Taiwan-Fujian, Hong Kong–Guangdong, Greater Shanghai, and south-central China—which by the twenty-first century will have surpassed South Korea's economic scale and become the new Asian Tigers.

To explore this prediction, we first depict China's economic growth up to 2020 according to three alternative scenarios: the high-growth potential based on the policy regime of economic deregulation and decentralization, the stable-growth potential based on an extrapolation of China's current policies and trends, and the low-growth scenario postulated on a reversion to an authoritarian socialist government. Under the stable-growth scenario, China will progress along the lines of gradualism by "groping for stones on which to cross the river." This will enable the Chinese economy to grow at a compound annual rate of 5.8 percent between 1997 and 2020. Under the socialist hard-liner postulation, the Chinese economy will grow more slowly at an annual rate of 4.3 percent in the same period. If China speeds up its efforts toward economic deregulation and decentralization, China will achieve its high-growth potential at an annual rate of 7.4 percent up to 2020. Should this take place, by 2020 an average Chinese mainlander will enjoy a living standard as high as that of Taiwan's residents at present.

After examining various limitations on China's future growth, we believe regionalization is indeed the probable trend that the vast Chinese economy will follow. Following this revealing trend, we proceed to examine the emerging regional economies within Greater China and conclude by presenting a regional economic integration strategy for the three apparently related but somehow independent economies: Taiwan, Hong Kong and Macao, and Mainland China. We believe that an integration strategy may actually benefit them all.

A Retrospective of China's Economic Prosperity

Since 1978, China has been transforming its economy through two lengthy processes of structural changes: industrialization and marketization. Industrialization has been transforming a rural agricultural society into an urban industrial one. In addition, efforts to adopt market mechanisms for all levels of decisionmaking have greatly been diminishing China's authoritarian command economy. These two major structural changes have generated tremendous productivity advancement, stimulating the Chinese economy to grow at an unprecedented speed.

China's average gross domestic product (GDP) growth of 9.7 percent per annum between 1978 and 1996 has been characterized by an unusually high savings rate of over 37 percent, a doubling of consumption, a 60 percent decline in the poverty rate (170 million of the 270 million Chinese living in absolute poverty were raised above the minimum poverty threshold), a decline in the infant mortality rate from 48 to 35 per 1,000 live births, and an increase in life expectancy to seventy-one years.[3] China's per capita GDP grew, on average, 8.4 percent a year from 1978 to 1996 (see Figure 11.1).[4] Although other studies show that official statistics may overstate the annual economic performance by as much as 1–1.5 percent,[5] alternative estimated growth rates still rank China together with Taiwan and South Korea as the three fastest-growing economies in the world. However, even with miraculous rates of growth, by the end of 1996 an average Chinese merely earned an income (GDP per capita) of US$678, which places China among the low-income countries in the world.[6]

Even if lower domestic price levels were taken into account, China's per capita GDP, after adjusting for international prices (i.e., the Purchasing Power Parity equivalence, or PPP), was about US$3,865 in 1986. That amount was about the same as Indonesia's. In 1996, Taiwan and South Korea had GDPs per capita (PPP) of US$14,295 and US$11,750, respectively.[7]

Economic Attributes

In 1978, after years of state control over all productive assets, the government embarked on a major program of economic reform, which stressed rapid structural changes. It encouraged privatization of agricultural production, formation of rural enterprises and private businesses, liberalization of foreign trade and investment regulations, relaxation of state control over some prices, and investment in industrial production and the education of its workforce. Though characterized by gradualism and experimentation, this reform strategy, which has emphasized decentralization, reliance on market forces, and openness to trade and foreign investment, has worked spectacularly well.

Throughout the 1970s and 1980s, agriculture reforms, such as privatization through the household responsibility system, allowed agricultural prices to increase to market prices and allowed production controls to relax, which in turn substantially increased rural income. It has been estimated that the privatization of agricultural production contributed nearly half of the growth in agricultural outputs between 1978 and 1984.[8] By the end of 1984, over 99 percent of Chinese farmers had adapted to the household responsibility system. Higher rural incomes generated markets for consumer goods and services that required relatively little advanced technology and capital to produce. The reforms also boosted agricultural productivity, freeing a huge volume of agrarian labor previously engaged in the commune system for industrial development. More important, institutional changes in government procurement policies on agricultural materials and rural industrial products led to a boom in rural industry. For example, in 1988 rural enterprises accounted for about 36 percent of industrial output.

Three major reforms opened China's economy to the world. First, in the early 1980s, the Chinese government first ended the state-owned trade companies' monopoly on international trade and gradually lifted control of

Figure 11.1   China's Economic Growth: 1978–1996
GDP per Capita in 1996 US$ and Annual Rate of Growth (%)

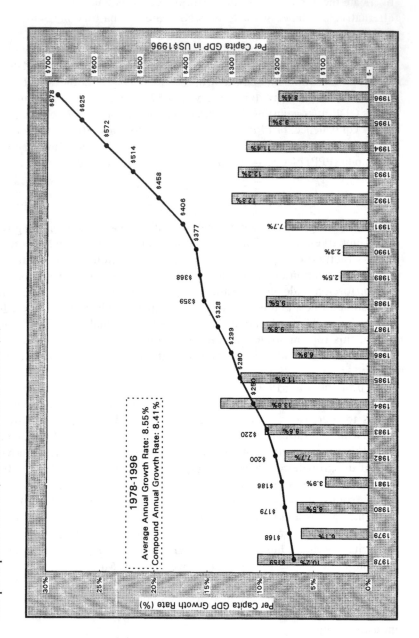

export products. Second, control over foreign exchange was also gradually relaxed: exporters were allowed to retain a portion of their foreign exchange from trading, and individuals were given some freedom to hold foreign currencies. Third, the government eased its intervention in foreign direct investment.

These three reforms have resulted in the rapid growth of foreign trade as well as in sharp increases in foreign direct investment, mostly in specially designated zones located in the nine coastal provinces. Foreign companies (including those invested in by overseas Chinese from Taiwan, Hong Kong, and all other parts of the world) have contributed not only financial capital, but also advanced technology as well as feasible (e.g., modern labor-intensive) production specialty, commercial expertise and management know-how, connections to foreign markets, and entrepreneurship. China's customs statistics show that 46.9 percent (US$152.6 billion) of China's total merchandise trade in 1997 was through foreign-investment enterprises (including joint ventures).

Noneconomic Attributes

Four noneconomic, exogenous factors have generated unusually strong impetuses to the economy and have distinguished China's economic growth from that of Latin American, East European, and Southeast Asian countries: (1) a relatively stable political and social environment, (2) sustained high savings, (3) effective reform policies with powerful administrative authority, and (4) the supportive international environment.

Relatively stable political and social environment. During the "open-door and reform" period, China has experienced a relatively stable political environment, free from political and social disorder. Nevertheless, in the 1980–1981 period, when the power base of Hua Guofeng, Mao's personally picked successor, diminished rapidly and was replaced by the regime of Hu Yaobun and Zhao Ziyang, the change was accompanied by a policy vacuum and political uncertainty. This political instability, compounded with the Sino-Vietnam border war and its aftermath, was the main reason for the economic downturn in 1981, when economic growth decreased by 40 percent from the previous year's 6.5 percent. Nearly a decade later, the 1989 student uprising and its aftermath resulted in two years of low growth in 1989 and 1990 (see Figure 11.1); however, they also helped cool down the otherwise uncontrollable inflation that had persisted for years prior to the 1989 Tiananmen incident.

China has, on the whole, experienced nearly twenty years of stable political and social development, which is indeed extraordinary, compared with the thirty-year history prior to the reform and open-door era. Except for the 1980–1981 and the 1989–1990 political impediments, political and social stability has provided a solid foundation for economic growth in the 1980s and 1990s.

Sustained high savings. Before 1978, under strict central planning, the government obtained most savings by maintaining agricultural and raw materials prices at artificially low levels and setting arbitrarily high prices for certain goods. The planning authorities for investment and capital accumulation then commandeered these profits. Low wages and high-priced consumer goods held down personal savings. Between 1965 and 1978, when national savings remained, as planned, at 33 percent of GDP, household savings on average accounted for merely 1 percent of the GDP.

Since the start of the reform era, household savings have risen to 21 percent of the GDP. By the mid-1990s, households had contributed about half of the total national savings. State-owned enterprises together with privately and jointly owned enterprises now contribute the other half of the national savings.[9]

Effective reform policies and governing system. The most direct exogenous impetus that has caused the Chinese economy to grow swiftly must have been those often unerring but also highly pragmatic development policies. However, successful development policies alone would not have sufficed if the Chinese government had not had strong leadership, firm determination, and powerful administrative authority to implement those policies. Nevertheless, China's governmental system did have a nondemocratic, top-down command system, resulting in endemic low productivity and inefficiency. It was highly bureaucratic and authoritative, discretionary and secret, politically oriented and prejudiced, and so on. The Chinese Communist Party (CCP) continues to play a vital role in all levels of public administration without democratic approval. Therefore, the success of the authorities in implementing efficient and effective policies ought to be viewed as being offset by the sacrifice of democracy, freedom, and human rights.

This sacrifice has allowed the central authority to use highly selective taxation policies and often-discriminatory regional development policies with minimum resistance. The authority has also allowed the regime to carry out major reform policies with no legislative restraint. In addition, the CCP's power over the police and military forces has ensured a stable political and social environment that has provided the foundation for rapid economic growth.

The supportive world environment. In the early 1980s, when China began economic reform, the Western world, together with international organizations such as the United Nations and the World Bank, provided financial and nonfinancial aid to support the reform. By the end of 1996, foreign capital inflows (loans plus investments) accumulated to a total of US$283.9 billion (since 1983).

In addition, China has attracted more foreign direct investment than any country in the world except the United States. With its special economic zones, coastal cities, and inland areas as favored locations for private foreign investment, China's foreign direct investment grew from US$1.8 billion in 1984 to US$41.7 billion in 1996. Investments from major multinational firms and, to a larger extent, from the Chinese diaspora also contributed to the Chinese economy by bringing in management know-how and international market connections.

China's Economic Prospects

China's Official Economic Plans

China's official development plans, the Ninth Five-Year Plan (1996–2000) and the Fifteen-Year Perspective Plan (1996–2010), outline an explicit short-term target of an average annual real GDP growth of 8 percent through the period of 1996 to 2000 and a long-term growth prospect of 7 percent a year up to 2020. The Ninth Five-Year Plan also calls for fiscal and financial sector reforms and macroeconomic spending restraints to curtail inflationary pressures. Except for laying out quantitative growth targets, these plans also unambiguously prescribe institutional reform objectives and targets. The plans call for growth by transforming past growth (mainly driven by input increases) into future intensive growth by improving efficiency through the advancement of science and technology. This advancement would be achieved by:

1. Developing the five key industries of machinery, electronics, petrochemicals, automobiles, and construction;
2. Gradually reforming state-owned enterprises (SOEs): the largest thousand SOEs will be reformed before the whole sector of SOEs is further reformed;
3. Developing social welfare and human resources by: (a) eliminating poverty by the year 2000 through economic growth and public expenditures (transfer payments to poor areas); (b) establishing primary health care systems on a provincial basis and expanding coverage of social security benefits; and (c) extending nine-year compulsory education to all children; and
4. Reinforcing agricultural infrastructure investment, land reform, and research and technology to improve the production of grain, cotton, and oilseed.

The World Bank's Prediction

With the aid of a multisector, neoclassic growth model, the World Bank's study of China's long-term economic growth suggests an average annual growth of 6.6 percent over the period of 1996 to 2020.[10] This predicted rate of growth is about 0.6 percent per year lower than China's official plan over the same period of twenty-five years. This prediction extrapolates China's past growth experience into the future. The World Bank's study also provides many model-estimated or model-simulated economic parameters that are invaluable in appraising growth potential. Table 11.1 lists the World Bank's simulation of China's long-term growth potentials that are based on alternative combinations of savings rates and productivity growth. An annual savings rate of 40 percent, combined with a high productivity advancement of 2 percent a year, may produce an annual economic growth of 7.9 percent. On the other hand, a relatively low annual savings rate of 20 percent, together with a low productivity growth of 1 percent a year, will result in an annual growth of 4.2 percent.

The above simulated growth potentials are based on the World Bank's multisector Solow growth model. Its parameters are summarized in Table 11.2. The model contains three sectors: agriculture, industry, and services. Each sector is assumed to have a constant-returns-to-scale production function with fixed factor input, two variable factor inputs of capital and labor, and a variable input of intermediate goods. Unity elasticity of substitution between factor inputs and intermediates, together with perfect competition in all markets, are also assumed. These assumptions essentially qualify the adopted production technology as one for the long run. Goods and services are either used as intermediates in the production of other goods and services, or for final consumption and investment.

On the consumption side, household aggregate demands for goods and services are derived from maximizing a constant-elasticity-of-substitution (CES) utility function of all the final goods and services subject to the

Table 11.1   China's Long-Term Economic Growth Potentials
(Annual Percentage GDP Growth)

		Total factor productivity growth		
		1.0%	1.5%	2.0%
	20%	4.2%	4.9%	5.5%
Savings-	25%	4.8%	5.5%	6.4%
GDP	30%	5.4%	6.1%	7.2%
ratio	35%	5.9%	6.6%	7.6%
	40%	6.4%	7.2%	7.9%

Source: World Bank, *China 2020: Development Challenges in the New Century* (Washington, DC: World Bank, 1997).

budget constraint of total output minus total savings. The demand for investment goods is also assumed as a CES technology of individual investment goods subject to the budget constraint of aggregate savings. With further assumptions of initial conditions and friction in the labor market, the World Bank team managed to obtain the parameters shown in Table 11.2.

China's Growth Potentials

Based on the prescribed World Bank long-run, steady-state, multisector growth model, we can further simulate China's future growth potentials by employing several qualitative assumptions. These assumptions include potential demographic changes (refer to Figure 11.4, p. 184), pace and depth of institutional reforms, degree of decentralization and progress of regionalization, productivity advancement, savings rates, and the international business environment (e.g., membership of the World Trade Organization). These assumptions can be used to generate three possible regimes of development policies that may be adopted for China's economic growth up to the year 2020. The scenarios are based upon the following general presumptions for the entire forecasting horizon up to 2020: there will be no large-scale conflicts or severe impediments in world trade and investment systems, international affairs will be conducted as usual under the rulings of the United Nations and the World Trade Organization, and China's social and political environments will be stable.

The stable-growth scenario. If Beijing's authority maintains the current pace in its pragmatic approach to future economic development (i.e., if the central authority gradually decentralizes its power over economic affairs and incrementally relaxes its interventions and controls over markets as observed in the reform era of the 1980s and early 1990s), the economy will grow steadily at a compound annual rate of 5.8 percent through the

Table 11.2   The World Bank's Long-Run Growth Model for China: Parameters

		Agriculture	Industry	Services
Output elasticity	Fixed factor	.10	.0	.0
	Capital	.20	.20	.27
	Labor	.34	.09	.24
	Intermediates	.36	.71	.49
Intermediate	Agriculture	.39	.10	.30
elasticity	Industry	.44	.72	.56
	Services	.17	.19	.42
Investment shares		.04	.88	.08
Consumption shares		.25	.35	.40

Source: World Bank, *China 2020* (Washington, DC: World Bank, 1997).

next twenty-four years (1997–2020). The growth path under this scenario is illustrated as the stable-growth scenario in Figures 11.2 and 11.3.

Under this "business as usual" scenario, the economy will produce US$3,137 billion (at 1996 price levels and exchange rates) in goods and services annually by 2020; or equivalently, the size of the Chinese economy will grow to 3.9 times of that of 1996. Because the population will also grow during this period (refer to Figure 11.4), the GDP per capita will be expected to grow at a compound rate of 4.9 percent a year. This will enable an average citizen to earn an annual income of US$2,153 at 1996 price levels in 2020. If the relativity of China's prices and international prices remains unchanged, China will have a GDP per capita of US$10,136 at 1996 Purchasing Power Parity. This average income will be about the same as Malaysia's or about 86 percent of South Korea's in 1996.[11]

The low-growth scenario. If China reverts to authoritarian central planning with intense government intervention, if it alters its reform and open-door progrowth policies, or if the CCP has to, for political reasons, reinforce strict socialist philosophy and policies, China's economy will grow at a much slower pace of 4.3 percent a year between 1998 and 2020. This "socialist hard-liner" scenario will retard the market mechanism and result in the inefficient allocation of resources and high economic transaction costs throughout the whole economy.

Under this scenario, people's propensities to work and to save will largely deteriorate and both domestic and international investment will be reduced. The economy will probably only experience a basic growth that is primarily generated by population growth and the slow accumulation of domestic capital. Consequently, by 2020, China's economic scale will merely be 2.7 times that in 1996 (refer to the low-growth path in Figures 11.2 and 11.3), or will only be two-thirds of that under the stable-growth scenario. The average person will earn about US$1,509 a year (at 1996 price levels) in 2020, or equivalently, US$7,104 at 1996 PPP. This income level will be about the same as the Mexicans' in 1996.

The high-growth scenario. The high-growth scenario postulates that, in the next decade, China will speed up institutional reforms and relax most of its central government intervention in regional economic affairs. Under this policy regime, China's economy will grow at an average rate of over 7.4 percent per annum up to 2020 (refer to the high-growth path in Figures 11.2 and 11.3). This would make the Chinese economy 5.6 times as large as it was in 1996. The total value of goods and services produced in 2020 will reach US$4,552 billion computed at the 1996 price level. Or equivalently, the GDP per capita in 2020 will reach US$3,133 at 1996 price levels, or US$14,752 at the 1996 PPP. This personal income level will even be slightly higher than Taiwan's US$14,295 in 1996. If China further intensifies

Figure 11.2a   China's Economic Growth Prospects: 1997–2020
Growth in Real GDP (%)

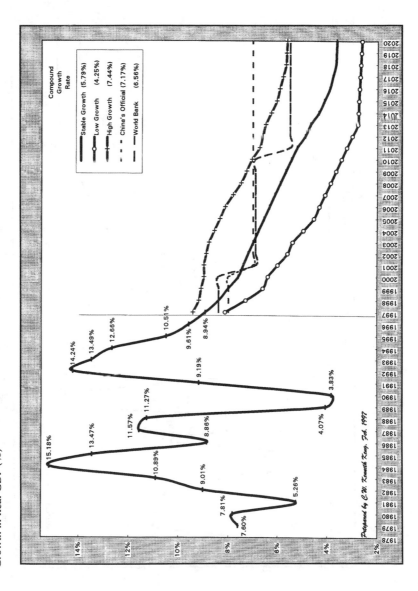

Figure 11.2b   China's Economic Growth Prospects: 1997–2020
                Growth in Real GDP per Capita (%)

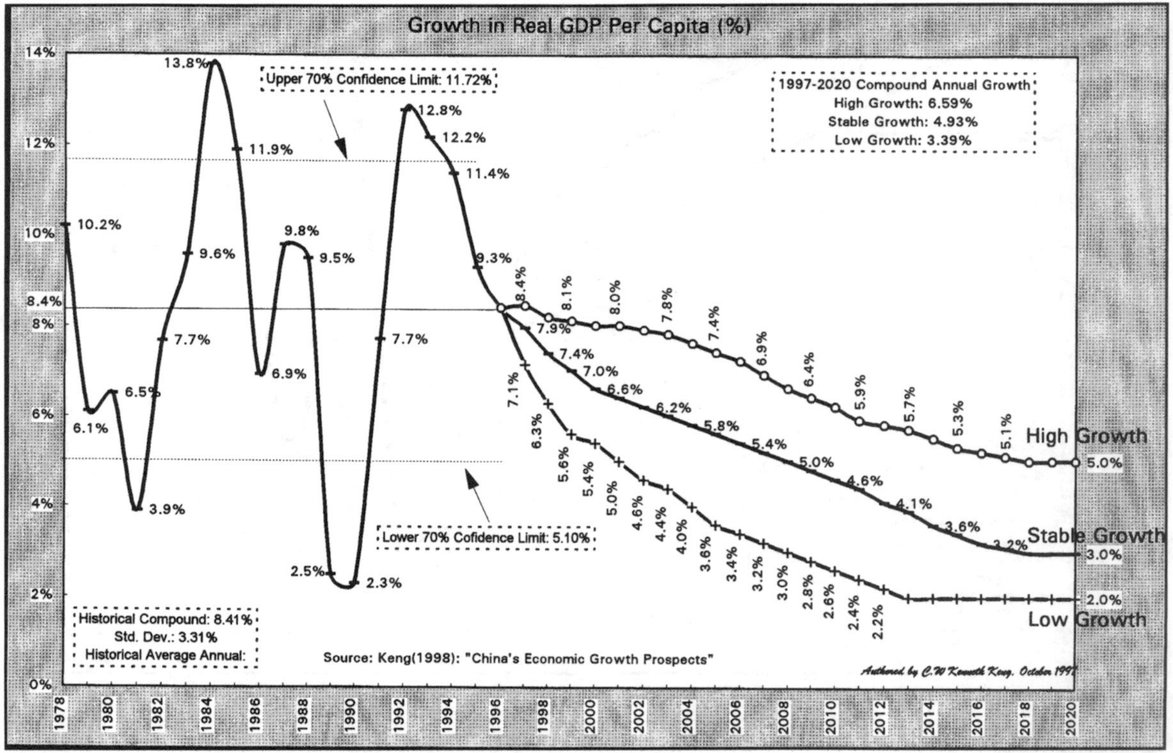

**Figure 11.3   China's GDP Growth Potentials 1997–2020
GDP in US$Billion 1996 Prices**

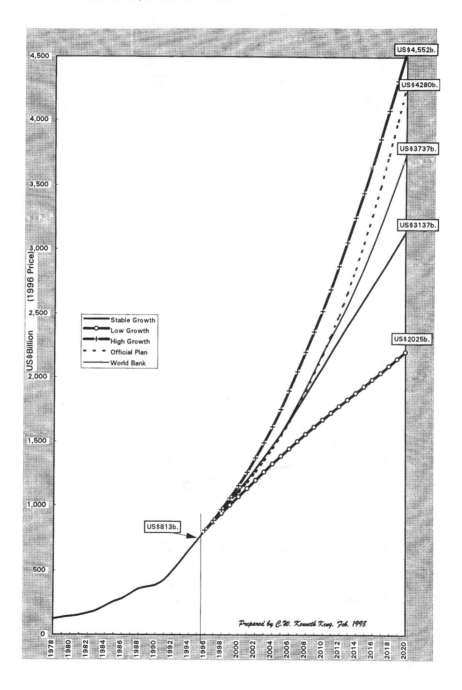

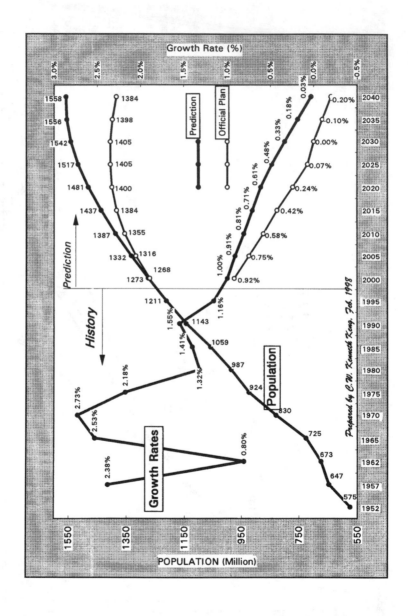

Figure 11.4   China's Population Growth Potentials 1952–2040

institutional reform and continues to open its markets, market forces, scale-economy impetus, and industry-structural optimization will continue to accelerate regionalization and productivity advancements. By 2020, China will be in the process of becoming one of the world's largest industrialized economies with an average living standard similar to that enjoyed by Taiwan today.

In order to build up internationally competitive industries for international exchanges for adequate food, materials, and energy resources to sustain a rapidly growing economy, China will have to accelerate its globalization process to accommodate a more liberal division of production, better capital movement, and freer international trade. This "decentralization and deregulation" policy regime provides China with an optimistic view of having a sustained growing economy in the future. Decentralization and regionalization will also create a free environment for interregional exchanges and competition. Regional economies with relatively independent industrial structures will emerge rapidly as a result of scale economy and market perfection. Free regional markets and competitive regional industries will attract more international investment and technology transfers. Meanwhile, the different regions will also invest abroad to secure their international sources of energy and materials as well as to sustain international markets for their products. These will lead to a more efficient use of capital and labor at lower transaction costs than in other scenarios. Market competition will guide resources to their optimal allocations with minimum transaction costs. Interregional competition will therefore ensure the best possible economic growth for the economy as a whole.

Under this scenario, China will enjoy high degrees of market openness and division of production. It will not only attract more overseas commercial investment, but will also likely induce Hong Kong and Taiwan to accelerate their economic integration with Chinese regions at large, and with the neighboring regions of the Pearl River Delta (Guangdong) and Fujian in particular. Since the industries of these two regions are already export-oriented and have been primarily based on investments from Taiwan and Hong Kong, it would be easy (in terms of transaction costs) for Taiwan and Hong Kong to optimize their production division by reallocating their existing and new production capacities to Guangdong and Fujian. To a large extent, Hong Kong's and Taiwan's capital, technology, commercial services, and managerial know-how will fuel Guangdong's and Fujian's economic development. These four regional economies will be in a much better position to integrate their industrial structures, capital and labor utilization, and market scale to attain maximum economic benefit.

Alternative Predictions and Probability Assessment

As shown in Figure 11.2a, the World Bank's prediction of China's future economic growth is, on average, about 0.78 percent higher than our prediction under the stable-growth scenario, and China's official plan is, on average, about 1.72 percent higher than ours. While, as indicated clearly in its report, the World Bank's prediction is an extrapolation based on China's past growth experience (mainly in the 1980s and the early 1990s), it did not incorporate qualitative information such as the extent of institutional reforms. However, the World Bank's study does provide many model-estimated or -simulated economic parameters, invaluable in appraising China's growth potentials.

Accounting for all possible outcomes and based on simulations using those parameters generated by the World Bank's model, our results show that the probability of China's future economic growth being between the high-growth and low-growth scenarios is about 80 percent. In other words, there is a 10 percent chance that China's future growth will either exceed the high-growth path or fall below the low-growth path. Accounting for uncertainties, the trend of China's economic growth in the next quarter century will most likely, with an 80 percent degree of confidence, fall in the range between our high-growth and low-growth predictions. In effect, our stable-growth scenario can be thought of as a representative prediction (the most likely forecast) of China's future growth potentials.

Limitations to China's Economic Growth

China has more than 20 percent of the world's population but only 7 percent of the world's arable land. In terms of a per capita resource base, China is among the most poorly endowed countries in the world. The 1992 World Bank study shows that China's per capita agricultural land is 28 percent of the world's average; range lands per capita are less than half the world's average, and forests and wilderness areas per capita are 15 percent of the world's average.[12] In addition, China's water resources are about one-third the world's average, and energy resources including coal on a per capita basis are also low.

This lack of natural resources could severely limit economic growth and welfare improvements if a more efficient use of resources and better production technology are not adopted. Although less government intervention, internationalization of markets, and globalization of industrial structures would enable China to resolve many of these natural-resource constraints by engaging in an international exchange of goods and services and a global division of production,[13] the relatively low per capita endowment of plains geography poses a critical limitation on China's future economic growth.

When demand for urban land rises with increasing urbanization and industrialization, land prices tend to rise relative to other prices. High costs together with government regulations (e.g., real estate property rights) on urban land use will impede the effort to build a national transportation system of highways and railroads with an even moderate capacity for interregional transportation. The limited supply of land for urban and rural housing, commerce, and industry will thus be a crucial physical limitation to China's economic development. The high cost of using land will be a crucial challenge to China's capital productivity and international competitiveness. Interested readers are referred to Tables 11.6–11.8 at the end of this chapter for a concise discussion of China's limitation on growth: the shortage of plains.

The low per capita endowment of plains areas will compel China to diversify its national economy into regional ones. Each of them will have its own relatively independent industrial structures and market system, so that the need for cross-regional long-distance land transportation will be reduced and the use of the scarce plains for transit systems will also be decreased. In this way, transportation costs, which constitute a major portion of the transaction costs of almost all economic activities, can be minimized. The economy as a whole will therefore use fewer resources for transportation to produce the same level of outputs; hence, macroeconomic productivity gains will be enjoyed. As a matter of fact, had there been no central planning and had China relied completely on market forces to allocate its resources, regionalization would have been the natural outcome.

Along this line of thought, the China State Planning Commission (SPC) study on regional and industrial development concludes that China will have to adopt Japan's model of regionalization of industrial structures so that the use of long-range transportation corridors can be economized.[14] The SPC study also calls for establishing metropolitan economies (an economic region centered in large metropolises and surrounded by scattered cities) so that the plains can be utilized intensively. These metropolises, connected with surrounding satellite cities, will form an urban net on which a multisector industrial system can be developed. Ideally, the metropolitan areas will be the regional centers of industries and services, while satellite cities may house specific industries. The regional industrial structure will be formed (under market mechanisms) so that a major portion of goods and services produced in the region can be consumed within the region; as a result, the need for long-range interregional transportation can be reduced.

Emerging Chinese Regional Economies

Considering China's history, geographic-economic characteristics, and the current status of regional economic development, many believe that in the first decade of the twenty-first century at least nine regional economies will emerge in Mainland China.[15] The emergence of these regional economies may be partly attributed to economic decentralization and market deregulation. Under market mechanisms, resources tend to be intensively utilized by being allocated toward urban centers where infrastructure and business services provide economic units with comparative advantages (lower transaction costs). As a result, regional markets and industrial systems, each with a network of geo-economic affiliated cities, will emerge and become relatively independent. This process of regionalization is essentially what Japan has experienced in the last thirty years.

The Trend Toward Economic Regionalization

To maintain economic growth, China needs to advance its industrial structure and economic efficiency as rapidly as possible so that its relatively limited natural resources (on a per capita basis) may be utilized to the maximum extent. To meet the demands of a future with an expected population of over 1.5 billion by 2020, China needs to perfect its manufacturing capacity and raise its productivity so that it can afford to import grains, raw materials, oil, capital equipment, advanced technology, and so on. Because of transportation costs (transit infrastructure construction and shipping costs), limited petroleum resources, and inadequate plains for building land transit systems and urbanization, China cannot rely on a singular national division of production, but instead must focus on regional systems of production and consumption. Regional economic development must then be a national priority for economic growth.

Traditionally, large portions of agricultural goods and services have been produced and consumed within regions. A World Bank study indicates that in the early 1990s, more than two-thirds of China's agricultural products were consumed within the local counties and towns where they had been produced.[16] Another study shows that even in 1994, interregional economic activities between neighboring regions were surprisingly small. Using railway shipments as a measure, for example, only 10 percent of Liaoning's shipments were to and from the neighboring Capital region—consisting of Beijing, Tianjin, and the whole province of Hebei—and the Shandong region across the Bohai Bay; and less than 12 percent of Shandong's interregional shipments were to and from the Capital and Liaoning regions. These three neighboring regions around the bay area of the Bohai Sea consist of large economies (Shandong and the Capital region's population is over 85 million, and Liaoning's exceeds 40 million) with adequate natural resources. Each has developed its own relatively independent industrial structure and its own market. Needs for interregional shipments of industrial goods are relatively small.[17] In other words, due to the structures of industries and markets, the Bohai Bay area in effect consists of three relatively independent economic regions.

On the development-policy side, the central government has delegated more power and responsibility to the regions. In 1995, the state transferred one of its key powers, grain (food-security) policy, to the provinces. It has always been a key policy objective of China's central government to maintain a nationwide balance of demand and supply of grain. One of the few economic achievements during the CCP era has been "providing food security to one-fifth of the world's population." However, under the new "governor's responsibility system,"[18] provincial governments assumed the responsibility of balancing their own provincewide grain supply and demand through interprovincial grain trade. This trade established an interprovincial wholesale market to replace centrally planned interprovincial grain transfers. It also replaced the nationwide grain security policy with provincial policies.[19]

Provinces have already shouldered the responsibility of all primary and secondary education and a large portion of postsecondary education. China's latest plan for reform of the education system calls for the "sale" of a large portion of those traditionally state-financed universities and colleges to the provinces. Production of human capital in the future and the investment decisions concerning human capital will be the responsibility of the provinces. Due to the diversity in economic development among the regions, China has in effect started to and will most likely continue to rely on the provinces to institutionalize their social welfare and pension systems, which so far have yet to be established.

If such key pillars of the socialist market economy as the food-security system, the social security system, and the education system can be delegated to the provinces, there is no reason that other economic decisions cannot be decentralized. For example, recent trends have strongly suggested that China's banking system will be reorganized to form regional (multiprovincial) central banks (similar to the Federal Reserve Banks in the United States) and regional commercial banks serving areas not bounded by administrative regions (e.g., provinces). Once the Chinese economic regions have their economic sovereignty within the framework of a national market (or even an international market), different regional socioeconomic systems will emerge. Economic regionalization may eventually lead to plural social and political subsystems in China.

Nine Emerging Regional Economies

If China's central authority maintains the current trend of market-based institutional reform and steadily decentralizes its economic power to regional authorities, many regional economies with relatively independent industrial structures and markets will consequently emerge. Regionalization may even be accelerated if Chinese macroeconomic strategic planners take into account the natural-resource constraints on growth and accelerate economic decentralization and regionalization. Jian Wang[20] and other authors[21] suggest that there will likely be nine or ten regional economies with metropolitan centers. If this occurs, China will probably enjoy its highest growth potential, with a compound annual growth of over 7 percent up to 2020.

Table 11.3 lists the nine metropolitan economies identified by State Planning Commission studies,[22] as well as their geographic and economic data. These nine economic regions together comprise 67 percent of China's population, 74 percent of its plains, and 71 percent of its GDP in 1996. Among them, five are coastal regions. Liaoning, the Capital, and Shandong regions are located around the Bohai Sea on China's northern coast, whereas Greater Shanghai comprises the vast area of the Yangtze and the Qientang River Deltas, while the Pearl River Delta is located on the southern coast. There is one near-coastal region: West Jiangsu and Anhui, where 10,000-ton ships can travel via the Yangtze River. Finally, there are three inland regions: Jilin-Heilongjiang at the northeast corner neighboring with North Korea and Russia, Hunan-Hubei-Jiangxi (or the south-central region) at the center of Mainland China, and Sichuan in the midwest.

At present, these regions have built or are building relatively modern intraregional land transportation systems. In addition, they have either developed their own regional markets with relatively independent industrial structures, or they are developing their own industrial systems. Nevertheless, interregional transportation relies heavily on frequently congested railways that are inadequate for meeting the shipping needs of a nationwide industrial system for a population of 1.5 billion.

These regional economies have emerged or are emerging as a natural consequence of urbanization and marketization. Their development pattern is surprisingly similar to Japan's regional development. Japan's regional economies typically have an area of 200 to 300 kilometers in radius (126,000 km^2 to 283,000 km^2) with a population over 30 million. A network of urban centers with a relatively independent system of industries characterizes each region. The urban network consists of a group of geoeconomically affiliated cities containing one or two metropolitan areas, such as manufacturing and commercial service centers complemented by a number of smaller satellite cities that may specialize in specific industries. Connected by well-developed interurban transit systems, the metropolitan centers and satellite cities with their surrounding rural areas constitute an independent production and consumption system or regional economy. Market forces impel the allocation of the regions' resources toward constructing localized industrial structures so that maximum production efficiency and therefore the greatest economic benefits can be enjoyed. Interregional activities are engaged in only when comparative advantages exist.

Table 11.3   Nine Emerging Metropolitan Economies in China, 1996

Major Regional Economies	Population (million) 1996 Year end	Share in Total Population %	Area (1,000 km²)	Share in Total Area %	Per Capita Plains (m²)	Plains (1,000 km²)	Share in Plains %	Major Metropolitan Areas or Cities	Regional GDP (US$billion)²	Share in National GDP %	Per Capita GDP (US$)²
Capital Region	86.91	7.10%	216	2.25%	1,070	93.0	8.07%	Beijing, Tianjin, Shijiazhuang	74.261	9.13%	854
Liaoning	41.16	3.36%	146	1.52%	1,214	50.0	4.34%	Shenyang, Dalian	37.999	4.67%	923
Jilin-Heilongjiang	63.38	5.18%	656	6.83%	3,679	233.2	20.24%	Changchun, Harbin	45.003	5.54%	710
Shandong	87.38	7.14%	153	1.60%	1,122	98.0	8.51%	Jinan, Qingdao	71.726	8.82%	821
Hunan-Hubei-Jiangxi	163.58	13.37%	564	5.88%	868	142.0	12.33%	Wuhan, Changsha, Nanchang	85.856	10.56%	525
Sichuan	114.30	9.34%	567	5.91%	123	14.0	1.22%	Chengdu, Chongqing	50.722	6.24%	444
Pearl River Delta	69.61	5.69%	186	1.94%	603	42.0	3.65%	Guangzhou, Shenzhen, Zhuhai	78.449	9.65%	1,127
West Jiangsu and Anhui	78.70*	6.43%*	191	1.99%	915	72.0	6.25%	Nanjing, Yangzhou, Hefei	54.227*	6.67%*	689
Greater Shanghai	83.78*	6.79%*	184	1.92%	1132	109.9	9.54%	Shanghai, Suzhou, Hangzhou, Ningbo, Wuxi, Changzhou	114.8*	14.12%*	1,370
Subtotal	816.52	66.72%	2,869	29.8%	932	854.1	74.14%		579.343	71.26%	1,370
Other Regions	407.13	33.26%	6,737	70.2%	726	297.9	25.86%		233.650	28.74%	574
China	1,223.89	99.98%¹	9,600	100%	941	1,152.0	11.98%³		812.993	100.0%	664

Sources: China National Statistics Bureau, *China Statistical Yearbook, 1996 and 1997* (Beijing: Zhongguo tongji ju, 1997 and 1998); *A Strategic Study of China's Regional Development*, State Planning Commission, 1996.

Notes: 1. Military personnel are not included.
2. 1996 mid-year US$–RMB$ exchange rate = 1:8.31.
3. Plains share in total area.
*Estimates based on provincial data.

Although the central government may use macroeconomic policies through a national fiscal system to transfer resources interregionally and to protect national interests, most interregional economic exchanges should rely on the market mechanism. This regional development model of the metropolitan economy is the trend most Chinese regions have followed. It is probably the least costly method for China's future economic development.

Four Emerging World-Class Economies: The Chinese Tigers

Fujian, a southeast coastal province (located between the regions of Greater Shanghai and the Pearl River Delta, with a population of 30.2 million), has been "left out" from the SPC's study of nine metropolitan economies in the mainland,[23] but can be easily integrated with its newly industrialized neighbor, Taiwan, across the Taiwan Strait (about 150 kilometers in average width) to become an export-oriented regional economy. Due to its physical-geographical characteristics, Fujian is relatively isolated from its neighbor provinces of Zhejiang, Jiangxi, and Guangdong by mountains and hills. But historically, Fujian has been the forerunner of international contacts via the sea since its ports were opened to international trade with Southeast Asian countries, India, and Arabian countries in the fifteenth century. The Pearl River Delta, or Guangdong, can also be easily integrated with Hong Kong and Macao to become another export-oriented economy.[24]

If integrated with Fujian and Guangdong, Taiwan, Hong Kong, and Macao will benefit from higher returns on their existing capital stocks as well as from new investment opportunities. Integration will provide Taiwan and Hong Kong with scale economy, abundant supplies of primary labor, and cheaper food and materials. It will also expand markets for their manufactured goods, modern technology, and commercial services. These institutional and structural changes will essentially enable the aggregate production of these newly industrialized economies to enjoy a return to a scale greater than unity for a certain period of time. That is, with the same amount of factor inputs, they would produce more outputs if they got free access to Fujian's and Guangdong's vast resources and commodity and service markets. Or, in other words, the real marginal returns to Taiwan's and Hong Kong's labor and capital would be raised. This will eventually propel their real per capita GDP (or the average real income) to grow faster. All of these economic advantages are estimated to generate as much as 2–4 percent economic growth annually in the next two decades in addition to Taiwan and Hong Kong's normal growth.[25]

On the other hand, if economically integrated with Hong Kong and Taiwan, Guangdong and Fujian will enjoy injections of Hong Kong and Taiwan capital, technology, and commercial know-how. Since Taiwan and Hong Kong will supply the capital and technology required for Guangdong's and Fujian's economic development, China would then direct its scarce capital resources to the economic development of other regions. Taiwan-Fujian and Hong Kong–Guangdong will become new regional economic powers with economic scales (in terms of GDP) even greater than their neighboring regions—Greater Shanghai (Shanghai, Zhejiang, and southern Jiangsu) and south-central China (Hunan, Hubei, and Jiangxi), with significantly larger populations.

Once Fujian and Guangdong start to integrate with Taiwan and Hong Kong and become open economies, their industrial structures will also evolve toward industrial and service orientation. There will be structural changes in Fujian and Guangdong: less-productive labor will flow to higher-paid industries, and therefore further productivity gains will occur. Hong Kong and Taiwan's quality commercial services and international connections will also lead Fujian and Guangdong into the international market. As a result, Fujian and Guangdong will not only become more productive but will also become more integrated with international markets.

Because the required capital and technology for Guangdong's and Fujian's economic development will be sufficiently supplied by Taiwan and Hong Kong, China may then direct its scarce capital resources to the economic development of other regions. A quarter century from now, there will emerge at least four new world-class regional economic powers within Greater China: Taiwan-Fujian, Hong Kong–Guangdong, Greater Shanghai (Shanghai, southern Jiangsu, and Zhejiang), and the south-central region (Hunan, Hubei, and Jiangxi). These four regions will experience higher growth than the rest of the Chinese economic regions.[26] Furthermore, we anticipate that by 2020, the Taiwan-Fujian and Hong Kong–Guangdong economies will have surpassed the size of South Korea's and will have become the new Asian Tigers in the twenty-first century (refer to Table 11.4 and Figure 11.5).

As shown in Table 11.4, in 1996 Taiwan and Fujian had a combined population of over 50 million and a total GDP of greater than one-third of China's. Taiwan's manufacturing capacity and technology, human and financial capitals, degree of internationalization, and commercial expertise will sustain its integration with Fujian's less skilled labor force and natural resources. In addition, Hong Kong and Guangdong had a combined population of over 75 million and a total GDP of US$224.6 billion in 1996, which was more than a quarter of China's GDP. Hong Kong's 6.3 million people speak the same dialect as the people of Guangdong, and over the past two decades almost all of Hong Kong's manufacturing plants have been moved to the Pearl River Delta area. As a result, Hong Kong, with its advanced financial systems, international commercial expertise, and modern transportation and communication facilities and technology, has become a port city servicing southern China.

Table 11.4 also shows that if fully economically integrated with Fujian and Guangdong, Taiwan and Hong Kong may grow at a rate of 8 percent

Table 11.4 Chinese Tigers Versus Asian Tigers: Present and Future

Economy	Population Million	1996 GDP US$Billion (1996 Dollar)	1996 GDP (PPP) US$Billion (1996 Dollar)	1996 GDP Per Capita US$ (1996 Dollar)	1996 GDP Per Capita US$ (PPP) (1996 Dollar)	Compound Annual Growth Rate	2020 GDP US$Billion (1996 Dollar)	2020 GDP Per Capita US$ (1996 Dollar)
				Status Quo Scenario				
Korea	44.8	451.4	526.4	11,750	13,702	5%	1,456	33,793
Taiwan	21.6	264.9	308.8	12,265	14,298	5%	854	35,274
Hong Kong	6.3	146.2	150.5	23,200	23,882	4%	375	58,111
Singapore	3.1	81.8	73.1	26,400	23,592	4%	210	66,127
China	1,223.9	825.4	4,486.2	678	3,685	6%	3,187	2,187
Guangdong	68.8	78.4	426.4	1,145	6,222	7%	398	3,692
Fujian	32.61	31.4	170.5	979	5,321	7%	159	3,158
Macao	0.4	7	6.7	17,475	16,726	4%	18	43,771
				Economic Integration Scenario				
Taiwan-Fujian	54.2	296.3	479.3	5,407	8,747	8.3%	1,989	30,252
Taiwan	21.6	264.9	308.8	12,265	14,298	8.0%	1,680	69,578
Fujian	32.6	31.4	170.5	979	5,321	10.0%	309	7,745
HK-Guangdong	75.5	224.6	576.9	2,911	7,475	8.3%	1,514	15,967
Hong Kong	6.3	146.2	150.5	23,200	23,882	7.0%	742	93,935
Guangdong	69.61	78.4	426.4	1,145	6,222	10.0%	773	9,056
Greater Shanghai	83.8	114.8	623.9	1,370	7,446	8.5%	813	7,771
South-Central China	163.6	85.9	466.6	525	2,853	8.5%	608	2,977

Sources: China National Statistics Bureau, *China Statistical Yearbook, 1997* (Beijing: Zhonggou tongji ju, 1998); "A Study in Regional Development Strategies of China," *Asiaweek*, September 1996.

Notes: US$ and RMB$ exchange rate = 1:8.31 (mid-year rate).
PPP Price Factor: In 1996, US$1.00 worth of goods and services in China was assumed to be equivalent to US$5.435 (PPP).
1996–2020 Population Growth Assumptions: Taiwan: 0.5%; Hong Kong and Macao: 0.1%; China: 1.0%.

Figure 11.5 Asian Tigers and Chinese Tigers: 1996 Versus 2020

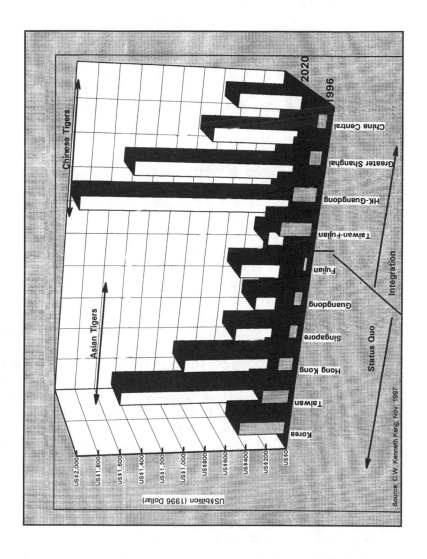

and 7 percent, respectively, from the present to 2020. Otherwise, Taiwan and Hong Kong will only grow, at best, by 5 percent and 4 percent per annum, respectively.

Benefits of Regional Integration

Taiwan and Hong Kong will attain higher productivity if integrated with Fujian and Guangdong. For example, Taiwan's prices for industrial-use land are between two to three times Japan's average, and Hong Kong's land cost is even higher than Taiwan's. If integrated with Fujian, Taiwan will probably restructure its industries so that low-productivity sectors such as agriculture and less technology-intensive manufacturing industries can be moved to Fujian, where land prices, water resources, and labor costs are much lower. Taiwan's investment in the Fujian agricultural sector will generate a much higher return. In addition, Taiwan's downsized agricultural sector will release valuable land as well as huge capital and labor to industrial and commercial sectors for producing outputs with much higher added values. These changes will also help Taiwan to re-strengthen its environment.

Taiwan's labor market will also be restructured. Professionals and technicians can assist in Fujian's economic development, which will certainly reduce Fujian's need for skilled labor and quality professionals and will lower its investment in human capital. Meanwhile, Fujian's abundant and inexpensive labor can largely ease Taiwan's shortage of less-skilled laborers (e.g., construction workers, assembly-line operators, steel mill workers, etc.). Taiwan's well-educated and trained manpower can then be better utilized for higher productivity. Labor mobility between Taiwan and Fujian will not only raise the productivity of both economies, but will also lower their real unit labor costs; hence both economies will enjoy greater competitiveness in international markets. Moreover, if integrated with Fujian, Taiwan will also gain access to the mainland markets of food and raw materials. Therefore, material prices for Taiwan's production and the cost of living for its whole population will be lowered. This will definitely improve the competitiveness of Taiwan products in international markets.

Since Fujian is a part of the mainland, enterprises in Fujian that are invested in by Taiwan will produce "domestic" products to which the vast market of China will have access. These investments will not only greatly increase the market share of Taiwanese enterprises on the mainland, but will also enable them to optimize their production scales. Hence, an expansion of production and an improved productivity would generate additional growth for Taiwan's economy. These economic advantages are estimated to generate as much as 2–4 percent economic growth in addition to normal growth.[27] Table 11.5 provides estimates of productivity gains and additional growth that Taiwan will enjoy if it is integrated with Fujian.

Table 11.5 Taiwan's Additional Growth Resulting from Integration

	Productivity Gain	Additional Growth
Sectoral Shift of Labor	0.5%–1.5%	0.5%–1.5%
Larger Market & Scale Economy	0.5%–1.0%	0.5%–1.5%
Deletion of Tariffs & Other Trade Barriers	0.5%–1.0%	0.5%–1.0%
Lower costs of factor inputs and materials	0.5%–1.0%	0.5%–1.0%
Production Division	1.0%–2.0%	0.5%–1.0%
Total		2.5%–6.0%

Economic Integration: A Win-Win Strategy

Having been arch enemies for almost forty years (1949–1987) and then having experienced ten years of cultural and commercial exchanges, Taiwan and Mainland China have reached a stage where they may reopen the semiofficial talks that were suspended unilaterally by the mainland following President Tenghui Lee's visit to the United States in the summer of 1995. For the foreseeable future, a political resolution of the "One China" issue is unlikely. Meanwhile, many strategists suggest this issue may simply be tabled or downplayed so that other mutually beneficial issues can be dealt with. At present, a politically unified China remains a distant goal rather than a realistic objective. Yet, Taiwan's and Hong Kong's economic integration with China plays a crucial role in accelerating China's economic growth. In effect, it will propel China's future growth toward its highest potential. The speed and the scale of Taiwan's and Hong Kong's economic integration with China will decisively affect China's economic growth course in the next two decades. On the other hand, Taiwan and Hong Kong may also benefit from a fast-growing Chinese economy.

Hong Kong's reversion to China, recent developments across the Taiwan Strait, the increasing capabilities resulting from the Asia Pacific Economic Cooperation (APEC), China's and Taiwan's progress toward joining the World Trade Organization, and President Clinton's visit to China have all created a spirit of optimism concerning affairs cross the Taiwan Strait. As discussed in the last section, there are clear advantages to economically integrating Taiwan and Hong Kong with the neighboring Chinese regions of Fujian and Guangdong. These two integrated economies (Taiwan-Fujian and Hong Kong–Guangdong) may not only become two new "Asian Tigers" in the new century, but will also propel other Chinese regional economies to robust and sustainable growth.

However, from nearly a century ago to the present, the economies of Taiwan, Hong Kong, and Macao have been politically and socially different from that of China. While the benefit of this integration can clearly and easily be seen, it may not be easily conducted when the huge differences in various dimensions between the involved economies are taken into account. These difficulties will make this integration a long process of market integration and industrial restructuring that will require extensive cooperation and coordination in almost all aspects of the socioeconomic systems. It indeed presents a real challenge to the political wisdom of the people on both sides of the Taiwan Strait. Furthermore, this integration is not merely a "domestic" affair; it also has international dimensions: it will affect all those nations having investment and trade relations with the involved economies. It is hence crucial to search for a practical approach that may be accepted by people on both sides of the Taiwan Strait.

Economic Integration Models

Many social and economic systems have been developed to provide frameworks to coordinate the economic affairs of member nations without affecting the fundamental rules governing their political relationships. Economic integration of states or regions can take a variety of forms, ranging from open economy, free trade area, custom union, common market, and economic union, to complete integration. Although these models of economic integration may not readily apply to the Taiwan-China case, they nevertheless can be considered as possible starting points. Instead of analyzing hypothetical models, we proceed with an examination of the following realized integration models:

The commonwealth model. The member economies of a commonwealth recognize a common goal but have no formal political accords or detailed agreements on economic affairs. Each member may still exercise its own political sovereignty and economic powers. The model is essentially feasible for cultural exchanges between Taiwan and Mainland China. It is indeed in accord with the short-term phase of exchanges and reciprocity under the Republic of China's *Guidelines for National Unification.* It is also consistent with China's long-announced policy of increased people-to-people exchanges with Taiwan. Under this framework, Taiwan and Mainland China may progress to some solid cooperation toward cultural integration. For example, Taiwan may participate in China's efforts toward hosting the 2008 Olympic Games in exchange for hosting a part of the games in Taiwan. China may also support Taiwan's effort toward hosting future Asian Games. Taiwan and China may also form joint committees to work on all kinds of cultural integration issues such as the unification of computer codes for Chinese systems, interconnection of on-line library systems, publication of textbooks and ancient Chinese books, joint investigations into traditional Chinese medicine and into historical concerns, the promotion of traditional Chinese philosophy, value systems, and language, and much more.

The NAFTA (North American Free Trade Agreement) Model. Each member signs an agreement that states that within a certain time frame, every member economy will amend its domestic laws and regulations so that free trade and fair competition within the joint territory of all members will be attained. While each member retains its own sovereignty, all free trade–related disputes (such as dumping, counterfeiting, intellectual property rights, compatibility of social welfare systems, and environmental standards) are resolved by joint governmental or public agencies. This model is readily applicable to provide security and fairness for cross–Taiwan Strait trade and investment that have been desperately awaited by Taiwan businesspeople and investors. It is worth stressing that a free-trade agreement is not merely a commercial trade agreement. It can essentially be viewed as a potential systematic approach to the realignment of all economic, social, and legal standards in Taiwan and China so that the free movement of goods, services, capital, and personnel is achieved. Such an agreement actually involves a lengthy process during which both sides can gradually adapt to a full cooperation that facilitates free trade.

We acknowledge that the free-trade negotiation may essentially constitute a milestone or serve as an unavoidable step toward unification. Only economic cooperation works; therefore, we hope that regions on both sides of the Taiwan Strait will proceed further toward cooperation and coordination in government regulations and policies, which are necessary steps in achieving social and political unification. The negotiation of a free-trade agreement between Taiwan and China is essentially a logical and pragmatic process that can lead toward greater integration.

The European Union Model. While each member may still execute its own discretionary policies in domestic and foreign affairs, the European Union (EU) model provides a united front on almost all external economic issues. Free trade, common external tariffs, and free mobility of production factors are gradually attained, along with an integrated economy that has a centralized monetary authority issuing a single currency. Military cooperation and strategic/security partnerships (e.g., NATO) are also strengthened but not included in the EU framework. Each member nation may still exercise its own political powers and assert its own international sovereignty. However, each member also has to cooperate with other member nations (or even be coordinated by the European Council and Commission) for those policies with overlapping common interests of other member countries (e.g., monetary and taxation policies). The EU model essentially provides a policy coordination system that is governed by the European Council that represents governments of member countries, and is administered by an executive body, the European Commission, that is independent of the governments of member countries. The EU model presents a big leap forward from the NAFTA model because it necessitates joint governmental maneuvers in policy coordination, which clearly articulate a certain form of political integration.

The Chinese Model

While none of these models may apply directly to the Taiwan-China case, the commonwealth model of cultural exchanges and the NAFTA model of interregional free trade provide common ground that may, to a certain extent, be acceptable to regions on both sides of the Taiwan Strait as intermediate phases toward ultimate unification. By the end of the twentieth century, the world will have witnessed the German reunification and also the dissolution of the Soviet Union. German reunification essentially provides a model of political resolution for a bisected nation. Yet, given the incomparable sizes of Taiwan, Hong Kong, and Mainland China, and with the huge structural differentials in their current political systems, the German reunification model could hardly be applied. Taiwan, Hong Kong, and Macao may, with reason, be concerned about being "devoured" by the vast Chinese mainland if an immediate political reunion were actualized. To ease this legitimate concern, we suggest that an adaptive process toward ultimate unification be established.

The process can be adaptive in the sense that all parties can, in a step-by-step manner and at their own discretion, negotiate a common agreement with the others. The adaptive nature of this process may enable the gradual establishment of a socioeconomic framework within which all their economic affairs may be eventually coordinated. Once such a framework has been established, people on both sides of the Taiwan Strait may then be ready to proceed toward political integration. Or, by that stage, the economies on both sides of the Taiwan Strait may readjust their priorities according to the interests of the majority of their peoples. Another striking feature of this adaptive process is that it does not necessarily need to follow any predetermined timetable. Different rounds of discussion can adapt or proceed according to agreements reached in previous rounds of negotiations. This adaptive process would in essence follow the mainland's philosophy used throughout its reform era: "groping for stones on which to cross the river."

Our suggested process is divided into three phases: the phase of cultural and nongovernmental exchange, the phase of free trade and common external tariffs, and the phase of monetary and economic union. We estimate that this process of economic integration may take as long as two to three decades to accomplish.

Phase I: The Chinese Commonwealth. Before a free trade agreement is negotiated, Taiwan, Hong Kong, Macao, Mainland China, and even Tibet and Mongolia may form a nongovernmental and nonpolitical commonalty of cultural cooperation and coordination: the Chinese Commonwealth. Within this Chinese Commonwealth, every member maintains its economic, political, and social status quo but may engage in cooperation and coordination in all aspects of cultural and nongovernmental affairs. This cultural cooperation and coordination may include joint efforts toward hosting the Olympic Games and other international cultural/sports events, joint memberships in international nongovernmental organizations and in academic and professional associations, coordination in unifying computer technology for Chinese applications, cooperation in humanity and science researches, and/or joint development of Chinese library and other information systems. During the commonwealth phase, members may also engage in free-trade agreement negotiations.

Phase II: The Chinese Free-Trade Area. Once the free-trade agreement is reached among Mainland China, Taiwan, Hong Kong, Macao, and others, the parties may attain greater cooperation and coordination in economic affairs and may then proceed to engage in forming a common economic front that would maximize their economic benefits internationally. Coordination in economic affairs may include not only free movement of goods and services within the free-trade area, but may also include freer movement of factor products such as capital, labor, information, and technology. The member economies may also start negotiations that would establish a common external tariff before proceeding toward a common market. During this phase, member economies may gradually readjust their industrial structures, production divisions, and market concentrations to achieve a better overall economic blend. Their industrial and engineering standards, health and environmental protection codes, transportation and communication regulations, social security requirements, business legal systems, and so on, may also be gradually aligned to facilitate a free flow of economic activities within the free-trade area.

During this phase, it is clear that direct communication and commercial relations across the Taiwan Strait will be established, which will accommodate China's immediate objectives. It is also clear that during this phase, mutual trust and cooperation between Taiwan and China will also be developed. This is consistent with the objective of the intermediate phase specified in the Republic of China's *Guidelines for National Unification.*

Phase III: The Chinese Union. When free movements of goods and services and a common external tariff within the free-trade area have been attained, the member economies will be ready for a more extended economic integration: financial and monetary coordination, free interregional mobility of production factors, and governmental coordination of an elected economic policies council for governing interregional affairs, and so on. These characteristics of economic integration will enable member economies to move toward a much greater breadth of coordination among governments not only in economic affairs but also in legal and political aspects. The European Union's formative experiences may provide tremendous assistance to the formation of the Chinese Union.[28]

A Time Frame for Integration

Once Chinese economies reach complete economic integration, they are ready to decide whether or not a political union in the form of a confederation, a federation, or a unity state should be constituted. However, given the fact that after signing the NAFTA treaty it may take up to fifteen years for the United States, Canada, and Mexico to complete their free-trade commitments, and also considering that it took more than four decades for European countries to negotiate and ratify the European Union accord, Chinese economic integration may take at least the same length of time in view of the differences in social systems and economic policies and the need to turn political antagonism into harmony.

If China tries to industrialize its economy by 2010, as its first fifteen-year long-term plan calls for, its first priority then should be to develop a stable economy as fast as possible by incorporating all potential resources. Taiwan's capital and technological and international commercial know-how will be valuable resources, for it is clear that China needs not only capital but also technological and commercial know-how. On the other hand, if Taiwan's priority is to provide a stable and secure business environment for its advancement toward a technologically oriented economy, it must resolve any security issues stemming from the unstable China-Taiwan relations. Neither can Taiwan afford to lose the vast market of China. It is also clear that Taiwan needs not only China's markets, but also China's less-skilled labor (Taiwan has already imported a great number of primary laborers from Southeast Asian countries). Taiwan and China may therefore be economic complements to each other. The NAFTA model provides a perfect starting point for regions on both sides of the Taiwan Strait to negotiate for better flows of capital, goods, and services.

If it takes the regions on both sides of the Taiwan Strait the next five years to negotiate a free-trade agreement similar in extent to the NAFTA, that will allow signed partners ten to fifteen years to reduce their customs duties to zero. It will take as long as twenty years for Taiwan and China to complete their free-trade agreement. Our expectation is that in the foreseeable future, or by 2020, Chinese economies may, at the fastest, have been ready to engage in negotiations toward forming the Chinese Union. By 2020, most of the prewar-born Chinese will have retired, and the regimes of the regions on both sides of the Taiwan Strait will be in the hands of those born long after the Chinese civil war. The political environment may then be largely different from what it is perceived to be at present. And by then, the Chinese economies of Taiwan, Hong Kong, Macao, and the mainland may have reduced the differences in their economic and social systems. When diversities between the regions on both sides of the Taiwan Strait diminish, Chinese reunification will no more be a problem, or, perhaps, it will no longer be an issue at all.

Conclusion

Sustainable economic growth is necessary for China's future stability. Clearly, sustainable growth depends on continued commitments to institutional reform and economic deregulation. China's relaxation of government intervention in economic activities has led to decentralization of the central governmental authority over economic planning and control. This decentralization will consequently lead to the emergence of regional economies in Mainland China. In the next two decades, there will likely be ten regional economies with relatively independent industrial structures emerging in Greater China as a result of economic decentralization.

There are three prospects for China's economic growth: (1) low-growth scenario postulated on a reversion to an authoritarian socialist government, (2) stable-growth potential based on an extrapolation of China's current policies and trends, and (3) high-growth potential based on the policy regime of economic deregulation and decentralization. Under the stable-growth scenario, China will progress along lines of gradualism by "groping for stones on which to cross the river." This will enable the Chinese economy to grow at a compound annual rate of 5.8 percent between 1997 and 2020. In contrast, under the socialist hard-liner postulation, the economy will grow more slowly at an annual rate of 4.3 percent in the same period. If China speeds up its efforts toward economic deregulation and decentralization, it will achieve its high-growth potential at an annual rate of 7.4 percent up to 2020. Should this take place by 2020, mainlanders will enjoy a living standard as high as that enjoyed by Taiwan residents at present.

Given the fact that a politically unified China remains a distant goal, the strategy of an economic union of Greater China is probably an optimal and realistic approach for all parties across the Taiwan Strait to work toward. The theoretical Chinese Economic Union, as a multiregional conglomerate with different institutional arrangements of economic, social, and political systems, may result in a dynamic process that works toward the goal of unification. The strategy will essentially combine Taiwan and Hong Kong economic forces to impel China's economic growth to its highest potential. It will in turn benefit Taiwan and Hong Kong. This strategy has a win-win prospect in the sense that no party will sacrifice its political objective for economic integration, while all parties will benefit from it. Free mobility of Taiwan's and Hong Kong's financial and human capitals as well as goods and services within the integrated southeastern coast of Greater China will propel these economies to another plateau of economic growth. A rapidly growing southeastern Greater China will not only provide new investment, commercial expertise, and industrial technology to the Chinese inland regions, but will also generate huge market demand for the materials, goods, and services of inland regions. China's economic growth will hence be durable and sustainable.

Appendix

Physical Limitation on China's Growth: The Shortage of Plains

China consists of 9.6 million square kilometers (km^2) of which less than 12 percent (1.15 million km^2) are plains. According to a recent survey, China has about 1,988 million mu[29] (1.32 million km^2) of cultivated land,[30] which account for about 13.8 percent of its total area. Of the cultivated land, 1,290 million mu (859,269 km^2) are on plains (with a gradient not exceeding 8 degrees), which account for 75 percent of China's plains area. This leaves merely 25 percent of the plains (290,000 km^2) for urban, industrial, and land transportation development, infrastructure construction, and other nonagricultural uses.

The per capita area of plains for nonagricultural use in 1996 was 238 square meters (m^2). In the coming quarter century, China's population will grow to 1.5 billion. This per capita statistic will then "shrink" to 194 m^2 if China maintains its agricultural use of plains to the extent it does today. On the other hand, if in the next quarter century China keeps its present standard of per capita nonagricultural use of plains, its agricultural use of plains will have to be reduced to accommodate the growing urban population and industrial and commercial developments. In this case, by 2020 China will have to have released an area as large as 40 percent of the current area of agricultural plains for nonagricultural uses. This will create problems such as an inadequacy of the domestic food supply, insufficiency of domestic production of food, impaired environment, and so on. These problems are considered as priority national security issues in China. There is little chance that the Chinese authorities would lower the announced food sufficiency level below 90 percent (the current level is 95 percent). Therefore, there is a severe limitation to releasing China's agricultural land for other uses.

Table 11.6   China's Limitation of Plain Lands for Economic Development

Year	Population (Million)	Plain Area (1000 km²)	Per Capita Plain Area (m²)	Plains Per Capita for Nonagricultural Use (m²)	Plains for Nonagricultural Use (1000 km²)
1996	1,223.89	1,152	941	238	290,811
2020	1,502	1,152	766	194*	356,893+

Notes: * Based on the 1996 plains area for nonagricultural uses.
+ Based on the 1996 per capita plain area for nonagricultural uses.

Use of Plains for Transportation

In 1992, Japan had a per capita plains area of 792 m² and the United States enjoyed over 25,000 m² of plains per capita. China's per capita plains area in 1997 was 941 m², and it is expected to decline to 767 m² by 2020 when the population grows to 1.5 billion. If the span (extensiveness) of land is taken into account, China's land transportation use of plains areas should be much larger than Japan's. This is because China's area is 25.3 times Japan's, and only one-third of China's provinces are coastal. Therefore, China needs much more long-distance land transportation than Japan does. Land transportation, due to construction technology and costs, should mostly take place on plains. High demand for long-distance land transportation means more highways and railroads should be built.

In 1997, China had 133,339 kilometers of railways and 1,185,789 kilometers of highways. If, on average, each kilometer of railroad occupies 0.004 km² of land and each kilometer of highway occupies 0.005 km² of land,[31] the land required for transportation totals an area of 56,299 km². China's per capita transportation land in 1997 can thus be estimated at 46.1 square meters. This is about half as much as Japan's 90 m² in 1992. Furthermore, if 80 percent of this land transportation system had been constucted on the plains, 45,039 km² of China's plains in 1997 would have been used, which would have been over 3.8 percent of its total area of plains.

Between 1996 and 2020, China will probably have to accommodate an additional 276 million in population. If it is assumed that the per capita transportation use of plains will not increase in the next quarter century, China still will need more than an additional 10,000 km² of plains to build new land transportation to accommodate the economic activities generated by the additional 276 million people. By 2020, the total area of plains used for land transportation would be over 55,000 km², which is 4.8 percent of the national total. This estimate may serve as the lower limit of what will be needed for land transportation by 2020 because it is based on China's actual present experience. A quarter century from now, China's economy may expand to at least over three times the size it is today with an additional population of over 276 million. The much larger economy will certainly generate much more demand for land transportation. As a result, per capita transportation use of land will increase significantly.

Alternative estimates based on different assumptions of per capita use of land for land transportation reveal the following data. It would take 9.4 percent of the plains areas if China constructed a land transportation system by 2020 similar to Japan's today. As an island nation, Japan has an area of merely 4 percent that of China. And unlike China, Japan imports most of its required energy, natural resources, and materials to its major industrial regions located along its coast. This means that Japan's demand for long-distance land transportation is relatively low. In contrast, 90 percent of China's required energy and natural resources and 95 percent of its required grains are domestically produced. Even in the future, when China fully participates in the international division of production, it will still have to produce the vast majority of goods and services by itself.

Given China's geographically unbalanced distribution of natural and energy resources, the future demand for land transportation to support its growing economic activities should be significantly greater than that of Japan at present. Jian Wang has argued that 1.5 times Japan's present per capita transportation use of land, that is, 135 m^2, will be needed as the basis to estimate that of China in 2020.[32] This means that 155,250 km^2 of land will be needed for China's future land transportation, which accounts for about 1.6 percent of the national area and 13.5 percent of the national plains. There is also an alternative estimate based on the present experience of the United States. More than a half of China's plains would be required to build a system of highways and railroads similar to that of the United States. Even based on a half of the U.S. standard at present, more than 25 percent of China's plains would be required.

Use of Plains for Urbanization

If China's urbanization reaches 60 percent by 2020, there will be 900 million people living in urban areas. The total land required will exceed 40,000 km^2, given Tokyo's 50 m^2 per capita urban use of land in 1994 as the benchmark. The total land needed for China's urbanization will take up about 3.5 percent of China's plains area. If 70 percent of the rural population's houses were also on the plains, rural housing would require 17,190 km^2 of plains. China's total urbanization and rural housing needs for plains would then be estimated at 45,840 km^2, which would account for about 0.5 percent of China's total area and 4.0 percent of the total area of plains. This estimate is conservative because it is based on statistics from the most-densely populated metropolitan center, Tokyo, with extremely high prices for land.

An alternative estimate is based on Japan's per capita urban use of land. If all cities are taken into account, Japan's per capita urban use of

Table 11.7 Estimates of China's Land Transportation Use of Plains

Year or Country	Land Used for Land Transportation (Per Capita)	Area Used for Land Transportation (National Total)	Plains Used for Land Transportation (National Total)	Share of Total Plains	Additional Area of Plains Needed
1996	46 m^2	56,299 km^2	45,039 km^2	3.9%	
2020	46 m^2	69,000 km^2	55,200 km^2	4.8%	10,161 km^2
2020*	135 m^2	202,500 km^2	162,500 km^2	14.1%	117,461 km^2
Japan	90 m^2	135,000 km^2	108,000 km^2	9.4%	62,961 km^2
USA	496 m^2	744,000 km^2	535,200 km^2	51.7%	490,161 km^2

Note: *Based on 1.5 times Japan's figure.
Source: U.S. and Japanese figures are from J. Wang, "Regional Development Issues in China's Ninth Five-year Plan," in *The Role of Foreign Capital in China's Industrial and Regional Development.* Beijing: China Macroeconomics Society, State Planning Commission, 1997.

land was 115 m² in 1992. If we use this as the standard, by 2020 China will need 172,500 km² of land for urban development; that is, China will need 1.8 percent of its total land area and 15.0 percent of its total plains area. If 90 percent of urban cities are on the plains, the actual use of plains for urbanization by 2020 will be 155,250 km², accounting for about 1.6 percent of China's total area and 13.5 percent of its plains.

Other cities have offered potential comparisons in the urban use of land. At present, Shenzhen is the only large city in China that was constructed according to modern urban planning. However, Shenzhen has so far accommodated mainly light industries and is still far from being fully commercialized. Therefore, its per capita urban use of land tends to fall short of that of a metropolitan area of the future. As a result, Shenzhen is not a representative city to be used as the benchmark for future metropolitan areas. Neither can Beijing and Shanghai, where most of the streets, houses, and business areas were built more than fifty years ago, be used as representative cities. There are very few areas in these cities that have been rebuilt under modern urban planning. Hence, their statistics even more seriously underestimate the future land requirement for an average metropolitan center.

The State Planning Commission estimates that by 2010 China's urbanization will reach 60 percent and will occupy 1 percent of its total area, and that transportation will occupy 1.3 percent of its area if China adopts Japan's "metropolitan model" to develop its economy. That is, China would not and could not plan for a nationwide division of production because a nationwide industrial structure like that of the United States requires extensive use of land transportation in order to move materials and goods. China does not have enough plains to build a minimum capacity of modern land transportation to accommodate a nationwide industrial structure for a population of 1.5 billion. Even if China adopts merely half of the U.S. standard on a per capita basis to build its land transportation system, such a system would still take up more than 25 percent of its plains. As a result, there will be conflicting demands for plains for environmental protection, food production, transportation, and urbanization. The problem will be compounded by China's low per capita reserve of petroleum, the principal fuel for both highway and railroad transportation in the foreseeable future.

The low per capita endowment of plains areas should compel China to diversify its national economy into regional ones. Each will have its own relatively independent industrial structure and market system, so that the need for cross-regional, long-distance land transportation will decrease and the use of plains for transit systems will also be reduced. In this way, the transportation costs that constitute a portion of the transaction costs of almost all economic activities can be minimized. The economy as a whole will therefore use fewer resources for transportation to produce the same level of outputs, and macroeconomic productivity gains will be enjoyed.

Table 11.8   Estimates of China's Urban Use of Plains by 2020

Alternative Models	Urban Use of Land* (Per Capita)	Urban Use of Land (National Total)	Urban Use of Plains (90% of the total urban use of land)	Urban Share of Plains	Rural Housing Use of Plains	Rural Share of Plains	Total Share of Plains
Japan Average	115 m^2	172,500 km^2	155,250 km^2	13.5%	34,500 km^2	3.0%	16.5%
Tokyo	50 m^2	45,000 km^2	40,500 km^2	3.5%	10,500 km^2	1.3%	4.8%
Shenzhen	30 m^2	27,000 km^2	24,300 km^2	2.1%	9,000 km^2	0.8%	2.9%
Beijing	20 m^2	18,000 km^2	16,200 km^2	1.4%	6,000 km^2	0.5%	1.9%

Source: *Figures in this column are cited from J. Wang, "China's Macroeconomic Strategy of Regional Economic Development," in *The Role of Foreign Capital in China's Industrial and Regional* Development. Beijing: China Macroeconomics Society State Planning Commission, 1997.

This use of resources essentially provides an economic rationale to decentralize resource allocation power to regions. Possible productivity gains from this strategy have been estimated to be as high as 1.5 percent a year through 2020. Had there been no central planning and had China relied completely on market forces to allocate its resources, regionalization would already have been the natural outcome.

Notes

1. The author has benefited from discussions with and comments from the editors of this book and from Chu-yuan Cheng, Cheng Hsiao, Ronald Mitchell, and Hung-Tao Tai on an earlier version of this chapter. Financial and administrative support from the China Development Fund, the Rotman School of Management at the University of Toronto, and the faculty of Business at the University of Victoria as well as research assistance from Everett Barclay, Iris Chen, and Robin Potter are gratefully acknowledged.

2. By Greater China, we unambiguously mean the neighboring economic areas of Hong Kong, Macao, Taiwan, and Mainland China.

3. Unless otherwise indicated, the World Bank reference cited in this section is from the World Bank, *China 2020: Development Challenges in the New Century* (Washington, DC: World Bank, 1997).

4. Unless otherwise indicated, statistics cited in this chapter are based on China's latest official statistics. The author acknowledges the potential existence of data deficiencies in official Chinese statistics and has made every effort to compare them with alternative statistics when necessary.

5. Eduardo Borensztein and Jonathan Ostry, "Accounting for China's Growth Performance," *American Economic Review Papers and Proceedings* 86, no. 2 (1996): 224–228.

6. World Bank, *China 2020.*

7. According to *Asiaweek*'s September 27, 1996, issue, the 1996 GDP per capita calculated at PPP of the following countries was, in U.S. currency: United States: $26,825; Japan: $22,220; South Korea: $11,750; Taiwan: $14,295; Hong

Kong: $23,892; Macao: $16,840; Singapore: $23,565; Malaysia: $9,470; Russia: $5,260; Thailand: $7,535; Mexico: $7,188; India: $1,385; and China: $2,935. Because *China Statistical Yearbook 1997* shows that China had a GDP per capita of renminbi (RMB) $5,634 in 1996 and the official RMB$ and US$ exchange rate in July 1996 was 8.31, this equates China's GDP per capita in 1996 to US$678, which is much higher than the GNP per capita of US$540 used in *Asiaweek*. (This may be due to differences in the base year and in exchange rates adopted.) Accordingly, we adjust China's 1996 GDP per capita at PPP to US$3,685. In this study, we use 5.435 as the 1996 PPP factor to adjust China's price level to the international one.

8. Justin J. Lin, "Rural Reforms and Agricultural Growth in China," *American Economic Review* 82 (January 1992): 34–51.

9. For further analysis of this dramatic shift in household savings, interested readers are referred to C. W. Kenneth Keng, "China's Economic Prospects in the New Century," Working Paper, Rotman School of Management, University of Toronto.

10. The World Bank's predictions for China's long-term average annual GDP growth rates are: 8.4 percent for 1996–2000, 6.9 percent for 2001–2010, and 5.5 percent for 2011–2020. These average to 6.6 per annum for 1996 to 2020. See World Bank, *China 2020*.

11. See note 7.

12. World Bank, *World Development Report 1992: Development and the Environment* (New York: Oxford University Press, 1992).

13. The World Bank's most recent studies convincingly document evidence that China's shortage of agricultural and energy resources will not significantly affect international energy and food prices in the foreseeable future. See World Bank, *At China's Table: Food Security Options* (Washington, DC: World Bank, 1997), and *Clear Water, Blue Skies: China New Environment in the New Century* (Washington, DC: World Bank, 1997).

14. Wang Jian, "Zhongguo quyu jingji fazhan de zongti silu" ["China's macroeconomic strategy of regional economic development"], in *Zhongguo de chanye diqu fazhan yu waici de zuoyong* [*The role of foreign capital in China's industrial and regional development*], (Beijing: Guojia jiwei Zhongguo hongguan jingji xuehui, 1997), pp. 1–19.

15. See, for example, Guojia jiwei [State Planning Commission], *Zhongguo de jingji fazhan zhanlue yu guoji xieli* [*China's economic development strategy and international cooperation*] (Beijing: Guojia jiwei Zhongguo hongguan jingji xuehui, 1997).

16. The World Bank, *At China's Table: Food Security Options.*

17. Wang Jian, "Guanyu woguo gediqu jiuwu jihuazhong de ruogan wenti" ["Regional development issues in China's ninth five-year plan"], in *Zhongguo de chanye diqu fazhan,* pp. 20–24.

18. The governor's responsibility system is less popular than its nickname: "The Rice Barrel Project." Under it, every provincial governor is personally responsible for the balance of demand and supply of grain (or rice) at the wholesale level in his own province, and each city or county mayor is personally responsible for the supply and demand of secondary foods (vegetables, meats, oil, eggs, sugar, etc.) in the retail markets within his or her jurisdictional territory. This "mayor responsibility system" also has the popular nickname of "The Vegetable Basket Project."

19. Under the decentralized grain security system, provinces are free to trade grains and to subsidize farmers' inputs and consumers' purchases. But provinces must meet the provincial stock responsibility; that is, surplus-producing provinces must maintain a three-month supply of grain stocks, while deficit provinces must maintain a six-month supply. The state retains the power to collect the grain quota,

and provincial quotas of grain at lower-than-market price must be delivered to grain bureaus at designated locations. The state also continues to maintain the national stock and the international grain trade monopoly. Private traders and provincial grain enterprises are not allowed to procure grain in the countryside until state grain quotas have been filled. This decentralization of grain security policy by itself did not have a direct impetus on grain production. However, its consequence, the deregulation of grain prices, has stimulated grain production. In 1997, the government procured grain quotas at "government unified" market prices and discontinued consumption subsidies through the grain enterprises.

20. Ping Wang and Yuan-li Wu, "Learning From the EC: The Implications of European Economic Integration for China and Taiwan," *American Journal of Chinese Studies* (1996): 205–224.

21. C. W. Kenneth Keng, *China's Regional Economic Development: Status, Strategy and Prospects*, Research Monograph, Rotman School of Management at University of Toronto, 1997, C. W. Kenneth Keng, "An Economic China: A Win-Win Strategy for Both Sides of the Taiwan Strait," *American Journal of Chinese Studies* 2 (October 1998): 182–215.

22. Guojia jiwei jingji yanjiusuo ketizu (State Planning Commission Economic Research Institute Topic Group), "Zhongguo quyu jingji fazhan zhanlue yanjiu (zhubaogao) ["Studies in China's regional economic development strategies (main report)"], unpublished mimeograph, April 1996.

23. Fujian has traditionally been ad hoc excluded from most of China's regional studies mainly due to military and political sensitivities.

24. C. W. Kenneth Keng, *China's Regional Economic Development* (Toronto: Research Monograph Series, Rotman School of Management at University of Toronto, 1997).

25. Ibid.

26. Ibid.

27. We acknowledge that more detailed quantitative studies are needed to qualify this claim. Figures listed in Table 11.4 are estimated by analogy using NAFTA, WTO, and EU experiences. See, for example, references included in notes 20 and 21 above, as well as Z. Wang and F. C. Tuan, "The Impact of China's and Taiwan's WTO Membership in World Trade—A Computable General Equilibrium Analysis," *American Journal of Chinese Studies* III, no. 2 (1996): 177–204.

28. Interested readers are referred to the following publications for details: Council of the European Union, *Treaty on European Union* (Luxemburg: Office for Official Publications of the European Communities, 1992); T. Hitiris, *European Community Economics*. 3rd edition (Hertfordshire, England: Harvester Wheatsheaf, 1994).

29. *Mu* is a traditional Chinese measuring unit for land area. One *mu* = 666.1 square meters = 7,200 square feet = 0.164 acre.

30. China's cultivated land area, based on its official statistical survey, was 949,700 km^2 in 1996. This is significantly smaller by as much as 28 percent than the area calculated from China's new satellite survey of 1.32 million km^2. In *China Statistical Yearbook 1997,* it is noted that the statistical survey may underestimate the actual area of cultivated land. In our study, we adopt the satellite survey data because we believe that statistical survey data tend to underestimate the actual area, evidently because China's agricultural taxes are essentially based on its official (statistical) survey of cultivated land. Farmers and local governments have all kinds of reasons to report lower cultivated areas of their land.

31. Here, we assume that railroads take, on average, a 40-meter-wide strip of land, and highways take a 50-meter-wide strip of land. This assumption is based

essentially on "Chinese characteristics." For example, in the United States, the width of a strip of land occupied by a modern highway is at least twice as much as what is assumed here.

32. Wang Jian, "Jiuwu he dao 2010 nian Zhongguo jingji fazhan zhanlue de zhongdian mianlin de zhuyao wenti" ["China's economic development problems in the ninth five-year plan and in the long-term plan to 2010"], in Guojia jiwei, *Zhongguo de jingji fazhan zhanlue,* pp. 1–11.

The Contributors

Gene Hsin Chang is associate professor of economics at the University of Toledo and associate editor of *China Economic Review.* He has published more than sixty articles and chapters in academic journals and books.

Jie Chen is associate professor of political science at Old Dominion University in Virginia. His major research interests are Chinese politics and Sino–U.S. relations.

Xiaonong Cheng is a Ph.D. candidate in sociology at Princeton University. He has published more than thirty articles both in the United States and China. His writings cover a variety of economic, social, and political issues. He is chief-editor of an academic journal, *Modern China Studies,* sponsored by the Center for Modern China in Princeton, New Jersey.

Hungdah Chiu is professor of law and director of the East Asian Legal Studies Program at the University of Maryland School of Law in Baltimore. He has published numerous papers and books in the areas of international law, Chinese legal development, and U.S.–China relations. He has been elected president of the International Law Association.

Zhaohui Hong is associate professor of history at Savannah State University in Georgia. He has published five books and more than forty research articles on China's reform, comparative modernization, U.S.–China relations, and U.S. economic history.

C. W. Kenneth Keng is professor of economics at the University of Toronto, Canada. With numerous papers in areas of econometrics, energy economics, operation management, and industrial strategies, he is currently doing research in Asia-Pacific economic development with special emphasis on Greater China.

Shaomin Li is associate professor at the City University of Hong Kong. His research interests include strategic management, international business, and political economy. He has published over twenty research articles and eight books. He is coeditor of the *China Industrial Markets Yearbook*. He recently published *Business Operations in China's Transition* (with Xiaofeng He and Oliver H. M. Yau).

Hong Liang is an economist at the International Monetary Fund. She earned her Ph.D. in economics from Georgetown University. Her research areas cover exchange-rate regimes, capital flows, and commodity trade.

Andrew J. Nathan is professor of political science at Columbia University and former director of its East Asian Institute. He is a member of the board of directors of the Center for Modern China and chair of the board of editors of the *Journal of Contemporary China*. His recent books include *China's Transition* and (with Robert S. Ross) *The Great Wall and the Empty Fortress: China's Search for Security*.

John M. Scheb II is professor of political science at the University of Tennessee. His major research interests include judicial politics and American government.

Steven R. Smith is professor of history at Savannah State University in Georgia. He has published more than a dozen articles, most of which have been on topics in the social history of early modern England. He has served as visiting professor at Northeast Normal University and Xinzhou Teachers College in China.

Yi Sun is assistant professor of East Asian history at the University of San Diego. Her areas of research include modern China, women in Asia, and Sino-American relations.

Guoqiang Tian is professor of economics at Texas A&M University. He is the author or coauthor of over eighty publications. He has written a book and edited fourteen books. His research interests include economic mechanism design, mathematical economics, general economic theory, dynamic optimization, game theory, transitional economics, and Chinese economies.

Guoguang Wu is assistant professor of political science at the Chinese University of Hong Kong. He is the author of numerous articles and seven books on Chinese politics. His current research interests cover China's political change in the reform years and U.S.–China relations in the post–Cold War era.

Jason Z. Yin is associate professor of strategy management and international business at the W. Paul Stillman School of Business, Seton Hall University. He has published three books and edited twelve books on technology and modern business management. He also published numerous papers in areas of strategic management of technology, international trade, technology transfer, and intellectual property rights.

Wei Yu is assistant research professor of medicine at Boston University School of Medicine. His research interests include public finance, health care financing, cost-effective analysis in medical treatment, and the economic impact of aging. He has written articles for several finance and economics journals in both the United States and China.

Yang Zhong is associate professor of political science at the University of Tennessee. His major research interests include comparative study of political system transformation in communist and former communist countries, local government in China, and foreign relations in East Asia.

Selected Bibliography

Boisot, Max, and John Child. "From Fiefs to Clans and Network Capitalism: Explaining China's Emerging Economic Order." *Administrative Science Quarterly* 41 (1996): 600–628.

Borenztein, Eduardo, and Jonathan Ostry. "Accounting for China's Growth Performance." *American Economic Review Papers and Proceedings* 86, no. 2 (1996): 224–228.

Bothwell, J. L., and T. E. Keeler. "Profits, Market Structure, and Portfolio Risk." In R. T. Masson and P. D. Qualls, eds., *Essays on Industrial Organization in Honor of Joe S. Bain.* Cambridge, MA: Ballinger, 1976, pp. 71–88.

Brosseau, Maurice, Kuan Hsin-chi, and Y. Y. Kueh, eds. *China Review 1997.* Hong Kong: The Chinese University Press, 1997.

Brugger, Bill, and David Kelly. *Chinese Marxism in the Post-Mao Era.* Stanford, CA: Stanford University Press, 1990.

Bunce, Valerie. *Do New Leaders Make a Difference? Executive Succession and Public Policy Under Capitalism and Socialism.* Princeton, NJ: Princeton University Press, 1981.

Caporaso, James A., and David P. Levine. *Theories of Political Economy.* Cambridge: Cambridge University Press, 1992.

Chai, Joseph C. H., and George Docwra. "Reform of Large and Medium State Industrial Enterprises: Corporatization and Restructure of State Ownership." In Maurice Brosseau, Kuan Hsin-chi, and Y. Y. Kueh, eds., *China Review 1997.* Hong Kong: The Chinese University Press, 1997, pp. 161–180.

Chang, Gene Hsin. "What Caused Hyperinflation at Big Bang: Monetary Overhang or Structural Distortion?" *China Economic Review* 6 (1995): 137–147.

Chang, Gene Hsin, and Jack Hou. "Structural Inflation and the 1994 'Monetary' Crisis in China." *Contemporary Economic Policy* (July 1997): 73–81.

Cheng, Xiaonong. "Fanrong cong he er lai?—Zhongguo jingji xianzhuang he qushi de fenxi" ["The Puzzle of China's Economic Prosperity: Problems and Perspectives"]. *Dangdai zhongguo yanjiu (Modern China Studies)* 3 (October 1996): 31–36.

———. "Gaige zhong de hongguan jingji: Guomin shouru de fenpei yu shiyong" ["The Macroeconomic in the Process of Reform: Distribution and Use of National Income"]. *Jingji Yanjiu (Economic Research Journal)* (August 1987): 16–28.

———. "Gaige zhong guomin jingji shouru liucheng de bianhua" ["Changes in Distribution of National Income in the Process of Reform"]. *Zhongguo:*

Fazhan yu gaige (China: Development and Reform) (August 1987): 17–24.
China National Statistics Bureau. *Zhongguo gongye renkou tongji, 1995 [Chinese Industrial Census, 1995]*. Beijing: Zhongguo tongji ju, 1995.
———. *Zhongguo tongji nianjian, 1993, 1994, and 1996 [China Statistical Yearbook 1993, 1994, and 1996]*. Beijing: Zhongguo tongji ju, 1994, 1995, and 1997.
China Reform Foundation. *Xianshi de xuanze [Reality's Choice]*. Shanghai: Shanghai yuandong Chubanshe, 1997.
Collier, David, ed. *The New Authoritarianism in Latin America*. Princeton, NJ: Princeton University Press, 1979.
Cook, Linda J. *The Soviet Social Contract and Why It Failed: Welfare Policy and Workers' Politics from Brezhnev to Yeltsin*. Cambridge, MA: Harvard University Press, 1993.
Council of the European Union. *Treaty on European Union*. Luxemburg: Office for Official Publications of the European Communities, 1992.
Deng, Dasong, Zhu Shifan, and Song Shunfeng. "Lun Zhongguo shehui baozhang shuishou zhidu jiqi gaige wanshan de silu yu duice" ["Concepts and Policies of China's Social Safety Tax Structure and Its Reform"]. In Xu Dianqing and Li Yanjin, eds., *Zhongguo shuizhi gaige [China Tax System Reform]*. Beijing: Zhongguo jingji chubanshe, 1997, pp. 250–264.
Deng, Xiaoping. *Deng Xiaoping jingji lilun xuexi gangyao [Deng Xiaoping's Economic Theory: A Study Outline]*. Beijing: Remin chuban she, 1997.
———. *Deng Xiaoping wenxuan 1975–1982 [Selected Works of Deng Xiaoping]*. Beijing: Renmin chunbanshe, 1983.
Deyo, Frederic C., ed. *The Political Economy of the New Asian Industrialism*. Ithaca, NY: Cornell University Press, 1987.
Dicey, A. V. *Introduction to the Study of the Law of the Constitution*. 10th ed. London: Macmillan & Co., Ltd., 1961.
Ding, X. L. *The Decline of Communism in China, Legitimacy Crisis, 1977–1989*. New York: Cambridge University Press, 1994.
Dittmer, Lowell. "Patterns of Élite Strife and Succession in Chinese Politics." *The China Quarterly* 123 (September 1990): 405–430.
Dong, Yiyu, and Shi Binhai, eds. *Zhengzhi de Zhongguo—Mianxiang xintizhi xuanze de shidai [Political China—Facing the Era of New System Selection]*. Beijing: Jinri Zhongguo chubanshe, 1998.
Dunne, Michael J. "The Race Is On." *Chinese Business Review* (March–April 1994): 16–23.
Esherick, Joseph W., and Elizabeth J. Perry. "Leadership Succession in the People's Republic of China: 'Crisis' or Opportunity?" *Studies in Comparative Communism* 16, no. 3 (autumn 1983): 171–177.
Feng, Zirui. "Jiang Zemin yiyu xingcheng 'chuangxin siwei'" ["Jiang Zemin Intends to Establish His 'Creative New Ideas'"]. *Jingbao (The Mirror)* 256 (November 1998): 24–26.
Feng, Runsheng. "Wo zhege shizhang xianzai mang xie shenmo?" ["As a Mayor, What Am I Busy with Now?"]. *Juece cankao (Policy References)* 28 (1997): 27–28.
Fewsmith, Joseph. "Chinese Politics on the Eve of the 15th Party Congress." In Maurice Brosseau, Kuan Hsin-chi, and Y. Y. Kueh, eds., *China Review 1997*. Hong Kong: The Chinese University Press, 1997, pp. 1–32.
Finnis, John. *Natural Law and Natural Rights*. Oxford: Clarendon Press, 1980.
Forney, Matt, and Nigel Holloway. "In Two Minds." *Far Eastern Economic Review* (June 19, 1997): 66–71.

Fuller, Lon. *The Morality of Law*. New Haven, CT: Yale University Press, 1969.
Gereffi, Gary, and Donald L. Wyman, eds. *Manufacturing Miracles: Paths of Industrialization in Latin America and East Asia*. Princeton, NJ: Princeton University Press, 1990.
Goldman, Merle. *Sowing the Seeds of Democracy in China: Political Reform in the Deng Xiaoping Era*. Cambridge, MA: Harvard University Press, 1994.
Gong, Ting. *The Politics of Corruption in Contemporary China*. Westport, CT: Praeger, 1994.
Goodman, David S. G. "Collectives and Connectives, Capitalism and Corporatism: Structural Change in China." *The Journal of Communist Studies and Transition Politics* 11, no. 1 (March 1995): 12–32.
Grossman, Stanford, and Olive D. Hart. "Cost and Benefits of Ownership: A Theory of Vertical and Lateral Integration." *Journal of Political Economy* 94 (1986): 691–719.
Gunter, Frank R. "Capital Flight from the People's Republic of China: 1984–1994." *China Economic Review* 7, no. 1 (spring 1996): 77–96.
Hannan, Kate. "Reforming China's State Enterprises, 1984–93." *The Journal of Communist Studies and Transition Politics* 11, no. 1 (March 1995): 33–55.
Hansen, Gary S., and Biger Wernerfelf. "Determinants of Firm Performance: The Relative Importance of Economic and Organizational Factors." *Strategic Management Journal* 10 (1989): 399–411.
Hay, Donald A., and Derek J. Morris. *Industrial Economics: Theory and Evidence*. Oxford: Oxford University Press, 1986.
Hayek, F. A. *The Constitution of Liberty*. Chicago: Henry Regnery Co., 1960.
Fuller, Lon. *The Morality of Law*. New Haven, CT: Yale University Press, 1969.
He, Qinglian. *Zhongguo de xianjing [China's Perplexity]*. Hong Kong: The Mirror Books, 1997.
Hitiris, T. *European Community Economics*. 3rd ed. Hertfordshire, England: Harvester Wheatsheaf, 1994.
Hong, Zhaohui. "The Shareholding Cooperative System and Property Rights Reform of China's Collective Township-Village Enterprises." *Asian Profile* 23 (October 1995): 359–369.
———. "Shehui gaige yu Zhongguo de xiandaihua" ["Social Reform and China's Modernization"]. *Zhonggong yanjiu (Studies on Chinese Communism Monthly)* (May 1994): 63–69.
———. "Lun Denghou Zhongguo de zhixu chongjian yu Jiang Zemin de jiang zhengzhi" ["The Reconstruction of Social Order in Post-Deng China"]. *Dangdai Zhongguo yanjiu (Modern China Studies)* (January 1997): 60–76.
———. *Shehui jingji bianqian de zuti [The Themes of Socio-Economic Transition: Reinterpretation of Modernization]*. Hangzhou, China: Hangzhou University Press, 1994.
———. "The Subordinate Men and Social Stability in Twentieth-Century China." *Asian Thought and Society* 60 (September–December, 1995): 70–89.
Hu, Shuli. "Zhongce xianxiang: guanyu yinzi gaizao de jiexi he sikao" ["The Phenomenon of 'China Strategy': Analysis and Thinking of Restructuring State Enterprises Through Foreign Investors"]. *Gaige (Reform Journal)* 3 (1994): 74–85.
Huntington, Samuel P. *The Third Wave: Democratization in the Late Twentieth Century*. Norman: University of Oklahoma Press, 1991.
Jiang, Zemin. *Gaoju Deng Xiaoping lilun weida qizhi, ba jianshe you Zhongguo tese shehui zhuyi shiye quanmian tuixiang ershiyi shiji [Hold High the Great Banner of Deng Xiaoping's Theory for All-Round Advancement of the Cause*

of Building Socialism with Chinese Characteristics into the 21st Century: Report Delivered at the 15th National Congress of the Communist Party of China on September 12, 1997]. Beijing: Renmin chubanshe, October 6–12, 1997.

———. "Guanyu jiang zhengzhi" ["Reemphasis on Politics"]. *Qiu Shi (Searching for Truth)* 13 (1996): 1–3.

———. *Lingdao ganbu yiding yao jiang zhengzhi* [*Leadership Must Stress Politics*]. Beijing: Renmin chubanshe, 1996.

———. "Shenru xuexi Deng Xiaoping lilun—Jinian Deng Xiaoping tongzhi shishi yi zhounian" ["Promoting Studies of Deng Xiaoping's Theory at the One-Year Anniversary of the Death of Comrade Deng Xiaoping"]. *Renmin ribao (People's Daily, Overseas Edition)*, February 18, 1998.

———. "Zhengque chuli shehui zhuyi xiandaihua jianshe zhong de ruogan zhongda guanxi" ["Correctly Managing Some Great Relationships in Socialist Modernization Construction"]. *Renmin ribao (People's Daily)*, October 9, 1995.

Keng, C. W. Kenneth. "An Economic China: A Win-Win Strategy for Both Sides of the Taiwan Strait." *American Journal of Chinese Studies* 2 (October 1998): 182–215.

Khalilzadeh-Shirazi, J. "Market Structure and Price-Cost Margins in U.K. Manufacturing Industries." *Review of Economics and Statistics* 56 (1974): 67–76.

Kong Zi (Confucius). *Lun yu* [*Analects of Confucius*]. Beijing: Hua jiaoxue chubanshe, 1994.

Kornai, Janos. *Economics of Shortage*. Amsterdam: North-Holland, 1980.

———. "Transformational Recession: A General Phenomenon Examined Through the Example of Hungary's Development." *Economic Appliquee* XLVI, no. 2 (1993): 181–227.

Kwong, Julia. *The Political Economy of Corruption in China*. Armonk, NY: M.E. Sharpe, 1997.

Lam, Willy Wo-lap. "Leadership Changes at the Fourteenth Party Congress." In Joseph Cheng Yu-shek and Maurice Brosseau, eds., *China Review 1993*. Hong Kong: The Chinese University Press, 1993, pp. 2.1–2.50.

Li, Cheng, and Lynn White. "Élite Transformation and Modern Change in Mainland China and Taiwan: Empirical Data and the Theory of Technocracy." *The China Quarterly* (1990): 1–35.

———. "The Thirteenth Central Committee of the Chinese Communist Party: From Mobilizers to Managers." *Asian Survey* 28, no. 4 (April 1988): 371–399.

Li, Shaomin. "Success in China's Industrial Market: An Institutional and Environmental Approach." *Journal of International Marketing* 1 (1998): 56–80.

Li, Shenzhi. "Ye yao tuidong zhengzhi gaige" ["Promoting Political Reform Too"]. *Dangdai Zhongguo yanjiu (Modern China Studies)* (April 1998): 17–19.

Li, Yining. "Zhuanxing fazhan lilun" ["The Theory of Transitional Development"]. *Xinhua wenzhai (New China Digest)* (July 1997): 49–51.

Lieberthal, Kenneth. *Governing China: From Revolution Through Reform*. New York: W. W. Norton & Co., Inc., 1995.

Lin, Justin J. "Rural Reforms and Agricultural Growth in China." *American Economic Review* 82 (January 1992): 34–51.

Lin, Justin J., Fang Cai, and Zhou Li. "Qiye gaige de hexin shi chuangzao gongping jingzheng de huanjing" ["Creating an Environment for Fair Competition Is the Core of Enterprise Reform"]. In Xu Dianqing and Wen Guanzhong, eds., *Zhongguo guoyou qiye gaige* [*Reform of State Owned Enterprises in China*]. Beijing: Zhongguo jingji chubanshe, 1996, pp. 49–89.

Lin, Yusheng. *The Crisis of Chinese Consciousness: Radical Anti-Traditionalism in the May Fourth Era*. Madison: University of Wisconsin Press, 1979.

Lin, Zijun. *Chenfu—Zhongguo jingji gaige beiwanglu* [*The Ups and Downs—The Memorandum of China's Economic Reform*]. Shanghai: Dongfang chuban zhongxin, 1998.

Liu, Allen P. L. *Mass Politics in the People's Republic: State and Society in Contemporary China*. Boulder, CO: Westview Press, 1996.

Ludlam, Janine. "Reform and the Redefinition of the Social Contract under Gorbachev." *World Politics* 43 (January 1991): 284–312.

Luo, Rongqu. *Xiandaihua xinlun xupian—Dongya yu Zhongguo de xiandaihua jincheng* [*Reinterpretations of Modernization—East Asian and China's Process of Modernization*]. Beijing: Beijing daxue chubanshe, 1997.

Ma, Licheng, and Ling Zhijun. *Jiaofeng: Dangdai Zhongguo sanci sixiang jiefang shilu* [*Crossing Swords: The Chronicle of Three Mind Emancipations in Contemporary China*]. Beijing: Jinri Zhongguo Chubanshe, 1998.

Mao, Zedong. "Lun shida guanxi" ["On the Ten Great Relationships"]. In *Mao Zedong xuanjji* [*Selected Works of Mao Zedong*]. Beijing: Renmin chubanshe, 1977, vol. 5.

McGahan, Anita M., and Michael E. Porter. "How Much Does Industry Matter, Really?" *Strategic Management Journal* 18 (1997): 15–30.

McKenzie, Paul D. "China's Application to the GATT: State Trading and the Problem of Market Access." *World Trade Journal* 24 (October 1990): 133–158.

Meade, James. *Alternative Systems of Business Organization and of Workers' Remuneration*. London: Allen & Unwin, 1986.

———. "Different Forms of Share Economy." In Susan Howson, ed., *The Collected Papers of James Meade*. Volume II: *Value, Distribution and Growth*. London: Unwin Hyman, 1988.

Montinola, Gabriella, Yingyi Qian, and Barry R. Weingast. "Federalism, Chinese Style: The Political Basis for Economic Success in China." *World Politics* 48 (October 1995): 50–81.

Nathan, Andrew J. *China's Crisis: Dilemmas of Reform and Prospects for Democracy*. New York: Columbia University Press, 1990.

———. "Even Our Caution Must Be Hedged." *Journal of Democracy* 9 (January 1998): 60–64.

Naughton, Barry. *Growing out of the Plan: Chinese Economic Reform, 1978–1993*. New York: Cambridge University Press, 1995.

Nee, Victor. "Organizational Dynamics of Market Transition: Hybrid Forms, Property Rights and Mixed Economy in China." *Administrative Science Quarterly* 37 (1992): 1–27.

Nee, Victor, and David Stark, eds. *Remaking the Economic Institutions of Socialism: China and Eastern Europe*. Stanford, CA: Stanford University Press, 1989.

———. "Toward an Institutional Analysis of State Socialism." In Victor Nee and David Stark, eds., *Remaking the Economic Institutions of Socialism: China and Eastern Europe*. Stanford, CA: Stanford University Press, 1989.

North, Douglass C. *Institutions, Institutional Change and Economic Performance*. Cambridge: Cambridge University Press, 1990.

Park, Seung Ho, Shaomin Li, and David K. Tse. "Determinants of Firm Performance in a Transition Economy: Institutional vs. Economic Effects in China." Paper presented at the 1997 Meeting of the Academy of International Business, Monterrey, Mexico, 1997.

Pei, Minxin. *From Reform to Revolution: The Demise of Communism in China and the Soviet Union*. Cambridge, MA: Harvard University Press, 1994.

Powell, Thomas C. "How Much Does Industry Matter? An Alternative Empirical Test." *Strategic Management Journal* 17 (1996): 653–664.

Rocca, Jean Louis. "Corruption and Its Shadow: An Anthropological View of Corruption in China." *China Quarterly* (June 1992): 402–416.

Ruan, Ming. "Jiang Zemin de yishi xingtai" ["Jiang Zemin's Ideology"]. *Kaifang (Open Magazine)* 134 (February 1998): 39–41.

Rumelt, Richard P. "How Much Does Industry Matter?" *Strategic Management Journal* 12 (1991): 167–185.

Schmalensee, Richard. "Do Markets Differ Much?" *American Economic Review* 75 (1985): 349–365.

Schurmann, Franz. *Ideology and Organization in Communist China*, enlarged edition, Berkeley: University of California Press, 1968.

Shambaugh, David. "The CCP's Fifteenth Congress: Technocrats in Command." *Issues & Studies* 34, no. 1 (January 1998): 1–37.

Shirk, Susan. *The Political Logic of Economic Reform in China*. Berkeley: University of California Press, 1993.

Shively, W. Phillips. *Power and Choice*. 4th ed. New York: McGraw-Hill, 1995.

Sjoberg, Orjan, and Zhang Gang. *Soft Budget Constraints in Chinese Township Enterprises*. Stockholm: Stockholm School of Economics, 1996.

Sun, Yan. *The Chinese Reassessment of Socialism, 1976–1992*. Princeton, NJ: Princeton University Press, 1995.

Survey Department of Household Income, State Bureau of Statistics. "Woguo cheng xiang shouru chaju wenti yanjiu" ["On Urban-Rural Income Gap in China"]. *Jingji Yanjiu (Economic Research Journal)* (December 1994): 30–45.

Swaine, Michael D. "China Faces the 1990s." *Problems of Communism* (September–October 1989): 20–35.

Tian, Guoqiang. "State-Owned Enterprise Reform and Smooth Institutional Transition in China—A Three-Stage Economic Reform Method." In G. J. Wen and D. Xu, eds., *The Reformability of China's State Sector*. New York: World Scientific Publisher, 1996, pp. 220–240.

———. "Zhongguo guoyou qiye de gaige yu jingji tizhi pingwen zhanggui de fangshi he buzou" ["The State-Owned Enterprise Reform of China and the Mode—Steps for Transforming Economic System Smoothly"]. *Jingji yanjiu (Economic Research Journal)* 319 (1994): 3–9.

———. "Zhongguo xiangzhen qiye de chanquan jieguo yu gaige" ["Property Rights Structure and Reform of China's Rural and Township Enterprises"]. *Jingji yanjiu (Economic Research Journal)* 323 (1995): 35–39.

Tilly, Charles. "Does Modernization Breed Revolution?" *Comparative Politics* 5, no. 3 (April 1973): 425–447.

Tucker, Robert C., ed. *The Lenin Anthology*. New York: W. W. Norton, 1975.

———. *The Marx-Engels Reader*. 2nd ed. New York: W. W. Norton, 1978.

U.S. Social Security Administration. *Social Security Programs Throughout the World—1995*. Washington, DC: GPO, 1996.

Varian, Hal R. *Intermediate Microeconomics*. New York: W. W. Norton, 1996.

Wade, Robert. *Governing the Market: Economic Theory and the Role of Government in East Asian Industrialization*. Princeton, NJ: Princeton University Press, 1990.

Walder, Andrew G. *Communist Neo-Traditionalism: Work and Authority in Chinese Industry*. Berkeley: University of California Press, 1986.

———. "Local Governments as Industrial Firms: An Organizational Analysis of China's Transitional Economy." *American Journal of Sociology* 101 (1995): 263–301.

Wang, Hengfu, and Shi Zheng. *Wenhua jingji lungao* [*Theory of Cultural Economy*]. Beijing: Renmin chubanshe, 1995.

Wang, Huning. *Mingren riji: Zhengzhi de rensheng [VIP's Diary: Political Life]*. Shanghai: Shanghai renmin chubanshe, 1995.

Wang, Jue, ed. *Laozhe you qigu: suoyouzhi gaige yu Zhongguo jingji luntan [The Share to the Workers: Forum of Reform and Chinese Economy]*. Nanning: Guangxi renmin chubanshe, 1997.

Wang, Ping, and Yuan-li Wu. "Learning from the EC: The Implications of European Economic Integration for China and Taiwan." *American Journal of Chinese Studies* (1996): 205–224.

Wang, Zhi. "China and Taiwan Access to the World Trade Organization: Implications for the U.S. Agriculture and Trade." *Agricultural Economics* 17 (1997): 239–264.

Wang, Zhi, and F. C. Tuan. "The Impact of China's and Taiwan's WTO Membership in World Trade—A Computable General Equilibrium Analysis." *American Journal of Chinese Studies* III, no. 2 (1996). 177–204.

Weber, Max. *Economy and Society: An Outline of Interpretive Sociology*. Guenther Roth and Claus Wittich, eds. Berkeley: University of California Press, 1978, vol. 1.

Weng, Jieming, Zhang Ximing, Zhang Tuo, and Qu Kemin, eds. *Yu zongshuji tanxin [Discussion with General Secretary of the CCP]*. Beijing: Zhongguo shehui kexue chubanshe, 1996.

White, Gordon. "Corruption and the Transition from Socialism in China." *Journal of Law and Society* (March 1996): 149–169.

White, Stephen. "Economic Performance and Communist Legitimacy." *World Politics* 38 (April 1986): 462–482.

World Bank. *Bureaucrats in Business*. Washington, DC: World Bank, 1997.

———. *At China's Table: Food Security Options*. Washington, DC: World Bank, 1997.

———. *China 2020: Development Challenges in the New Century*. Washington, DC: World Bank, 1997.

———. *China Engaged: Integration with the World Economy*. Washington, DC: World Bank, 1997.

———. *China: Pension System Reform, The World Bank Country Report, Report No. 15121-CHA*. Washington, DC: World Bank, 1996.

———. *Clear Water, Blue Skies: China's New Environment in the New Century*. Washington, DC: World Bank, 1997.

———. *World Development Report 1992: Development and the Environment*. New York: Oxford University Press, 1992.

Xu, Heping. *Zhucheng qiye gaige tantao [Studies of Zhucheng's Enterprise Reform]*. Beijing: Jingji guanli chubanshe, 1996.

Xu, Ming, ed. *Guanjian shike—Dangdai Zhongguo jidai jiejue de 27 ge wenti [The Critical Moment—The 27 Urgent Issues for Contemporary China]*. Beijing: Jinri zhongguo chubanshe, 1997.

Yang, Mayfair Mei-hui. *Gifts, Favors, and Banquets: The Art of Social Relationships in China*. Ithaca, NY: Cornell University Press, 1994.

Yang, Peng. *Dongya xinwenhua de xingqi [The Emergence of East Asia's New Culture]*. Kunming, Yunnan: Yunnan jiaoyu chubanshe, 1997.

Yang, Y. Z. "China's WTO Membership: What's at Stake?" *World Economy* 19 (1996): 661–682.

Yin, Jason Zunsheng. *Jishu guanli: kaifa he maoyi [Technology Management: R&D and Trade]*. Shanghai: Shanghai renmin chubanshe, 1995.

Yuan, Hong. "Hong Zhaohui de sanmian yinbi lilun" ["Zhaohui Hong's Theory of the Three Sided Coin"]. *Huaren (Today's Chinese)* (November 1997): 23–25.

Zhang, Erzheng. "Qianxi woguo guanshui xiatiao de jingji yingxiang" ["The Economic Impact of the Reduction of Tariff Rates"]. *Guoji maoyi wenti (International Trade Issues)* 6 (1996): 25–31.

Zhang, Weiying. "Decision Rights, Residual Claim and Performance: A Theory of How the Chinese State Enterprise Reform Works." *China Economic Review* 8, no. 1 (spring 1997): 67–82.

Zhao, Hui. "Zhongguo dalu zhengfu jigou gaige de yinhuang" ["The Potential Crises of China's Administrative Reform"]. *Jing Bao (The Mirror)* 249 (May 1998): 49–51.

Zhao, Ziyang. "Yanzhe you Zhongguo tese de shehui zhuyi daolu qianjin: zai Zhongguo Gongchan Dang di shisan ci quanguo daibiao dahui shang de baogao" ["Advancing Along the Road of Socialism with Chinese Characteristics: Report to the 13th National Congress of the Chinese Communist Party"]. In *Zhongguo Gongchan Dang di shisan ci quanguo daibiao dahui wenjian huibian [Documentaries of the 13th National Congress of the CCP]*. Beijing: Renmin chubanshe, 1987, pp. 34–49.

Zhou, Xueguang. "Unorganized Interests and Collective Action in Communist China." *American Sociological Review* 58 (February 1993): 54–73.

Index

About the Book

As China enters a stage of economic reform more challenging and risky than any that has gone before, the pressure for political liberalization grows apace. This volume explores the dilemmas of this new phase of complex change.

The authors—most of whom write with the insight that comes from having lived and worked within the Chinese system—analyze how the evolution of China's economic reforms is likely to affect its political system. Most counsel continued transformation of the economy in its present direction; but to follow this path without disorder, they caution, it will be necessary both to reshape an entire belief system and to reconstruct the social welfare system. Though the obstacles are considerable, they conclude that the post-Deng leadership does have the opportunity to offer China a comprehensive ideological, economic, and political "new deal."

Andrew J. Nathan is professor of political science at Columbia University; among his publications, the most recent are *China's Transition* and (with Robert S. Ross) *The Great Wall and the Empty Fortress: China's Search for Security*. **Zhaohui Hong** is associate professor of history at Savannah State University of Georgia; his recent publications include *The Themes of Social Economic Transition* and (with Jixuan Hu and Eleni Stavrou) *In Search of a Chinese Road Toward Modernization*. **Steven R. Smith** is professor of history at Savannah State University; he has taught at Northeast Normal University in Changchun and at Xinzhou Teacher's College.